4th edition

MATHEMATICS
FOR ELEMENTARY TEACHERS

AN ACTIVITY APPROACH

4th edition

MATHEMATICS
FOR ELEMENTARY TEACHERS

AN ACTIVITY APPROACH

Albert B. Bennett, Jr.
University of New Hampshire

L. Ted Nelson
Portland State University

WCB
McGraw-Hill

Boston, Massachusetts   Burr Ridge, Illinois   Dubuque, Iowa
Madison, Wisconsin   New York, New York
San Francisco, California   St. Louis, Missouri

WCB/McGraw-Hill

A Division of The McGraw·Hill Companies

MATHEMATICS FOR ELEMENTARY TEACHERS: AN ACTIVITY APPROACH

This book is printed on acid-free paper.

1 2 3 4 5 6 7 8 9 0 QPD QPD 9 2 0 1 0 9 8 7

ISBN: 0-07-006298-6

This book was set in Caslon by The Clarinda Company.
The editors were Jack Shira, Karen M. Minette, and David A. Damstra; the production supervisor was Elizabeth I. Strange.
The design was by Keithley & Associates
Quebecor–Dubuque was printer and binder.

Library of Congress Cataloging-in-Publication Data

Bennett, Albert B.
    Mathematics for elementary teachers :   an activity approach /
Albert B. Bennett, Jr., L. Ted Nelson. — 4th ed.
      p.   cm.
    Includes bibliographical references.
    ISBN 0–07–006298–6
    1. Mathematics.   I. Nelson, Leonard T.   II. Title.
QA39.2.B4763   1998
372.7—dc21
                                                        97-5914

http://www.mhhe.com

About the Authors

It was at the University of Michigan that Albert Bennett and L. Ted Nelson and their families first met. Bennett and Nelson had been invited to participate in a National Science Foundation sponsored program of graduate studies in mathematics. Ten years later while on sabbaticals at the University of Oregon they collaborated in writing lessons to actively involve prospective teachers in learning the mathematical concepts they would be teaching. These lessons eventually lead to the publication of the first editions of *Mathematics for Elementary Teachers: A Conceptual Approach* and *Mathematics for Elementary Teachers: An Activity Approach.*

Albert Bennett completed his undergraduate and masters degrees at the University of Maine in Orono. He taught mathematics at Gorham State College and became active in the summer mathematics institutes that were sponsored by the Association of Teachers of Mathematics in New England. An early bias that was reflected in his teaching of these institutes was the need to encourage intuition in the teaching and learning of mathematics. He received his doctorate in mathematics from the University of Michigan in 1966 and joined the mathematics faculty at the University of New Hampshire to teach mathematics to prospective teachers. There he organized a mathematics lab and started writing laboratory activities for teachers. In the next few years his efforts led to the publication of Fraction Bars, Decimal Squares, and articles and textbooks for elementary and middle school teachers. These publications support methods of using models and concrete materials in the teaching of mathematics.

Ted Nelson is professor of mathematics and education at Portland State University. He taught junior and senior high school mathematics after graduating from St. Cloud State University, and then continued mathematical studies at Bowdoin College and the University of Michigan, where he received his doctorate in 1968. After serving four years as the first mathematics department chair at Southwest Minnesota State University he moved to Oregon to follow his interest in teaching mathematics to teachers. Currently, his main goal is to continue development of three lab-based courses for prospective elementary teachers and eight additional lab-based courses for middle school teachers. His teaching and curriculum efforts led to a faculty achievement award for outstanding university teaching in 1988. Over the past fifteen years he has written curriculum materials and given workshops designed to bring more concrete materials, visual models, and problem solving investigations into the elementary and middle school mathematics curriculums.

CONTENTS

CHAPTER 6

DECIMALS: RATIONAL AND IRRATIONAL

CHAPTER 7

ALGEBRA AND FUNCTIONS

Puzzlers
170, 188

Puzzlers
197, 209

Puzzlers
219, 225, 231

MATERIALS CARDS

1 Rectangular Grid (1.3)
2 Isometric Grid (1.3)
3 Attribute-Game Grid (2.1)
4 Two-Circle Venn Diagram (2.1)
5 Three-Circle Venn Diagram (2.1, 10.1)
6 Pica-Centro Recording Sheet (2.3)
7 Coordinate Guessing and Hide-A-Region Grids (7.2)
8 Table of Random Digits (8.1, 8.3, 9.1)
9 Two-Penny Grid (9.1)
10 Three-Penny Grid (9.1)
11 Geoboard Recording Paper (10.1)
12 Game of Hex Grids (10.2)
13 Perpendicular Lines for Symmetry (10.4)
14 Metric Measuring Tape (11.1)
15 Centimeter Racing Mat (11.1)
16 Pentomino Game Mat Grid (11.2)
17 Attribute Label Cards and Circles for Wheels (2.1, 2.2)
18 Logic Problem Clue Cards and People Pieces (Problem 1) (2.3)
19 Logic Problem Clue Cards (Problems 2 and 3) (2.3)
20 Logic Problem Clue Cards (Problems 4 and 5) (2.3)
21 Object Pieces for Logic Problem 5 (2.3)
22 Mind-Reading Cards (3.1)
23 Decimal Squares* (6.1, 6.2)
24 Decimal Squares (6.1, 6.2)
25 Decimal Squares (6.1, 6.2)
26 Decimal Squares (6.1, 6.2)
27 Rectangular Geoboard Template (6.4, 10.1, 11.2)
28 Algebra Pieces (7.1)
29 Algebraic Expression Cards (7.1)
30 Simulation Spinners (9.2)
31 Trick Dice (9.2)
32 Metric Ruler, Protractor and Compass (10.1, 11.1, 11.3, 12.1, 12.2, 12.3)
33 Circular Geoboard Template (10.1)
34 Regular Polyhedra (10.3)
35 Regular Polyhedra (10.3)
36 Cube Patterns for Instant Insanity (10.3)
37 Pentominoes (11.2)
38 Prism, Pyramid, and Cylinder (11.3)
39 Hypsometer-Clinometer (12.3)

*Decimal Squares® is a registered trademark of Scott Resources.

PREFACE

The primary purpose of *Mathematics For Elementary Teachers: An Activity Approach* is to engage prospective elementary and middle school teachers in mathematical activities that will enhance their conceptual knowledge and simultaneously model the kind of mathematical learning experiences that they will be expected to provide for their students.

The National Council of Teachers of Mathematics' *Curriculum and Evaluation Standards for School Mathematics,* which establishes the direction of school mathematics as we turn to a new century, strongly asserts that students learn mathematics well only when they construct their own mathematical thinking. Mathematical information can be transmitted but mathematical understanding and knowledge come from within the learner as that individual explores, discovers, and makes connections.

The National Council of Teachers of Mathematics' *Professional Standards for Teaching Mathematics* presents a vision of mathematics teaching that "redirects mathematics instruction from a focus on presenting content through lecture and demonstration to a focus on active participation and involvement. Mathematics instructors do not simply deliver content; rather, they facilitate learners' construction of their own knowledge of mathematics."

This book provides instructors with activities and materials to actively engage students in mathematical explorations. It provides prospective elementary and middle school teachers the opportunity to examine and learn mathematics in a meaningful way.

Reasons for Mathematical Activities

Current views about the learning of mathematics are summarized well in *Everybody Counts: A Report to the Nation on the Future of Mathematics Education* (National Research Council, pp. 58–59):

Effective teachers are those who can stimulate students to *learn* mathematics. Educational research offers compelling evidence that students learn mathematics well only when they *construct* their own mathematical understanding. To understand what they learn, they must enact for themselves verbs that permeate the mathematics curriculum: "examine," "represent," "transform," "solve," "apply," "prove," "communicate." This happens most readily when students work in groups, engage in discussion, make presentations, and in other ways take charge of their own learning.

Mathematics for Elementary Teachers: An Activity Approach is a book of inductive activities for prospective teachers. It provides the instructor with the resources to make students' mathematical activity the focus of attention. The instructor is then free to interact with small groups, pose questions, and encourage reflective thinking and class discussions. The book enables students to experience mathematics directly by using models which embody concepts and promote mathematical thinking.

This book reflects the beliefs that

- Students who learn mathematics constructively through the appropriate use of manipulatives, models, and diagrams are more likely to develop a solid conceptual basis.
- A concrete approach diminishes the mathematical anxiety often accompanying a more abstract approach.
- Tactile and visual approaches provide mental images which can be more easily retained than symbols and called forth as needed in mathematical thinking.
- Prospective teachers who learn mathematics by being actively involved in doing mathematics will be more likely to teach in the same manner.
- The best way to inform students of current mathematical reforms is to involve them in a learning environment which incorporates them.

Features

Mathematics for Elementary Teachers: An Activity Approach contains 12 chapters with 38 activity sets and accompanying materials to provide a self-contained mathematics laboratory. Here are the special features of this book.

Active Learning Each activity set uses physical materials or visual models to provide a context for understanding. The questions and activities in each activity set are sequentially developed to encourage discovery and to proceed with depth into the topic.

Cooperative Learning The activity sets can be done individually or in small groups. Activity Set 2.3, Logic Problems for Cooperative Groups, is designed for small-group interaction.

Individual Reflections Throughout the activity sets, students are encouraged to describe patterns, discuss their thinking, and write explanations of their reasoning.

Manipulative Kit and Material Cards The Manipulative Kit contains 12 common manipulatives that are used in the activities together with envelopes to organize them. The 39 additional material cards contain manipulatives, models, grids, templates, game mats, and other materials to be used in the activities.

Pedagogy The activity sets demonstrate ways that manipulatives and visual models can be used in classrooms to promote conceptual understanding and mathematical thinking. There are concrete or visual models for teaching the following:

reasoning	even and odd numbers
numeration	factors and primes
whole numbers	greatest common divisor
fractions	least common multiple
integers	geometry
decimals	length, area, and volume
percent	statistics and probability
patterns and sequences	story problems
algebraic expressions	metric measurement
indirect measurement	graphing curves

Metric System There are explorations, games, and activities for learning the metric system in Chapter 11. Metric units are used in several activities after that chapter.

Calculators The use of calculators is encouraged throughout the book. Several activities are designed to be carried out with calculators.

Just for Fun Thirty-seven of the activity sets are followed by Just for Fun activities. These are usually related to the topics of the activity sets but extend the ideas to recreational or artistic areas.

Classroom Ideas At the end of each chapter a Suggested Classroom Activity is given for students to try with children. All of the models and manipulatives are appropriate for use with children.

Readings for More Classroom Ideas Many creative teachers have written about activities they have successfully used in their classrooms. Also, the National Council of Teachers of Mathematics has sponsored many booklets which discuss reform issues for teachers. A selected list of readings appears at the end of each chapter.

Puzzlers These brain teasers are interspersed throughout the text to add variety and provide practice in problem solving.

Answer Section Answers to all puzzlers and to selected (★) activities are included in the back of the book.

Supplements

Activity Book Instructor's Manual The *Instructor's Manual for Mathematics for Elementary Teachers: An Activity Approach* contains answers for all activity sets, puzzlers, and Just for Fun activities. There is a sample test for each chapter of the activity book and blackline masters of various grids used throughout the book. In addition, there are blackline masters for producing transparencies of the manipulatives for use on the overhead projector.

Companion Text The text, *Mathematics for Elementary Teachers: A Conceptual Approach,* Fourth Edition, is a companion volume to this activity book. Like the activity book, the text contains 12 chapters and 38 sections. Each of these sections corresponds to an activity in the activity book. The text contains a math activity at the beginning of each section; a problem opener at the beginning of each section; a computer, calculator, or lab investigation at the end of each section (a disk, the *Mathematics Investigator,* is available for 14 computer investigations); and one or more problem-solving applications in each section of the text.

Class Formats

The familiar chapter headings in *Mathematics for Elementary Teachers: An Activity Approach* will be convenient for those who wish to use the activities with the companion text or their current mathematics textbook. Many of the activity sets are independent and may be selected out of sequence.

Mathematics for Elementary Teachers: An Activity Approach can be effectively used in several types of class formats:

- **A lab course** based on the activity sets with outside readings from a reference text or journals
- **A combination lab and recitation course** in which the activities are used as starting points, followed by discussions or lectures based on extensions of the ideas raised in the investigations
- **A traditional lecture/recitation course** with the activity sets as supplemental and used for outside assignments

To Prospective Teachers

In this course you are a student. However, this is an important time for you to begin to think like the teacher you are planning to become. This is the time to begin your thinking about the nature of mathematics and about teaching and learning mathematics. You can do this by monitoring your own thoughts and feelings as you explore and investigate, by keeping a personal journal during your course, by observing the way your classmates learn and "grapple" with math, by noting how you might change or adapt an activity to use in an elementary or middle school classroom, and by deciding why it is important that children study mathematics.

This book was written to help you experience the mathematical ideas you will be teaching and the way you will be expected to teach them to your students as you enter the twenty-first century. You will construct models, use manipulatives, work cooperatively, explore, investigate, discover, make conjectures, and form conclusions. The models and manipulatives that accompany this book can be used with children. We encourage you to try appropriate explorations with the children you know and, by observing and asking questions, try to understand how they are thinking about mathematics. Eleanor Duckworth used her observations of children learning in her book, *The Having of Wonderful Ideas and Other Essays on Teaching and Learning,* where she makes these comments on teaching and learning:[1]

So what is the role of teaching, if knowledge must be constructed by each individual? In my view, there are two aspects to teaching. The first is to put students into contact with phenomena related to the area to be studied—the real thing, not books or lectures about it—and to help them notice what is interesting; to engage them so they will continue to think and wonder about it. The second is to have the students try to explain the sense they are making, and, instead of explaining things to students, to try to understand their sense. These two aspects are, of course, interdependent: When people are engaged in the matter, they try to explain it and in order to explain it they seek out more phenomena that will shed light on it.

[1] New York: Teachers College Press, Columbia University, 1987, p. 123.

4th edition

MATHEMATICS
FOR ELEMENTARY TEACHERS

AN ACTIVITY APPROACH

CHAPTER 1

PROBLEM SOLVING

From the earliest grades, the curriculum should give the students opportunities to focus on regularities in events, shapes, designs, and sets of numbers. Children should begin to see that regularity is the essence of mathematics. The idea of a functional relationship can be intuitively developed through observations of regularity and work with generalizable patterns.[1]

ACTIVITY SET 1.1

SEEING AND EXTENDING PATTERNS

Purpose To recognize, describe, construct, and extend geometric patterns

Materials Pattern blocks from the Manipulative Kit

Activity Human beings are pattern-seeking creatures. Babies begin life's journey listening for verbal patterns and looking for visual patterns. Scientists in search of extraterrestrial intelligence send patterned signals into the universe and listen for incoming patterns on radio telescopes. Mathematics is also concerned with patterns. Many mathematicians and educators involved in reforming mathematics teaching and learning at the elementary and middle school levels are suggesting that the notion of mathematics as the study of number and shape needs to be expanded. Some suggest that "mathematics is an exploratory science that seeks to understand every kind of pattern."[2]

In this first activity set colored geometric shapes called pattern blocks will be used to recognize, study, and extend geometric patterns. The set of pattern

---

[1]*Curriculum and Evaluation Standards for School Mathematics* (Reston, VA: National Council of Teachers of Mathematics, 1989), 60.
[2]Lynn A. Steen, *On the Shoulders of Giants: New Approaches to Numeracy* (Washington, DC: National Academy Press, 1990), 1–8.

blocks consists of six different figures: a green triangle, an orange square, a red trapezoid, a blue rhombus, a white rhombus, and a yellow hexagon.

1. The pattern block figures shown here form the first five figures of a sequence. Use your green triangles to construct the sixth and seventh figures that you think extend the given pattern.

★ **a.** Describe in writing at least three ways that the seventh figure in your sequence differs from the sixth figure.

b. Describe in writing what the 15th figure in this sequence would look like so that someone reading your description could build the same figure. Give your written description to another person and ask him or her to build a figure according to your instructions.

2. Use your pattern blocks to construct the sixth and seventh figures of the sequence below.

a. Describe in writing how new figures are created as this sequence is extended.

b. Will the 10th figure in an extended sequence have a green triangle or a blue rhombus on the right end? Explain your reasoning.

★ **c.** How many triangles and how many rhombuses are in the 25th figure of the extended sequence? Explain how you arrived at your answer.

d. Write a statement that will enable readers to determine the number of triangles and rhombuses in any figure they choose.

3. The pattern block sequence started below uses three different types of pattern blocks. Use your pattern blocks to build the next two figures in the extended sequence.

1st   2d   3d   4th   5th

a. Describe in writing how new figures are created as this sequence is extended.

★ **b.** What pattern block will be on the right end of the 17th figure in this sequence? Explain how you arrived at your answer.

c. Determine the number of hexagons, squares, and rhombuses in the 20th figure of the sequence without building the figure. Explain how you thought about it.

★ **d.** Repeat part c for the 57th figure in the sequence.

4. Use your pattern blocks to build the sixth and seventh figures of the sequence shown here.

1st   2d   3d   4th   5th

   a. Determine the number of triangles and hexagons in the 10th figure of the extended sequence. Do the same for the 15th figure.

★ b. Devise a way to determine the number of triangles and hexagons in any given figure in this sequence. Write an explanation of your procedure so that readers can use it to determine the number of triangles and hexagons in any figure they choose.

5. The third and fourth figures of a sequence are given below. Use your pattern blocks to construct the first, second, and fifth figures in this sequence. Sketch diagrams of your figures in the space provided.

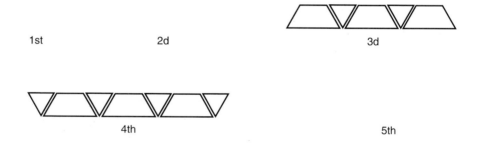

1st   2d   3d

4th   5th

   a. Describe how the odd-numbered figures differ from the even-numbered figures.

   b. Sketch the missing figures for the following sequence. Explain how you can determine the number of hexagons in any even-numbered figure of the sequence, then explain it for any odd-numbered figure.

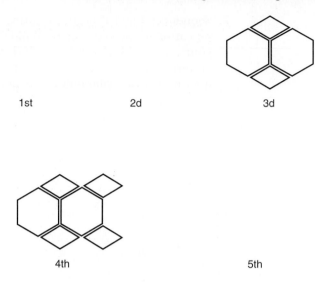

1st   2d   3d

4th   5th

★ **6.** The third term of a sequence is shown below. Create more than one sequence for which the given figure is the third term and sketch diagrams of the first, second, and fourth figures in the space provided. Write a rule for extending each pattern you create so that the reader is able to build the next few figures in the sequence. (You may wish to use the colored tiles from your Manipulative Kit for this activity.)

Sequence I

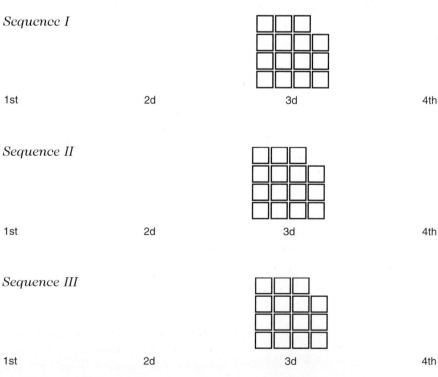

1st   2d   3d   4th

Sequence II

1st   2d   3d   4th

Sequence III

1st   2d   3d   4th

7. Sequences I and II begin repeating in the fifth figure and sequence III begins repeating in the sixth figure. Build the next two figures in each sequence with your pattern blocks. For the 38th figure in each sequence determine which pattern block is at its right end and how many of each type of pattern block it contains. Describe how you reached your conclusion in each case.

Sequence I

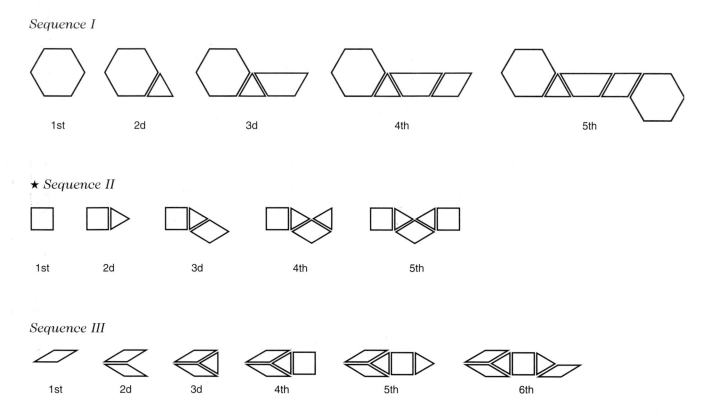

1st   2d   3d   4th   5th

★ *Sequence II*

1st   2d   3d   4th   5th

Sequence III

1st   2d   3d   4th   5th   6th

8. Devise your own sequence of figures with pattern blocks. Pose at least three questions about your sequence. Ask another person to build your sequence and answer your questions.

· ·

PUZZLER

By moving exactly two toothpicks, get the cherry out of the cup without changing the size and shape of the cup.

JUST FOR FUN

THE PEG-JUMPING PUZZLE

red pegs and vice versa. There are two legal moves: any peg can move to an adjacent empty hole, and a peg of one color can jump a single peg of another color if there is a hole to jump into. (You cannot jump over two or more pegs.)

A simple model for this puzzle uses black and red tiles from the Manipulative Kit on a puzzle grid drawn like the one here.

The official peg-jumping puzzle is shown here. A block of wood has seven holes in a row, with three movable black pegs in the holes at one end and three movable red pegs in the holes at the other end. The hole in the center is empty.

The challenge of the peg-jumping puzzle is to interchange the pegs between the right and left sides so that the black pegs move to the positions occupied by the

★ 1. Use three problem-solving strategies as you investigate this puzzle: using a model, simplifying the problem (start with one red and one black peg and three holes), and making a table (to record the numbers of moves).

2. What is the least number of moves required to solve the puzzle?

ACTIVITY SET 1.2

GEOMETRIC NUMBER PATTERNS

Purpose To use geometric patterns to represent number patterns and provide visual support for extending number sequences

Materials Colored tiles from the Manipulative Kit

Activity How long would it take you to find the sum of the counting numbers from 1 to 100?

$$1 + 2 + 3 + 4 + \cdots + 49 + 50 + 51 + \cdots + 97 + 98 + 99 + 100$$

Karl Friedrich Gauss (1777–1855), one of the greatest mathematicians of all time, was asked to compute such a sum when he was 10 years old. As was the custom, the first student to get the answer was to put his or her slate on the teacher's desk. The schoolmaster had barely stated the problem when Gauss placed his slate on the table and said, "There it lies."

No one knows for sure how the young Gauss obtained the sum so quickly. It is possible, however, that he, like many other creative thinkers, made a mental calculation by thinking of this number problem in a pictorial or visual way. Can you think of a picture or diagram that represents Gauss' sum?

Often in mathematics visual information can give valuable insights into numerical questions. Visual images can also help us remember mathematical ideas and concepts. In the following activities, geometric patterns will be used to generate number sequences. The visual information in the patterns will aid you in making numerical generalizations.

Karl Friedrich Gauss

1. Find a pattern in the following sequence and use your tiles to construct the sixth and seventh figures of the sequence.

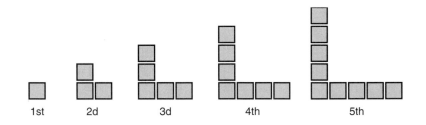

1st 2d 3d 4th 5th

a. By counting the number of tiles in each figure, we can see that the first seven figures represent the sequence of odd numbers 1, 3, 5, 7, 9, 11, and 13. Use your tiles to build the tenth figure in this sequence. Determine the tenth odd number by counting the tiles in the tenth figure.

b. Write a sentence or two describing precisely how you would build the 20th figure in this sequence. How many tiles would be needed? What is the 20th odd number?

★ c. Write a sentence or two describing what the 50th figure would look like and how many tiles it would contain.

d. Write a statement which will enable readers to determine the number of tiles in any figure they choose from this sequence.

2. The first three terms of the number sequence represented by the sequence here are 7, 12, and 17. Build the fourth figure. Sketch this figure, and beneath it record the number of tiles needed to build it.

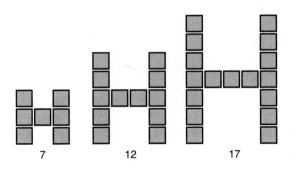

7   12   17

a. Write directions for constructing the eighth figure in the sequence. Ask someone to build the figure by following your directions.

b. How many tiles are in the eighth figure?

c. Determine the number of tiles in the 15th figure. (Imagine how you would construct that figure.)

d. Describe in words what the 50th figure would look like and how many tiles it would contain.

    e. Write a procedure using words or an algebraic expression to determine the number of tiles for any figure, given the figure number.

3. Here are three sequences and the number sequences they represent. Build the fourth figure in each sequence, and record the fourth number in each number sequence. Then determine the 10th number in each number sequence by imagining how you would construct the 10th figure in each geometric pattern.

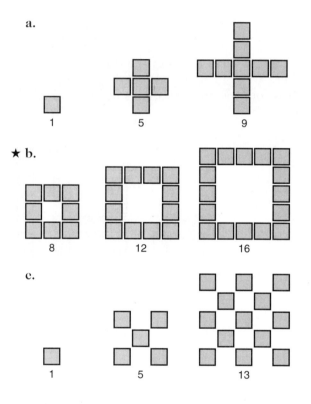

4. Using red and blue tiles, construct the fourth and fifth patterns in this sequence of rectangles and sketch your results. Determine the fourth and fifth terms of the corresponding number sequence.

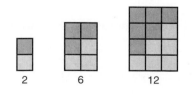

★ a. Describe the 10th rectangle in the sequence, including: height, width, total number of tiles, and number of red tiles and blue tiles.

b. Explain how you can determine the number of red tiles and the number of blue tiles in the 50th rectangle in the sequence.

5. The four figures in the following sequence have a stairstep pattern. Use your tiles to build the fifth figure in this sequence.

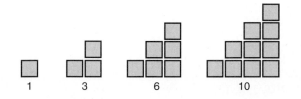

1   3   6   10

a. What number does the fifth stairstep represent? The 10th stairstep?

b. Use the results from activity 4 earlier to help you determine the number of tiles in the 50th stairstep.

★ **c.** Which stairstep corresponds to Gauss' sum $1 + 2 + 3 + 4 + \cdots + 99 + 100$?

d. What was Gauss' answer? Explain how you reached your conclusion.

e. Write a paragraph explaining how the sum of consecutive whole numbers from 1 to any given number can be obtained.

6. Suppose young Gauss had been asked to compute the sum

$$2 + 4 + 6 + 8 + 10 + 12 + 14 + \cdots + 78 + 80$$

How might he have computed this sum quickly? Devise a method of your own to compute the sum. (*Hint:* One way is to build a stairstep sequence similar to that in activity 5, except for the height of the steps.)

PUZZLER

Use 12 toothpicks to make this figure of squares. By repositioning exactly 3 toothpicks, form a figure with exactly 3 squares, all the same size.

JUST FOR FUN

FIBONACCI NUMBERS IN NATURE

The Fibonacci numbers 1, 1, 2, 3, 5, 8, 13, . . . occur in nature in a variety of unexpected ways. Following the first two numbers of this sequence, each number is obtained by adding the previous two numbers. What are the next five numbers in this sequence?

★ **1. Daisies:** Field daisies often have 21, 34, 55, or 89 petals. If you are playing the game "loves me, loves me not" with a daisy, which numbers of petals will result in a yes answer? The centers of daisies have clockwise and counterclockwise spirals. The numbers of these spirals are also Fibonacci numbers.

2. Sunflowers: The seeds of the sunflower form two spiral patterns, one proceeding in a clockwise direction and one in a counterclockwise direction. The numbers of spirals in the two directions are consecutive Fibonacci numbers. In the drawing, there are 34 counterclockwise and 55 clockwise spirals. In larger sunflowers, there are spirals of 89 and 144. Find a sunflower and count its spirals.

3. Cones and Pineapples: Pine, hemlock, and spruce cones have clockwise and counterclockwise spirals

of scalelike structures called bracts. Notice the two spirals that pass through the bract marked with an X in the pine cone diagram. The numbers of these spirals are almost always Fibonacci numbers. For example, the white pine cone has 5 and 8 spirals.

The sections of a pineapple are also arranged in spirals that represent Fibonacci number patterns. Count the spirals on a pineapple from upper left to lower right and from lower left to upper right.

PUZZLER

These toothpicks form five squares of the same size. Reposition exactly two toothpicks to get exactly four squares of the same size.

ACTIVITY SET 1.3

PATTERNS WITH COLORED TILES

Purpose   To search for and describe patterns

Materials   Colored tiles from the Manipulative Kit

Activity   "Mathematics is an exploratory science that seeks to understand every kind of pattern—patterns that occur in nature, patterns invented by the human mind, and even patterns created by other patterns. To grow mathematically, children must be exposed to a rich variety of patterns appropriate to their own lives through which they can see variety, regularity, and interconnections."[3]

In this activity, patterns created with colored tiles will be examined and extended. Then number pattern sequences will be written to record the numbers of colored tiles in the colored tile sequences. Finally, you will invent your own colored tile sequences and describe them with number sequences.

1. Here are the first six terms in a sequence of colored tile patterns. Below the figures are descriptions of how four different students described the pattern of yellow and green tiles numerically. For each student's observation:

   a. Briefly describe how you think the student obtained the numerical data from the figures in the sequence.

   b. Find a *pattern in the student's number pattern* and extend it to the seventh and eighth figures.

   c. Use the student's pattern to describe the number of yellow tiles and green tiles in the eleventh figure without building the ninth and tenth figures.

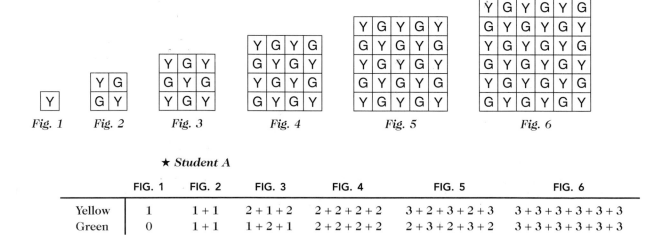

Fig. 1   *Fig. 2*   *Fig. 3*   *Fig. 4*   *Fig. 5*   *Fig. 6*

★ *Student A*

	FIG. 1	FIG. 2	FIG. 3	FIG. 4	FIG. 5	FIG. 6
Yellow	1	1 + 1	2 + 1 + 2	2 + 2 + 2 + 2	3 + 2 + 3 + 2 + 3	3 + 3 + 3 + 3 + 3 + 3
Green	0	1 + 1	1 + 2 + 1	2 + 2 + 2 + 2	2 + 3 + 2 + 3 + 2	3 + 3 + 3 + 3 + 3 + 3

[3]Lynn A. Steen, *On the Shoulders of Giants: New Approaches to Numeracy* (Washington, DC: National Academy Press, 1990): 8.

Student B

	FIG. 1	FIG. 2	FIG. 3	FIG. 4	FIG. 5	FIG. 6
Yellow	1	1 + 1	1 + 3 + 1	1 + 3 + 3 + 1	1 + 3 + 5 + 3 + 1	1 + 3 + 5 + 5 + 3 + 1
Green	0	2	2 + 2	2 + 4 + 2	2 + 4 + 4 + 2	2 + 4 + 6 + 4 + 2

Student C

	FIG. 1	FIG. 2	FIG. 3	FIG. 4	FIG. 5	FIG. 6
Yellow	$1^2 \div 2 + .5$	$2^2 \div 2$	$3^2 \div 2 + .5$	$4^2 \div 2$	$5^2 \div 2 + .5$	$6^2 \div 2$
Green	$1^2 \div 2 - .5$	$2^2 \div 2$	$3^2 \div 2 - .5$	$4^2 \div 2$	$5^2 \div 2 - .5$	$6^2 \div 2$

Student D

	FIG. 1	FIG. 2	FIG. 3	FIG. 4	FIG. 5	FIG. 6
Yellow	1	2	5	8	13	18
Green	0	2	4	8	12	18

2. Here are the first four terms of a sequence of colored tiles. Determine how the pattern is growing and then use your colored tiles to build the fifth figure in the sequence.

Fig. 1   Fig. 2   Fig. 3   Fig. 4

 a. Assume that this pattern continues and write a description of the 10th figure in the sequence so that a reader is able to build the figure from your description.

b. Find a pattern to determine the number of tiles of each color in each figure and record these numbers in the table below. Extend your pattern to the sixth figure.

	FIG. 1	FIG. 2	FIG. 3	FIG. 4	FIG. 5	FIG. 6
Yellow	_____	_____	_____	_____	_____	_____
Red	_____	_____	_____	_____	_____	_____

c. How many tiles of each color are in the 30th figure of the sequence?

d. Write a rule using words or symbols that will enable the reader to determine the number of tiles of each color in any figure that the reader chooses.

3. For each of the sequences I–IV of colored tiles that follow, construct the next figure in the sequence with your tiles and then do the following:

a. Determine a number pattern to describe the different colors in each of the figures and record it below each figure.

b. Use your number patterns to determine the number of tiles of each color in the 30th figure and show how you arrived at the result.

c. Write a rule using words, number symbols, or an algebraic expression that will enable the reader to determine the number of tiles of each color in any figure that the reader chooses.

Sequence I

Fig. 1   Fig. 2   Fig. 3   Fig. 4

★ *Sequence II*

Fig. 1   Fig. 2   Fig. 3   Fig. 4

Sequence III

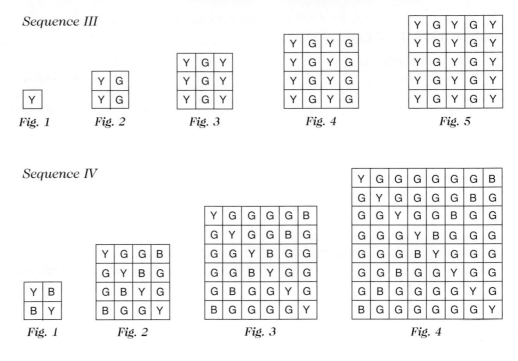

Fig. 1   Fig. 2   Fig. 3   Fig. 4   Fig. 5

Sequence IV

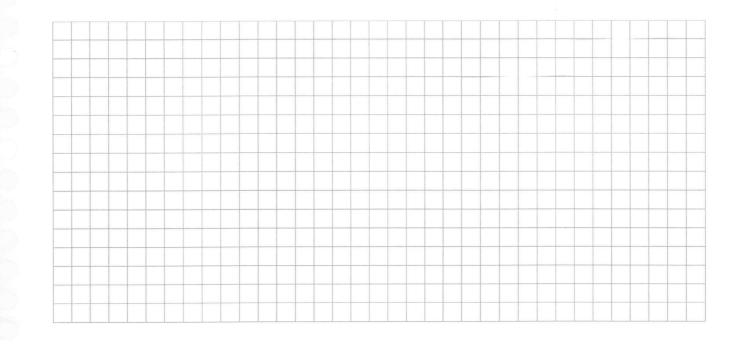

Fig. 1   Fig. 2   Fig. 3   Fig. 4

4. Create your own sequence of figures with colored tiles and sketch the first four figures of your sequence below. Answer parts a, b, and c from activity 3 for your sequence.

JUST FOR FUN

SPIROLATERALS

Spirolaterals are graphs of number sequences. The spirolateral shown in the accompanying diagram is the graph of 1, 2, 3, 4, 5. The following segments were drawn, starting at point *x*: a segment of length 1 in the east direction, a segment of length 2 in the south direction, a segment of length 3 in the west direction, and so on, repeating the number sequence with a 90° clockwise turn each time. After the sequence 1, 2, 3, 4, 5 has been repeated several times, the spirolateral will be *completed* in that it will have returned to its starting point and further use of the sequence will cause the same figure to be retraced. How many times was the sequence 1, 2, 3, 4, 5 used before the spirolateral was completed?

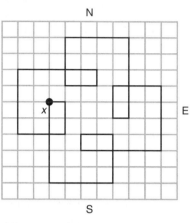

★ **1.** The number of numbers in a sequence is called the *order of the spirolateral*. Some spirolaterals cannot be completed but tend to wander off in some direction. Whether this happens depends on the order of the spirolateral. Sketch the following spirolaterals, beginning at the given starting points. Which two of these spirolaterals cannot be completed? What happens to the spirolateral if the numbers in its sequence are reversed? (For more graph paper, see Material Card 1.)

  a. 1, 2, 3   **b.** 1, 2, 3, 4   **c.** 1, 2, 3, 4, 5, 6

  d. 1, 3, 3, 1, 5, 2   **e.** 1, 2, 3, 4, 5, 6, 7, 3

2. In order for a spirolateral to be completed, the total movement in the east direction must equal the total movement in the west direction. Similarly, there must be a balance between total movement in the north and south directions. For the spirolateral 2, 5, 1, 3, 3, 1, the amount of movement in each of these directions is shown in the table above. The sums of numbers in the east-west directions are 6, and the sums of numbers in the north-south directions are 9. This spirolateral will close after the numbers have been used twice. Try it. Complete the following five tables for the spirolaterals that were graphed above. Two of these tables cannot be completed so that the sums in the columns balance.

E	S	W	N
2	5	1	3
3	1	2	5
1	3	3	1
6	9	6	9

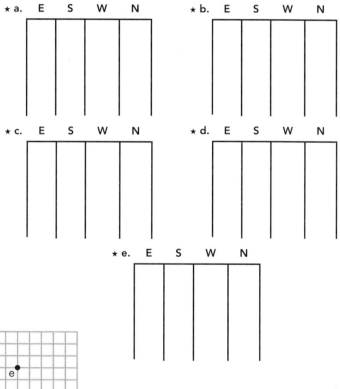

★ a.

E	S	W	N

★ b.

E	S	W	N

★ c.

E	S	W	N

★ d.

E	S	W	N

★ e.

E	S	W	N

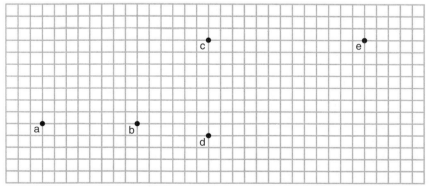

3. The only spirolaterals in the preceding examples that could not be completed were the two whose orders were multiples of 4. This suggests the following conjecture: if the order of a spirolateral is not a multiple of 4, the spirolateral can be completed. Test this statement with other spirolaterals. Try your telephone number or your Zip code.

At this point, you may be tempted to conclude that if the order of a spirolateral is a multiple of 4, the spirolateral cannot be completed. Before you do, try graphing the following spirolaterals:

1, 2, 1, 2   1, 2, 3, 4, 4, 3, 2, 1   1, 2, 4, 4, 4, 5, 1, 3

The spirolateral in the opening example, 1, 2, 3, 4, 5, was completed by using the numbers in its sequence 4 times. Try a few more spirolaterals to test the following conjecture: if the order of a spirolateral is odd, the number sequence will be used 4 times before the spirolateral is completed. (Note: Spirolateral 1, 2, 3, 4, 8, 2, 6 will return to its starting point after the sequence has been used only once. The spirolateral will not be complete at this point, however, because continuing the numbers will not cause the spirolateral to be retraced.)

Graph a few spirolaterals whose orders are even numbers but not multiples of 4. Form a conjecture about the number of times their sequences must be used before the spirolaterals are completed.

If a spirolateral can be completed, its sequence of numbers will be used 1, 2, or 4 times. Why?

4. Spirolaterals can also be graphed on isometric grids (Material Card 2). The graph of 1, 2, 3, 4 is shown here. The starting point is x, and each turn is 120° clockwise. Graph a few spirolaterals on your isometric grid, and form some conjectures about which ones can be completed. There are three directions on an isometric grid: east (E), southwest (SW), and northwest (NW). Try analyzing these spirolaterals by using a table—with three columns labeled E, SW, and NW.

Readings for More Classroom Ideas

Bennett, A., E. Maier, and L. Ted Nelson. "Seeing Mathematical Relationships." (Unit I). *Math and the Mind's Eye.* Salem, OR: The Math Learning Center, Box 3226, 1988.

Burns, Marilyn. *Problem-Solving Lessons: Grades 1–6.* Sausalito, CA: Math Solutions Publications, 1996.

Burns, Marilyn. *Writing in Math Class: A Resource of Grades 2–8.* Sausalito, CA: Math Solutions Publications, 1996.

Carey, Deborah A. "The Patchwork Quilt: A Context for Problem Solving." *Arithmetic Teacher* 40 (December 1992): 199–203.

Coburn, Terrence G., et al. *Patterns,* in the *Curriculum and Evaluation Standards for School Mathematics Addenda Series: Grades K–6.* Reston, VA: National Council of Teachers of Mathematics, 1993.

Farivar, S., and N. M. Webb. "Helping and Getting Help-Essential Skills for Effective Group Problem Solving." *Arithmetic Teacher* 41 (May 1994): 521–525.

Gill, Alice J. "Multiple Strategies: Product of Reasoning and Communication." *Arithmetic Teacher* 40 (March 1993): 380–387.

Jensen, Rosalie, and O'Neil, David R. "Let's Do It: Classical Problems for All Ages." *Arithmetic Teacher* 29 (January 1982): 8–12.

Norman, F. Alexander. "Figurate Numbers in the Classroom." *Arithmetic Teacher* 38 (March 1991): 42–45.

Silverman, F., K. Winograd, and D. Strohauer. "Student Generated Story Problems." *Arithmetic Teacher* 39 (April 1992): 6–12.

Van de Walle, John A., and Holbrook, Helen. "Patterns, Thinking, and Problem Solving." *Arithmetic Teacher* 34 (April 1987): 6–12.

Van de Walle, John A., and Thompson, Charles S. "Let's Do It: Promoting Mathematical Thinking." *Arithmetic Teacher* 32 (February 1985): 7–13.

Walter, Marion. "Frame Geometry: An Example in Posing and Solving Problems." *Arithmetic Teacher* 28 (October 1980): 16–18.

CHAPTER 2

SETS, FUNCTIONS, AND REASONING

A climate should be established in the classroom that places critical thinking at the heart of instruction. . . . Children need to know that being able to explain and justify their thinking is important and that how a problem is solved is as important as its answer. . . . Manipulatives and other physical models help children relate processes to their conceptual underpinnings and give them concrete objects to talk about in explaining and justifying their thinking.[1]

ACTIVITY SET 2.1

SORTING AND CLASSIFYING

Purpose   To use attribute pieces in games and activities for sorting and classifying, reasoning logically, formulating and verifying hypotheses, and introducing set terminology and operations

Materials   Attribute pieces from the Manipulative Kit, attribute label cards from Material Card 17, attribute game grid on Material Card 3, and the two-circle and three-circle Venn diagrams on Material Cards 4 and 5, respectively

Activity   "Mathematics is reasoning. One cannot do mathematics without reasoning. The standard does not suggest, however, that formal reasoning strategies be taught in grades K–4. At this level, the mathematical reasoning should involve the kind of informal thinking, conjecturing, and validating that helps children to see that mathematics makes sense.

"Manipulatives and other physical models help children relate processes to their conceptual underpinnings and give them concrete objects to talk about in explaining and justifying their thinking." Observing children interact with

---

[1]*Curriculum and Evaluation Standards for School Mathematics* (Reston, VA: National Council of Teachers of Mathematics, 1989), 29.

objects in this way allows teachers to reinforce thinking processes and evaluate any possible misunderstandings."[2]

In the late 1960s, sets of geometric figures called attribute pieces became a popular physical model for activities that promote logical thinking. These attribute pieces are also well suited for introducing ideas and terminology related to sets. The 24 attribute pieces used in this activity set vary in shape, color, and size. There are 4 shapes (triangle, square, hexagon, and circle), 3 colors (red, blue, and yellow), and 2 sizes (large and small). Each attribute piece differs from every other piece in at least one of the attributes of shape, color, or size. Many of the games and activities in this activity set can be adapted for use with children.

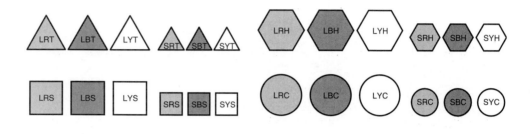

1. Place your *small blue square, small red square,* and *small yellow circle* on the indicated squares of the grid below. In the first row of the grid, the small blue square differs from the small red square in exactly one attribute—color. In the third column, the small red square differs from the small yellow circle in exactly two attributes—color and shape. Use your remaining small attribute pieces to fill the grid so that adjacent pieces in rows differ in exactly one attribute and adjacent pieces in columns differ in exactly two attributes. Record your results on the grid.

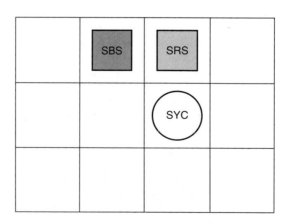

[2]NCTM's *Curriculum and Evaluation Standards for School Mathematics,* 29–30.

2. **Attribute Guessing Game** (2 players): To play this game, display all 24 attribute pieces on a flat surface. One player thinks of a specific attribute piece. The other player tries to determine that piece by asking questions that can be answered yes or no. Pieces that are ruled out by questions may be physically separated from the rest. The score is the number of questions needed to identify the piece. Low score wins. Players alternate roles.

★ a. If the player trying to guess the piece restricts all questions to the attributes of color, size, and shape, what is the minimum number of guesses necessary to ensure the identification of a randomly chosen piece? List the questions you would ask in order to identify a piece in the minimum number of guesses.

b. If the player guessing is allowed to use additional attributes of the pieces (like number of sides, size of angles, opposite sides parallel), can the minimum number of guesses be reduced? Explain.

3. **Attribute Grid Game** (2 or more players or teams, or solitaire): To begin this game, place any attribute piece on the center square of the grid (Material Card 3). The *large red hexagon* was used to start the game on the grid shown below. The players take turns placing an attribute piece on the grid according to the following conditions: the piece that is played must be placed on a square that is adjacent, by row, column, or diagonal, to a piece that has already been played; the adjacent attribute pieces in the rows must differ in one attribute (color, size, or shape); the adjacent pieces in the columns must differ in two attributes; and the adjacent pieces in the diagonals must differ in three attributes. A player's score on each turn is the total number of attributes in which the piece played differs from *all* adjacent attribute pieces.

Examples: The first piece played on the grid below was a *small blue square,* which differs in three attributes from the large red hexagon. The first player scored 3 points. The second player played the *small red hexagon.* This piece differs from the small blue square in two attributes and from the large red hexagon in one attribute. This player also scored 3 points. The game ends when no more pieces can be played on the grid.

Solitaire Version: Place an attribute piece on the center square. Try to place as many pieces as possible on the grid according to the rules. Record your results. Is it possible to place all 24 pieces on the grid?

Attribute-Game Grid

Rows, 1 difference (1 point)
Columns, 2 differences (2 points)
Diagonals, 3 differences (3 points)

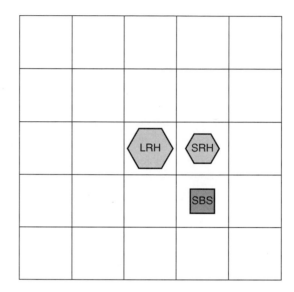

4. Label your two-circle Venn diagram (Material Card 4) with the attribute labels (from Material Card 17) RED and TRIANGULAR, as shown in the diagram below. In this diagram the *large red circle* is placed in the circle labeled RED and the *small blue triangle* is placed in the circle labeled TRIANGULAR. The *small red triangle* possesses both the red attribute and the triangular attribute, so it is placed in the intersection of the two circles. The *large yellow hexagon,* having neither attribute, is placed outside both circles. Place the same four pieces on your diagram. Distribute your remaining attribute pieces on the correct regions of the diagram.

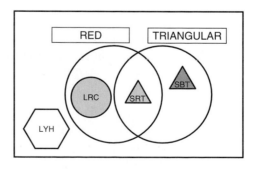

a. The attribute pieces that lie in the intersection of the two circles are described as being RED *and* TRIANGULAR. This set is called the *inter-*

section of the set of red pieces and the set of triangular pieces. Referring to your diagram, complete the following list of pieces in the intersection of the two sets.

Red *and* Triangular: SRT, _____

★ **b.** The attribute pieces that lie in the RED circle or the TRIANGULAR circle or both circles are described as being RED *or* TRIANGULAR. This set is called the *union* of the set of red pieces with the set of triangular pieces. Referring to your diagram, complete the following list of pieces in the union of the two sets.

Red *or* Triangular: LRC, SRT, SBT, _____

5. Label your two-circle Venn diagram as shown here. Distribute your attribute pieces in the appropriate regions.

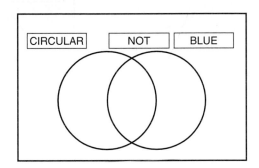

★ **a.** Record the set of attribute pieces in the *intersection* of the following two sets.

Circular *and* Not Blue: _____

b. Record the set of attribute pieces in the *union* of the following two sets.

Circular *or* Not Blue: _____

c. Using only words found on the attribute label cards, describe the pieces that are outside both circles in this diagram.

6. Mathematicians invent symbols for the purpose of abbreviating and representing ideas. In this activity the symbols NR, NL, T, NY, and NB will represent the NOT RED, NOT LARGE, TRIANGULAR, NOT YELLOW, and NOT BLUE sets of attribute pieces, respectively. The symbol ∪ will represent the *union of sets,* and the symbol ∩ will represent the *intersection of sets.* Use your labels and two-circle Venn diagram to determine and record the following sets of attribute pieces. (Each question calls for a different diagram.)

a. NR ∩ NL:

★ **b.** Using only words found on the attribute label cards, describe the pieces that are outside both circles in part a.

★ **c.** T ∪ NY:

d. NB ∪ NY:

7. Label your three-circle Venn diagram (Material Card 5) with the attribute labels shown in the diagram. There are eight different regions within the rectangle. Seven of the regions are enclosed by one or more circles, and one region is outside all three circles. Distribute the attribute pieces on the correct regions of your diagram.

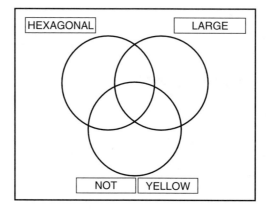

a. Record your solution by writing the abbreviation for each piece on the correct region of the diagram above.

b. The pieces LBH, LRH, and LYH are in the region H ∩ L. The pieces LBH and LRH are in the region (H ∩ L) ∩ NY. List the pieces in each of the following regions.

(1) H ∩ NY:

★ (2) (H ∩ NY) ∩ L:

(3) (NY ∩ L) ∪ H:

(4) (H ∩ L) ∪ H:

★ (5) H ∩ (NY ∪ L):

(6) (H ∩ NY) ∪ L:

PUZZLER

These three containers are all labeled incorrectly. But it is true that one contains two nickels, another two pennies, and another one nickel and one penny. How is it possible to determine the correct labels for all three containers by selecting one coin from one container?

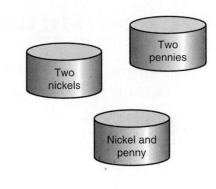

JUST FOR FUN

ATTRIBUTE IDENTITY GAME (2 teams or 2 players)

Draw three large circles and label them *X*, *Y*, and *Z*. Each circle represents a set of attribute pieces. The labeling team (or player) decides what the sets are to be, but does not tell the guessing team (or player). The descriptions of the sets should be written down. The guessing team selects an attribute piece, and the labeling team places that piece on the correct region of the diagram. The guessing team continues selecting pieces for placement until its members believe they have correctly identified sets *X*, *Y*, and *Z*. The labeling team answers yes or no to each guess and records the number of guesses. If part or all of a proposed identification is incorrect, the guessing team continues selecting pieces for placement until its members are able to guess all three sets.

After the guessing team correctly identifies the three sets, the teams reverse roles and play again. The winner is the team requiring the *fewest number of pieces (placed on the diagram) and guesses* to make an identification of all three sets.

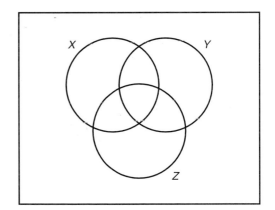

ACTIVITY SET 2.2

CURVES OF MOTION

Purpose To graph and interpret curves that describe motion

Materials Circles I, II, and III from Material Card 17

Activity As you ride a bicycle at a constant speed it is comfortable to think that you and all parts of the bike are traveling along at the same speed. However, there are parts of your bicycle wheels moving at vastly different speeds relative to the road, and some that momentarily stop! Such ideas about wheels intrigued early mathematicians. In 1658 the mathematician and philosopher Blaise Pascal diverted attention from a serious toothache by concentrating on the curve traced by a point on the circumference of a wheel rolling along a straight line—called a *cycloid*. His published reflections and solutions of problems related to the cycloid are said to have inspired Leibniz in his invention of calculus.[3] In this activity you will use models of wheels to graph curves that describe their motion.

1. **Bicycle Wheel Curve:** As a bicycle wheel moves along the road, a point on its tire traces out a curve called a cycloid. To see this curve, cut circle I from Material Card 17 and place it on the grid as shown below to represent a wheel. Mark several positions of point *P* as the wheel rolls along through one and one-fourth revolutions along the horizontal line. (Notice that as you roll the wheel along the horizontal axis the divisions on its circumference will match the divisions on the horizontal axis to help you accurately plot the location of point *P*.) Connect the points with a smooth curve. This curve, which shows the motion of a point on the circumference of a circle as it rolls along a line, is called a cycloid.

[3]D. M. Burton, *The History of Mathematics, an Introduction* (McGraw-Hill, Inc. 1985), 425–426.

a. On the graph above identify and label the following distances: the horizontal distance the wheel has moved forward after one revolution (d_1); the path that the point P traveled as the wheel made one revolution (d_2); the diameter of the wheel (d_3).

★ **b.** Using a piece of string and a ruler compare the following lengths and write a summary statement of your observations.

(1) Measure the diameter of the wheel (d_3) and the distance that the point P traveled along the arc in one revolution (d_2). Compute $d_2 \div d_3$. This number shows the relationship between the diameter of the wheel and the distance point P traveled.[4]

(2) Measure the length of the path of point P (d_2) and horizontal distance the wheel moved forward after one revolution (d_1). Compute $d_2 \div d_1$ to the nearest tenth. Explain what information this number gives you.

★ **c.** Using the value for $d_2 \div d_1$ from part b(2), determine the total distance that a point on your tire will have traversed (along its cycloid path) on a bike trip of 100 miles. Explain your thinking.

d. As your bicycle moves at a constant speed your wheels are turning at a constant speed. Yet, points on your tire are traveling at different speeds. The cycloid you constructed shows that in the same length of time that point A on your tire travels to position A_1, a point B on your tire is traveling to position B_1. Which point is traveling the fastest, A or B, and why?

[4]In 1658 the great architect Sir Christopher Wren determined that the length of one arc of the cycloid is a whole number times the diameter. (Do your measurements confirm this?) He thought that this curve had so many beautiful properties he called it the "Helen of Geometry."

★ **e.** There are points on the bike tire that momentarily come to a complete stop when the bike is moving forward. Indicate at what points on your cycloid you think this happens. Why do you think this happens?

f. Suppose that two ants climbed on the tires of a tricycle—one near the bottom edge of the front tire and the other near the bottom edge of the rear tire (which was half the diameter of the front). They hung on for dear life as the child pedaled the tricycle down the sidewalk. Write a convincing argument that their cycloid paths, while different, will be the same length. [*Suggestion:* Use the information from part b(1) to determine the lengths of the paths shown below.]

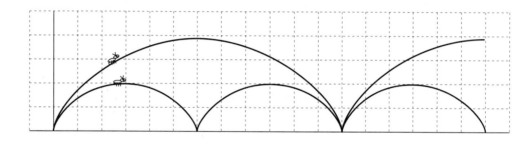

2. **Ferris Wheel Curve:**[5] On this Ferris wheel you enter a seat at midlevel as shown below. The wheel then rotates counterclockwise as the other seats are filled. Place circle II from Material Card 17 on the Ferris wheel as shown below and imagine you are seated at boarding level. Use the grid to plot your height above (or below) the entry level as the wheel turns. For example, point *A* shows where you start. Then when the seat after yours is being loaded the wheel will have turned one-twelfth of a revolution and you will have risen to the height indicated by point *B*. Plot the series of points which represent your height with respect to the entry level as the remaining seats are being filled and until the wheel turns through one complete revolution.

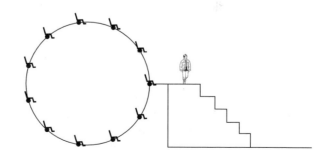

[5]For information on this curve and other similar functions see *Patterns and Functions* in the *Addenda Series, Grades 5–8* (Reston, VA: National Council of Teachers of Mathematics, 1991), 55–69.

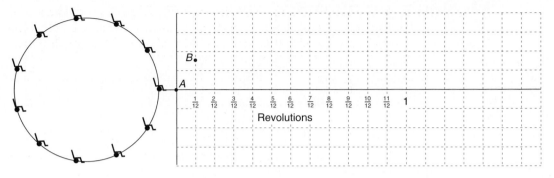

Revolutions

a. Draw a smooth curve through the points you plotted to represent your heights above the ground from the time you boarded until you made one complete revolution.

★ b. Extend your curve to represent $1\frac{1}{2}$ revolutions of the Ferris wheel and explain what the curve would look like as the wheel continues to revolve.

c. Assume that the Ferris wheel has a diameter of 50 feet (radius 25 feet). Make a scale on the vertical axis of your graph that shows the maximum distance you go above and below the entry level.

★ d. If the wheel makes one complete revolution in 24 seconds and you start at the entry level, use your graph to explain approximately how high you are above the ground after 34 seconds. After $2\frac{1}{2}$ minutes.

e. If your ride lasts 4 minutes, how many times will you be 20 feet below the entry level? Explain your answer in terms of your graph.

f. As the second seat was being boarded, you had risen to a height of 12.5 feet above the entry level as the wheel had rotated one-twelfth of a revolution. Use your graph to note after how much rotation you will be at that height again. Write a general statement which describes every time you will be at that same height if the wheel continues to rotate. (Remember, you are at that height going up and going down.)

3. If the Ferris wheel were twice as large as the one above, how do you think its graph would compare? Make a conjecture. Circle III on Material Card 17 has twice the diameter of circle II. Cut out circle III and use it to generate a curve on the grid below, using the same procedure as with circle II. Summarize your findings.[6]

---

[6]The curves that you have generated in activities 2 and 3 are the basic curve in trigonometry called the sine function. Edna E. Kramer says in her book, *The Nature and Growth of Modern Mathematics,* Vol. I, that "a thumbnail sketch would say that trigonometry is the study of the graph of the function $y = \sin x$." (Greenwich, CT: Fawcett Publications, 1970, p. 237).

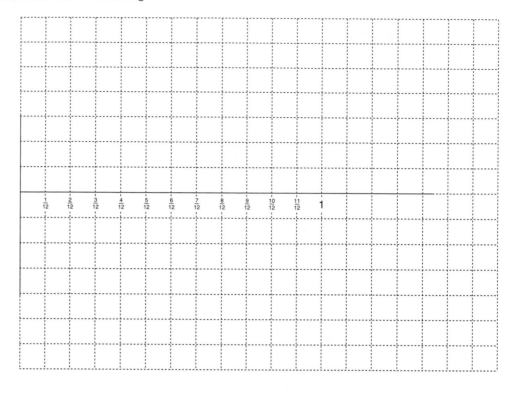

$\frac{1}{12}$ $\frac{2}{12}$ $\frac{3}{12}$ $\frac{4}{12}$ $\frac{5}{12}$ $\frac{6}{12}$ $\frac{7}{12}$ $\frac{8}{12}$ $\frac{9}{12}$ $\frac{10}{12}$ $\frac{11}{12}$ 1

JUST FOR FUN

THE CURVE OF ORBITING PLANETS

In the third century B.C. the Greek geometer Apollonius studied and wrote about the different curves that could be formed by cutting a cone. These shapes became known as *conics* or *conic sections*. One of the simplest and most beautiful of these curves, the ellipse, had a profound scientific importance hundreds of years later when Kepler discovered that planets move in orbits around the sun which are ellipses.

The ellipse may be more observable in everyday life than its simpler relative, the circle. If you look obliquely at any circular object around you, it will appear as an ellipse; a circular object viewed from an angle would be sketched as an ellipse; the beverage in a conical or cylindrical container forms an ellipse when tilted; and a ball resting on a table will often cast a shadow ellipse. Here are two ways to construct and intuitively understand an ellipse.

Drawing an Ellipse: Place a sheet of paper on a board (the top of a cardboard box works well) and place two tacks 4 inches apart. Cut a piece of string so that when the ends are tied the loop has a circumference of 11 inches. Place the string around the tacks and, keeping tension with a pencil, draw an ellipse.

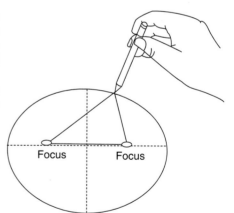

1. An *ellipse* is defined as a path (curve) such that the sum of the distances from any point on that path to two fixed points is a constant. For your curve the two fixed points are the tacks. What is the constant sum for your ellipse?

2. The two fixed points represented by the tacks are called the *foci* (singular, *focus*) of the ellipse. In the case of planetary motion, the sun sits at one focus and the earth travels in an elliptical orbit. Observe what happens to your ellipse as the foci move closer together or farther apart.

Folding an Ellipse: Draw a large circle on a sheet of paper and cut out the circle. Mark a point P somewhere inside the circle but not at its center. Fold the circle so that a point on its circumference falls on P and crease the paper along the fold line. Repeatedly fold 20 or more points around the circumference of the circle onto P. The more and sharper the creases, the better you will see that the crease lines appear to be touching the circumference of an ellipse.

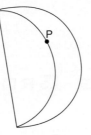

1. The point P is one of the foci of this ellipse. See if you can determine the location of the other focus and then pick a point which appears to be on the circumference of the ellipse and find the sum of the distances to the two foci. Check to see if this sum is approximately the same for other points on the circumference.

2. Experiment to see how the ellipse changes as the point P moves closer to, or farther from, the center of the circle.

ACTIVITY SET 2.3

LOGIC PROBLEMS FOR COOPERATIVE LEARNING GROUPS

Purpose To have cooperative learning groups use deductive reasoning to solve logic problems

Materials The logic problem clue cards and other materials for the five cooperative logic problems are on Material Cards 18, 19, 20, and 21.

Activity "In a cooperative learning situation, students' achievements of their shared goals are positively correlated; students perceive that they can reach their learning goals if and only if the other students in the learning group also reach their goals. Thus, students seek outcomes that are beneficial to all group members. When students work on mathematics assignments, they discuss the material with their group, explain how to complete the work, listen to each other's explanations, encourage each other to understand the solutions, and provide academic help and assistance."[7]

The logic problems in this activity set are designed to be solved cooperatively by a group of four people. Each member of the group will have a clue card that contains statements not found on any other person's card. No member of the group is allowed to read another member's card. The group is to work as a team to solve the problem cooperatively. When the activity begins, members of the group may read their clues to the group. The tasks of the group members are (1) to identify the problem that is to be solved; (2) agree on a process (Will there be one group recorder? Will the solution be arrived at mentally, or will diagrams, charts, or models be used?); (3) listen carefully when clues are read; and (4) make sure that all members of the group understand each step toward the solution.

Inductive reasoning is the process of forming conclusions on the basis of observations and experiments; it involves making an educated guess. *Deductive reasoning* is the process of deriving conclusions from given statements. The cooperative logic problems in this activity set will focus on deductive reasoning.

Cooperative Logic Problems

Form a team of four people. Follow these guidelines as you solve the problems:

Each team member takes one clue card. (If there are not enough people to form a group of four, some members may hold more than one card.)
Each person may read the clues aloud but may not show the clue card to another person.
The team is to identify the problem and agree on a method for solving it.

[7]David Johnson and Roger Johnson, "Cooperative Learning in Mathematics Education," in *New Directions for Elementary School Mathematics,* 1989 Yearbook (Reston, VA: National Council of Teachers of Mathematics, 1989), 235.

The team members are to solve the problem cooperatively by assisting each other.

The problem is solved when all team members understand the solution and agree that the problem has been solved.

After a problem has been solved, take a few minutes to record the solution in the blanks provided below. In the space for comments, record thoughts and feelings you had about the problem while they are fresh in your mind. What aids (models, diagrams, charts) did the team use in the solution? How did you feel about working with a team? Looking back and reflecting on the problem, can you see another approach to solving it?

1. **Nine in a Row:** The clue cards and people pieces are on Material Card 18. Use one set of clue cards and one set of people pieces in your cooperative group. Help each other arrange the people pieces as the clues are read.

_____ _____ _____ _____ _____ _____ _____ _____ _____
Shortest   Tallest

Comments:

2. **The Tennis Team:** The clue cards (Logic Problem 2) are on Material Card 19. Once you understand the problem, cooperatively devise a way to represent the problem so that you can solve it together.

Team members
for the road trip _____   _____   _____   _____

Comments:

★ 3. **The Prizes:** The clue cards (Logic Problem 3) are on Material Card 19. Devise a way to represent this problem that is acceptable to the entire group.

_____   _____   _____   _____
Math prize   English prize   French prize   Logic prize

Comments:

★ 4. **Who's Who:** The clue cards (Logic Problem 4) are on Material Card 20.

_____   _____   _____
Pilot's name   Copilot's name   Engineer's name

Comments:

5. **Five-House Puzzle:** The clue cards (Logic Problem 5) are on Material Card 20, and sets of objects referred to by the clues are on Material Card 21. Use one set of objects for your group.

House color _____   _____   _____   _____   _____

Nationality _____   _____   _____   _____   _____

Car make _____   _____   _____   _____   _____

Beverage _____   _____   _____   _____   _____

Pet _____   _____   _____   _____   _____

Comments:

- -

JUST FOR FUN

PICA-CENTRO (2 players)

In this game, one player chooses a three-digit number and the other player tries to discover it through logical deduction.

Preparation: Suppose that the chooser is player A and the guesser is player B. Player A begins by selecting a three-digit number, all of whose digits are different. (Zero may be used.) Player A records that number on a slip of paper and keeps it from the view of player B.

Player B uses the pica-centro recording sheet (Material Card 6) to record player B's guesses and player A's responses.

Play: Player B begins the process of deducing the identity of the number that player A has chosen by picking a three-digit number and recording that num-

ber on the recording sheet. A pica is a digit that is correct but not in the correct position; a centro is a digit that is both correct and in the correct position. Thus, player A might respond

- "One pica and no centros," which means that one digit has been correctly guessed, but it is in the wrong position
- "No picas and one centro," which means that the guess contains 1 correct digit and it is in the correct position
- "One pica and one centro," which means 1 correct digit in the wrong position and 1 correct digit in the correct position
- "No picas and no centros," which means that all digits are incorrect

Player B uses the clues to figure out other three-digit numbers to try. After each of player B's choices, player A responds with the appropriate number of picas and centros.

Example: Suppose player A chooses 471 and player B's first guess is 123. Player A responds, "You have one pica and no centros," and player B records that on the first line of the recording sheet, as shown below. One logical second choice for player B is 321. Player A responds, "You have no picas and one centro." Player B now deduces that either the 1 or the 3 is correct and in the correct position, but that 2 is not a digit in the number. (Why can player B deduce this?) Player B next chooses 541. Player A responds, "You have one pica

and one centro," which player B records on the sheet. Play continues in this manner until player B has deduced player A's number.

Ending: After player B has deduced player A's number, there will be a zero in the pica column and a 3 in the centro column. The players' roles are then reversed, with player B choosing the number and player A deducing the number. The winner is the player who requires the fewest number of turns to identify the number.

Variations: Four-digit, five-digit, or larger numbers can be used, as long as the players agree on the number of digits before playing.

Chosen number

4	7	1

GUESSES			RESPONSES	
Digits			Pica	Centro
1	2	3	1	0
3	2	1	0	1
5	4	1	1	1

- -

PUZZLER

Divide this parcel of land into two parts that each have the same size and shape (i.e., two congruent pieces).

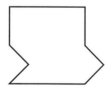

IDEAS FOR THE ELEMENTARY CLASSROOM
SUGGESTED CLASSROOM ACTIVITY: MATH COMMUNICATION

Two students sit on opposite sides of a barrier so that neither one can see the objects in front of the other.

Communication and Reasoning: Give each student a complete set of attribute pieces. One student selects a single piece and places it against the barrier. The other student attempts to identify that piece by asking questions that can be answered yes or no and by sorting his or her complete set of pieces to keep a record of which pieces have been ruled out (as in the Attribute Guessing Game). The students then reverse roles.

(continued)

(concluded)

Communication and Visualization: Give each student the same number of cubes. One student uses the cubes to build a structure and then gives verbal instructions to the other student as to how it is constructed. The other student builds according to the instructions. When the student is finished building, the barrier is removed and the structures are compared. If the structures are not identical, the students discuss statements that led to misunderstanding or confusion. The students then reverse roles.[8]

[8]See Glenda Lappan and Pamela Schram's "Communication and Reasoning: Critical Dimensions of Sense Making in Mathematics," in *New Directions for Elementary School Mathematics,* 1989 Yearbook (Reston, VA: National Council of Teachers of Mathematics, 1989), 14–30.

Readings for More Classroom Ideas

Cook, Marcy, "Ideas, Create a House Number." *Arithmetic Teacher* 36 (January 1989): 19–24.

Cruishank, Douglas E., "Sorting, Classifying, and Logic." *Arithmetic Teacher* 21 (November 1974): 588–598.

Edwards, Thomas G. "Students as Researchers: An Inclined-Plane Activity." *Mathematics Teaching in the Middle School* 1 (November-December, 1995): 532–535.

Goodman, Jan M. *Group Solutions: Cooperative Logic Activities, Grades K–4.* GEMS Series. Berkeley, CA: Lawrence Hall of Science, 1992.

Lappan, Glenda, and Pamela Schram. "Communication and Reasoning: Critical Dimensions of Sense Making in Mathematics." In *New Directions for Elementary School Mathematics,* 1989 Yearbook, edited by P. Trafton and A. Schulte. Reston, VA: National Council of Teachers of Mathematics, 1989, 14–30.

Phillips, Elizabeth, et al. *Patterns and Functions,* in the *Curriculum and Evaluation Standards for School Mathematics Addenda Series: Grades 5–8.* Reston, VA: National Council of Teachers of Mathematics, 1991.

Schwartz, James E. "'Silent Teacher' and Mathematics as Reasoning." *Arithmetic Teacher* 40 (October 1992): 122–124.

Scott, Thomas L. "A Different Attribute Game." *Arithmetic Teacher* 28 (March 1981): 47–48.

Warman, Michele, "Fun with Logical Reasoning," *Arithmetic Teacher* 29 (May 1982): 26–30.

Welchman-Tischler, Rosamond. "Making Mathematical Connections." *Arithmetic Teacher* 39 (May 1992): 12–18.

Whitin, David J., "Bring On the Buttons," *Arithmetic Teacher* 36 (January 1989): 4–6.

CHAPTER 3

WHOLE NUMBERS

Children come to understand number meanings gradually. To encourage these understandings, teachers can offer classroom experiences in which students first manipulate physical objects and then use their own language to explain their thinking. This active involvement in, and expression of, physical manipulations encourages children to reflect on their actions and to construct their own number meanings. In all situations, work with number symbols should be meaningfully linked to concrete materials.[1]

ACTIVITY SET 3.1

MODELS FOR NUMERATION

Purpose To use base-five number pieces and visual diagrams for other bases to introduce the concepts of grouping and place value in a positional numeration system

Materials Base-five number pieces from the Manipulative Kit

Activity The concepts underlying positional numeration systems—grouping, regrouping, and place value—become much clearer when illustrated with concrete models, and many models have been created for this purpose. Models for numeration fall roughly into two categories or levels of abstractness. *Grouping models,* such as bundles of sticks and Dienes blocks, show clearly how groupings are formed; *abacus-type models,* such as chip-trading or place-value charts, use color and/or position to designate different groupings.

---

[1]*Curriculum and Evaluation Standards for School Mathematics* (Reston, VA: National Council of Teachers of Mathematics, 1989), 38.

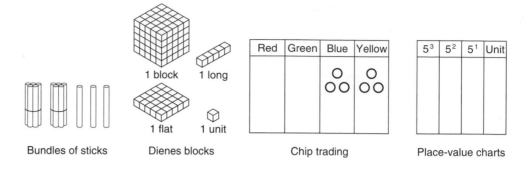

Red	Green	Blue	Yellow
		O	O
		O O	O O

Bundles of sticks   Dienes blocks   Chip trading   Place-value charts

5^3	5^2	5^1	Unit

The base number pieces shown here are in the Manipulative Kit. They are called base-five number pieces because each piece, other than the unit, has 5 times as many unit squares as the preceding piece.

Long-flat   Flat   Long   Unit

1. Use your base-five pieces to form the collection consisting of 8 units, 6 longs, and 5 flats, as shown in figure a. Exchange 5 units for 1 long, 5 longs for 1 flat, and 5 flats for 1 long-flat. This results in the collection shown in figure b. The two collections are *equivalent* because they both contain the same number of unit squares, but the second collection has fewer base-five pieces. (The first collection has 19 pieces, and the second has 7 pieces.)

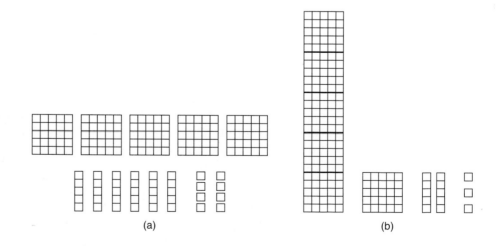

(a)   (b)

Use your base-five pieces to form each of the following collections. Make exchanges until you have an equivalent collection with the *minimum* number of base-five pieces. Record the number of long-flats, flats, longs, and units in your minimal collection in the table below.

a.

b.

c.

	LONG-FLATS	FLATS	LONGS	UNITS
a.	_____	_____	_____	_____
b.	_____	_____	_____	_____
★ c.	_____	_____	_____	_____

d. Explain why you never have to write a numeral greater than 4 in the table.

2. Using the base-five pieces, you can represent a collection of 28 units by a minimal collection of 1 flat, 0 longs, and 3 units. This is recorded in the table below.

Using base-five pieces to aid visualization, supply the missing entries in the following table:

	NO. OF UNIT SQUARES	LONG-FLATS	FLATS	LONGS	UNITS
a.	28	0	1	0	3
b.	31	_____	_____	_____	_____
★ c.	126	_____	_____	_____	_____
d.	200	_____	_____	_____	_____
e.	_____	0	1	2	3
★ f.	_____	3	3	0	3
g.	_____	4	4	4	4

3. Minimal collections of base-five pieces can be recorded without using tables. For example, the first entry in the table above can be written as 103_{five}. In doing this, we must agree that the positions of the digits from right to left represent the numbers of units, longs, flats, and long-flats. This method of writing numbers is called *positional numeration,* and 103_{five} is called a *base-five*

numeral. Write the base-five numerals for each of the other entries in the table in problem 2.

a. 103$_{five}$ b.   ★ c.   d.

e.   ★ f.   g.

4. The base-five pieces that represent the numeral 2034$_{five}$ are shown here. There are a total of 269 unit squares in these pieces.

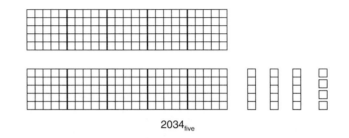

2034$_{five}$

Represent the following numbers with your base-five pieces, and determine the total number of unit squares in each.

	BASE-FIVE NUMERAL	TOTAL NUMBER OF UNIT SQUARES
a.	2304$_{five}$	_____
★ b.	1032$_{five}$	_____
c.	2004$_{five}$	_____

5. Here are the first three number pieces for base seven. Draw the first three number pieces for base three and base ten in the space provided below.

Base seven   Flat   Long   Unit

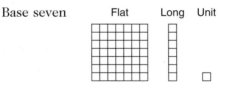

★ a. Base three

b. Base ten

6. Draw a diagram of the collection of base pieces representing each of the following numbers. Then determine the total number of unit squares in each collection.

    a. 122_{three} Total number of unit squares _____

    ★ **b.** 425_{seven} Total number of unit squares _____

    c. 157_{ten} Total number of unit squares _____

7. For each of the bases in parts a, b, and c, make a sketch of the minimal collection of base pieces that represents the collection of unit squares shown here. Then write the base numeral below the sketch.

    a. Base five

    ★ **b.** Base nine

    c. Base ten

JUST FOR FUN

The numbers 1, 2, 4, 8, 16, 32, and so on are called *binary numbers*. Following 1, each number is obtained by doubling the previous number. There are a variety of applications of binary numbers. Many of these applications provide solutions to games and puzzles, such as the intriguing mind-reading cards and the ancient game of Nim.

MIND-READING CARDS

With the five cards in Fig. 1, you can determine the age of any person who is not over 31. Which of these cards is your age on? If you selected card 4 and card 16, then you are 20 years old. If you selected cards 1, 2, and 16, then you are 19 years old.

1. The number in the upper left-hand corner of each of these cards is a binary number. Write your age as the sum of the fewest possible binary numbers. On which cards do the binary numbers that sum to your age appear? On which cards does your age appear?

★ 2. Write the number 27 as a sum of binary numbers. On which cards do these binary numbers occur? On which cards does 27 occur?

3. If someone chooses a number that is only on cards 1, 2, and 8, what is this number?

★ 4. Explain how the mind-reading cards work.

★ 5. The mind-reading cards can be extended to include greater numbers. The next card is card 32 (see Fig. 2). To extend this system to six cards, more numbers must be placed on the first five cards. For example, 33 = 32 + 1, so 33 must be put on card 1 as well as on card 32. On which cards should 44 be placed?

6. Write the additional numbers that must be put on cards 1, 2, 4, 8, 16, and 32 in Fig. 2 to extend this system to six cards.

7. Cut out the mind-reading cards from Material Card 22 and use them to intrigue your friends or students. Ask someone to select the cards containing his or her age, or to pick a number less than 64 and tell you which cards it is on. Then, amaze them by revealing that number.

16 21 26	8 13 26	4 12 22	2 11 23	1 11 21
17 22 27	9 14 27	5 13 23	3 14 26	3 13 23
18 23 28	10 15 28	6 14 28	6 15 27	5 15 25
19 24 29	11 24 29	7 15 29	7 18 30	7 17 27
20 25 30	12 25 30	20 30	10 19 31	9 19 29
31	31	21 31	22	31
Card 16	Card 8	Card 4	Card 2	Card 1

Fig. 1

32	16 21 26	8 13 26	4 12 22	2 11 23	1 11 21
	17 22 27	9 14 27	5 13 23	3 14 26	3 13 23
	18 23 28	10 15 28	6 14 28	6 15 27	5 15 25
	19 24 29	11 24 29	7 15 29	7 18 30	7 17 27
	20 25 30	12 25 30	20 30	10 19 31	9 19 29
	31	31	21 31	22	31
Card 32	Card 16	Card 8	Card 4	Card 2	Card 1

Fig. 2

GAME OF NIM (2 players)

The game of Nim is said to be of ancient Chinese origin. In its simplest form it is played with three rows of toothpicks or markers. On a turn, a player may take any number of toothpicks from any one row. The winner of the game is the player who takes the last toothpick or group of toothpicks.

Try a few rounds of this game with a classmate.

With a little practice, it is easy to discover some situations in which you can win. For example, if it is your opponent's turn to play and there is a 1-2-3 arrangement, as shown here, you will be able to win.

Sketch three more situations in which you will win if it is your opponent's turn to play.

Winning Strategy: A winning strategy for the game of Nim involves binary numbers.

1. On your turn, group the remaining toothpicks in each row by binary numbers, using the largest binary numbers possible in each row, as shown in this example.

2. Then remove toothpicks so that there is an *even number* of each type of pile left. In the example above, you will see an even number of 4s, an even number of 2s, and an odd number of 1s. So 1 toothpick must be taken from one of the rows. Show that the 1-2-3 arrangement above has an even number of binary groups.

★ 3. Assume it is your turn and you have the arrangement shown here. Cross out toothpick(s) so that your opponent will be left with an even number of binary groups.

★ 4. After the markers in each row have been grouped by binary numbers, there will be either an *even situation* (an even number of each type of binary group) or an *odd situation* (an odd number of at least one type of binary group). Experiment to see whether one turn will always change an even situation to an odd situation. Is it possible in one turn to change an even situation into another even situation?

Generalized Nim: Play the game of Nim with any number of rows and any number of toothpicks in each row. Try the strategy of leaving your opponent with an even situation each time it is his or her turn. Is this still a winning strategy?

ACTIVITY SET 3.2

ADDING AND SUBTRACTING WITH MULTIBASE PIECES

Purpose   To use multibase number pieces to visually illustrate addition and subtraction

Materials   A pair of dice and base-five number pieces from the Manipulative Kit

Activity   The operations of addition and subtraction are inverses of each other. *Addition* is explained by putting together sets of objects, and *subtraction* is explained by taking away a subset of objects from a given set. This dual relationship between subtraction and addition can be seen in the trading-up game, which introduces addition, and the trading-down game, which introduces subtraction.

    Algorithms for addition and subtraction are step-by-step procedures for adding and subtracting numbers. One of the best ways to gain insight into the addition and subtraction algorithms is by thinking the process through using manipulatives that represent other number bases. The base-five number pieces will be used in the following activities.

Addition

1. **Trading-Up Game** (2 to 5 players): Use your base-five pieces to play. On a player's turn, two dice are rolled. The total number of dots facing up on the dice is the number of base-five units the player wins. At the end of a player's turn, the player's pieces should be traded (regrouped), if necessary, so that the total winnings are represented by the fewest number of base-five pieces (minimal collection). The base-five numeral for the minimal collection should be recorded. The first player to get 1 long-flat wins the game.

   Example: On the player's first turn, shown below, the 8 units won were traded for a minimal collection and the corresponding base-five numeral was recorded.

       On the player's second turn, the 8 additional pieces won were added to the player's collection. After trading to get a minimal collection, the player recorded the base-five numeral for the total collection.

	Dice	Collection	Minimal collection	Record
1st turn	⚀ ⚅			13_{five}
2nd turn	⚄ ⚂			31_{five}

2. Answer the following questions for the trading-up game described in activity 1.

    a. What is the maximum number of longs and units you can win in one roll of the two dice?

    ★ **b.** By comparing the maximum collection for one turn (part a) to the long-flat, determine the fewest number of rolls in which a game can be won. Explain your reasoning.

    c. Determine the maximum number of turns it can take to obtain a long-flat. Explain how you arrived at your conclusion. (Hint: Compare the least possible winnings from one roll of the dice to the long-flat.)

    ★ **d.** If your total is 421_{five} after several turns, will it be possible for you to win on your next roll? Explain why or why not.

    e. Suppose your total score is 333_{five}. What is the fewest number of turns in which you can reach 1000_{five}? Explain how you reached your conclusion. (Hint: Use your base-five pieces to represent 333_{five}.)

3. Numbers written as base-five numerals can be added with base-five pieces. For example, $324_{\text{five}} + 243_{\text{five}}$ can be added by representing each number with base-five pieces, combining the collections, and trading (regrouping) to find the minimal collection, as shown below.

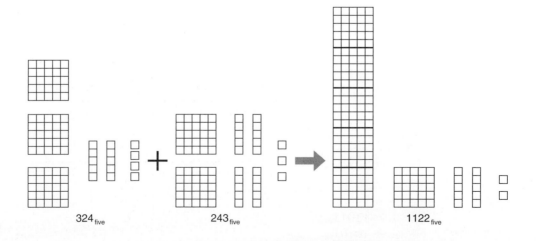

324_{five} 243_{five} 1122_{five}

Use base-five pieces to represent each of the following sums. Then regroup to obtain the minimal collection, and record the base-five numeral for this collection.

★ **a.** $43_{\text{five}} + 24_{\text{five}} =$ **b.** $313_{\text{five}} + 233_{\text{five}} =$

★ **c.** $304_{\text{five}} + 20_{\text{five}} + 120_{\text{five}} + 22_{\text{five}} =$ **d.** $1000_{\text{five}} + 100_{\text{five}} + 10_{\text{five}} =$

4. Numbers in other bases can be added mentally by visualizing the appropriate base number pieces or by making sketches of the appropriate base pieces. For example, in order to add $1221_{\text{three}} + 122_{\text{three}}$, the following diagrams show what regrouping must be done to obtain 2 long-flats, 1 flat, and 2 longs.

$$\begin{array}{r} 1221_{\text{three}} \\ +\ \ 122_{\text{three}} \\ \hline 2120_{\text{three}} \end{array}$$

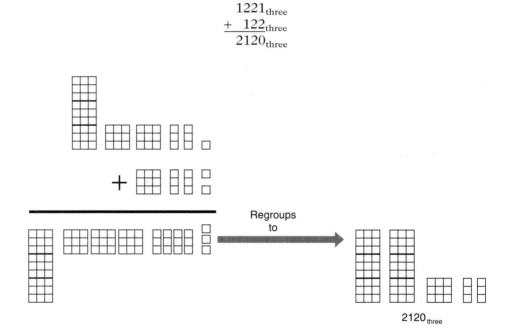

Make sketches of base number pieces representing the following sums and their regroupings (as above). Record the numeral for each sum.

★ **a.** $$\begin{array}{r} 201_{\text{three}} \\ +\ 102_{\text{three}} \\ \hline \end{array}$$

b. $$\begin{array}{r} 2312_{\text{four}} \\ +\ \ 203_{\text{four}} \\ \hline \end{array}$$

★ **c.** $$\begin{array}{r} 255_{\text{six}} \\ +\ 134_{\text{six}} \\ \hline \end{array}$$

d. $$\begin{array}{r} 11011_{\text{two}} \\ +\ 10101_{\text{two}} \\ \hline \end{array}$$

Subtraction

5. Trading-Down Game (2 to 5 players): Use your base-five pieces to play. Each player begins the game with 1 long-flat. On a player's turn, two dice are rolled. The total number of dots facing up on the dice is the number of units the player discards. The object of the game is to get rid of all base-five pieces. The first player to do so wins the game. On some turns the player will have to trade (regroup) in order to discard the exact number of pieces. At the end of a player's turn, the remaining pieces should be a minimal collection, and the base-five numeral should be recorded.

Example: On the player's first turn, shown below, the long-flat was traded for other base-five pieces so that 1 long and 2 units could be discarded. The numeral representing the remaining minimal collection was recorded.

On the player's second turn, 1 long was traded for units so that the correct number of pieces could be discarded. The base-five numeral for the remaining collection was recorded.

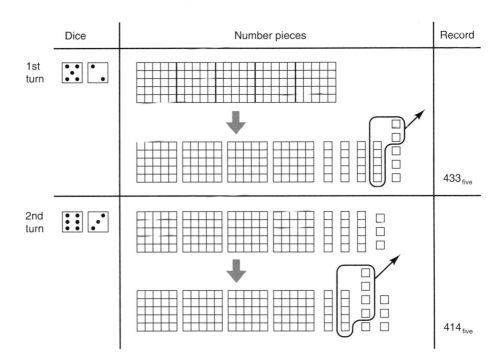

Dice	Number pieces	Record
1st turn		433_{five}
2nd turn		414_{five}

6. Answer the following questions for the trading-down game described in activity 5.

    a. Determine the fewest number of rolls in which a player can discard all pieces. Explain your conclusion.

★ **b.** If a player's total was reduced from 313_{five} to 242_{five} in one turn, what did the player roll on that turn? (Hint: Use your base number pieces to represent both scores.)

7. Here are three methods that students have been observed using to determine $232_{\text{five}} - 143_{\text{five}}$. Work through each method using your base number pieces. Then briefly explain the strategy or technique you believe was used in each method.

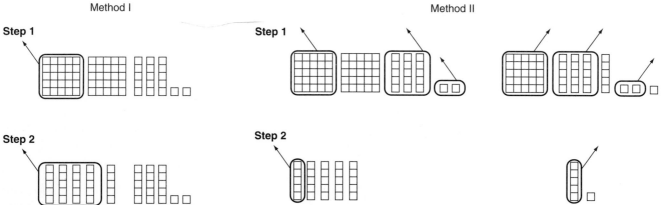

Method I

Step 1

Step 2

Step 3

Method II

Step 1

Step 2

Step 3

Method III

Step 1

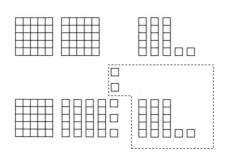

Step 2

8. Methods I and II in activity 7 are forms of the *take away* model for subtraction, and method III is called the *comparison* model. Use your base number pieces and one or more of these subtraction models to determine the following differences.

★ **a.** $1142_{five} - 213_{five}$ **b.** $2331_{five} - 124_{five}$ ★ **c.** $4112_{five} - 143_{five}$

9. Determine each of the following differences by drawing diagrams of the base number pieces that represent the numerals.

★ **a.** $1221_{three} - 122_{three}$

b. $2312_{four} - 203_{four}$

★ **c.** $1010_{two} - 101_{two}$

d. $101_{ten} - 11_{ten}$

JUST FOR FUN

FORCE OUT (2 players)

The whole numbers from 1 to 21 are listed as shown below. The players take turns crossing off one, two, or three consecutive numbers, starting with 1. For example, player A might cross off 1 and 2, player B might cross off 3, 4, and 5, and so forth. The loser is the player who is forced to cross off the last number, 21. Play the game a few times. Can you develop a strategy for winning?

1 2 3 4 5 6 7 8 9 10 11 12 13 14 15 16 17 18 19 20 21

★ *Winning Strategy:* With a little practice, you will see some "winning numbers." Suppose it is your turn to move and the numbers from 1 to 15 have been crossed off. If you cross off the number 16, you can win the game no matter what your opponent does. Why? What number preceding 16 must you cross off in order to guarantee that you will get to cross off 16? Work back-ward in this manner to develop a winning strategy. Can you always win if you start? Can you always win if your opponent starts?

Toothpick Variation: Twenty-one toothpicks are spread in a row, as shown below. One of the toothpicks is bent. The players take turns selecting 1, 2, 3, or 4 toothpicks from the row. The loser is the player who is forced to select the bent toothpick. Play the game a few times. Can you develop a strategy for winning?

| | | | | | | | | | | | | | | | | | | | | >

Other Variations: An arbitrary whole number is selected. The players take turns mentally subtracting 1, 2, 3, 4, or 5 from that number. The loser is the player who is forced to reach zero. Describe a strategy for win-ning this game. (*Hint:* Start with a number like 30 and play the game a few times.)

PUZZLER

Three cardboard disks are numbered on both sides. When the disks are dropped onto a table, the sum of the three visible numbers will be 6, 7, 8, 9, 10, 11, 12, or 13. What number is written on the back of each disk?

ACTIVITY SET 3.3

MULTIPLYING WITH MULTIBASE PIECES

Purpose   To use base-ten pieces to build a visual model for multiplication

Materials   Base-ten pieces from the Manipulative Kit

Activity   Multiplication is often thought of as repeated addition. For example,

$$4 \times 8$$

can be thought of as 4 copies of 8, or

$$8 + 8 + 8 + 8$$

If repeated addition is illustrated with 4 sets of 8 tiles, the tiles can be pushed together to form a rectangular array of squares with dimensions 4 by 8.

So, the conceptual model for multiplication will be a rectangle. The two numbers being multiplied are the dimensions of the rectangle, and the number of squares in the rectangle is the product. In this activity set, base-ten pieces will be used to illustrate the paper-and-pencil multiplication algorithm.

1. The product 7 × 12 can be represented with base-ten pieces as 7 copies of 12. When the pieces are pushed together, they form a rectangle with dimensions 7 × 12. By regrouping the base pieces to form a minimal collection of 8 longs and 4 units, we can determine that the product is 84.

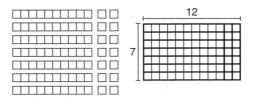

Determine the following products by forming rectangles with your base-ten pieces and then regrouping to obtain the minimal collection. Sketch each rectangle, and write the numeral representing the minimal collection beneath it.

a. 6 × 14

b. 7 × 23

★ **2.** Explain how it is possible, using base-ten number pieces, to multiply a one-digit number by a two-digit number without knowing any multiplication facts. For example, think of representing 7 × 64 with your base-ten number pieces. Draw a diagram to illustrate your explanation.

3. The product 12 × 13 is represented below with base-ten pieces. Several exchanges can be made without affecting the dimensions of the rectangle. Ten longs can be exchanged for 1 flat, and groups of 10 adjacent units can be exchanged for longs. The resulting rectangle is composed of 1 flat, 5 longs, and 6 units, so the product of 12 and 13 is 156.

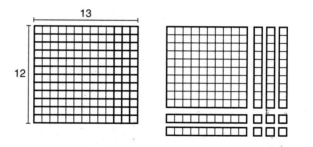

Use your base number pieces to determine these products. Make exchanges when possible, and use as few base pieces as you can when building your rectangle. Sketch each rectangle, and record the minimal set of base-ten pieces in the rectangle.

a. 13 × 13

★ **b.** 21 × 23

c. 17×12

★ 4. Explain how it is possible, using base-ten number pieces, to multiply a two-digit number by a two-digit number without knowing any multiplication facts. Draw a diagram to illustrate your explanation for a specific product.

5. The rectangle model for multiplication corresponds very closely to the usual paper-and-pencil algorithm for multiplication. Use your base-ten number pieces to form the rectangle representing 23 × 24.

★ a. Here is a paper-and-pencil procedure that uses four partial products for multiplication. Make a diagram of the base-ten number piece rectangle representing 23 × 24. Clearly match each partial product with the corresponding region of your diagram.

b. The following procedure uses two partial products for multiplication. Make another sketch of your number piece rectangle, and match the parts of the rectangle with the corresponding partial products.

6. Once you become familiar with the base-ten number piece model, it is easy to sketch diagrams of rectangles in order to compute products. For example, to compute 33 × 41, you would outline the rectangle as in the first sketch below and fill it with flats, longs, and units as in the second sketch. The product is obtained by counting the number pieces (12 hundreds, 15 tens, and 3 units) and adding.

For each of the following products,

    (1) Draw a number piece sketch like the one above.

    (2) Determine the product from the sketch.

    (3) Adjacent to each sketch, compute the product using the usual paper-and-pencil algorithm, and match the partial products to the corresponding parts of your sketch.

  a. 10 × 23

★ b. 22 × 43

  c. 45 × 45

JUST FOR FUN

CROSS-NUMBERS FOR CALCULATORS

Sit back, relax, and exercise your calculator's multiplication key with this cross-number puzzle. Not all answers are obtainable on a calculator, however. Clues for some of the numbers have been omitted, but no square is left blank.

Across

1. $[(18 + 2) \times 4] + 19$

5. $\dfrac{14 + 3}{9 + 8} \times 66$

6. $500,000,000 \div 9$ (Omit the decimal part of the number.)

8. The middle two digits of the product of $2 \times 2 \times 2 \times 2 \times 3 \times 37$

12. $\dfrac{(41 - 29) \times (63 - 23)}{95 \div 19}$

15. The sum of the digits in the product of $13 \times 9004 \times 77$

16. The sum of the first seven odd numbers

17. March 30, 1974: A "freeze model" in a department store posed motionless for 5 hours, 32 minutes. How many minutes in all did he pose?

23. $\dfrac{13,334 - 6566}{8 \times 9} \times \dfrac{992 \div 4}{17 + 14}$

27. $(10,000,000 \div 81) \times 100$ (nearest whole number)

28. Take the current year, subtract 17, multiply by 2, add 6, divide by 4, add 21, subtract $\frac{1}{2}$ of the current year.

29. First two digits of the product of 150×12

Down

3. $(34 \times 53) - (137 \times 2)$

4. Asphalt roof shingles are sold in bundles of 27. Three bundles cover 100 ft². How many bundles are needed for 11,700 ft² of roofing in a housing development?

5. $\dfrac{88,984 \times 493}{17 \times 392}$

7. $\dfrac{51 \times 153 \times 62 \times 57}{17 \times 969 \times 31}$

11. $\dfrac{(62 \times 21) + 23}{25} - 11$

14. The number of different combinations of U.S. coins into which a dollar can be changed. (This number is a palindrome, and the sum of its digits is 13.)

17. Remainder of $1816 \div 35$

18. $(343 \times 5 + 242) \times 2$

19. $4 \times [(37 \times 24) - 1]$

21. The number halfway between 7741 and 8611

26. $\dfrac{119 \times 207 \times 415}{23 \times 747}$

ACTIVITY SET 3.4

DIVIDING WITH MULTIBASE PIECES

Purpose To use base-ten number pieces to illustrate two physical interpretations of division and the long-division algorithm

Materials Base-ten pieces from the Manipulative Kit

Activity In this activity set we will begin by using base-ten pieces to look at two different ways to approach division. The *measurement* or *subtractive* approach to division is illustrated by answering the question "How many piles of 3 cards can you make from a total of 39 cards?"

The *sharing* or *partitive* approach to division is illustrated by answering the question "If 39 cards are separated into 3 piles, how many are in each pile?"

Each question can be answered by computing 39 ÷ 3. The answer to both questions is 13. With cards, however, the first answer would be obtained by repeatedly subtracting groups of 3 cards and counting the number of groups, the second by dealing the cards into 3 piles and counting the number of cards in each group.

Base-ten pieces also will be used to illustrate the inverse relationship between multiplication and division and to provide a concrete interpretation of the long-division algorithm.

36 ÷ 3 = 12
(12 in each of 3 equal groups)
Sharing

1. Using base-ten number pieces, we can determine the quotient 36 ÷ 3 by simple counting procedures. With the *sharing* method, 36 is shared equally among 3 groups. Each group has 1 long and 2 units.

The *measurement* approach to division asks how many groups of 3 can be formed from 36. In this case, all the longs must be traded for units so that groups of 3 can be formed.

36 ÷ 3 = 12
(12 groups of 3)

Measurement

a. Represent 24 as a minimal collection of base-ten pieces. Then, regrouping when necessary, determine 24 ÷ 6 using the measurement interpretation of division. Record your results with sketches of base-ten pieces.

★ **b.** Represent 132 as a minimal collection of base-ten pieces. Determine 132 ÷ 12 using the sharing interpretation of division. Record your results with sketches of base-ten pieces.

2. Many times division does not come out evenly, so there is a remainder. When we divide 20 by 3 using the measurement approach, there are 6 groups of 3 units and 2 remaining units. Dividing 20 by 3 using the sharing method, we have 3 groups of 6 with 2 remaining.

(6 groups of 3 with 2 remaining)   (6 in each of 3 groups with 2 remaining)
         Measurement   Sharing

Use base-ten pieces to determine each of the following quotients and record your results in a diagram.

a. 57 ÷ 4 (sharing approach)

★ **b.** 114 ÷ 12 (measurement approach)

3. When 36 was divided by 3 in activity 1, the answer 12 was obtained in two different ways. Notice that with either approach the base-ten number pieces can be pushed together to form a rectangular array of 36 squares with one dimension of 3. So *division can be thought of as finding the missing dimension of a rectangle when the total number of unit squares and one dimension are known.*

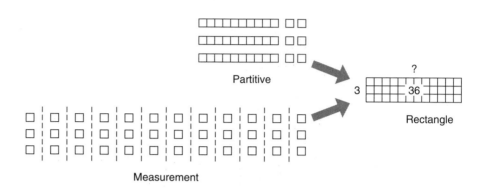

In each of the following activities, use the specified base-ten pieces to construct a rectangle with the given dimension. You may have to trade pieces for other pieces of equal value. Sketch a diagram of your result, and record the missing dimension of the rectangle.

a. Start with 9 longs and 6 units, and build a rectangle that has one dimension of 4 units.

★ b. Start with 2 flats, 7 longs, and 3 units, and build a rectangle that has one dimension of 13 units.

c. Start with 4 flats, 6 longs, and 2 units, and build a rectangle that has one dimension of 21 units.

4. To divide 143 by 11 using the base-ten number pieces, form the minimal collection of base-ten number pieces for 143. Then draw a line segment of length 11 units to represent one dimension of the rectangle. Finally, distribute the base pieces representing 143 (regrouping as necessary) until a rectangle has been formed. In this example we can see that the other dimension is 13, so 143 ÷ 11 = 13.

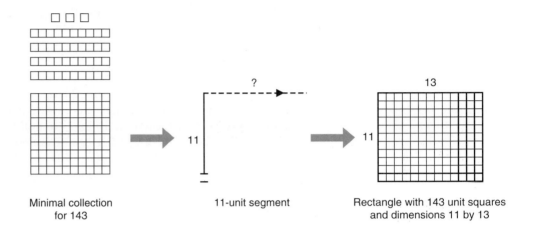

Minimal collection   11-unit segment   Rectangle with 143 unit squares
    for 143   and dimensions 11 by 13

In a similar manner, use your base-ten number pieces to determine each of the following quotients. Sometimes you may need to trade pieces. Draw a sketch of your results. (*Note*: If there is a remainder, you will get a rectangle with units left over.)

a. 221 ÷ 17

★ b. 529 ÷ 23

c. 397 ÷ 34

5. The paper-and-pencil algorithm for long division can be visualized using base-ten number pieces and the rectangle model. Suppose the goal is to compute 477 ÷ 14. Notice that the usual symbol for division, 14)‾477, suggests two sides of a rectangle, where the length of one side is 14, the total number of units is 477, and the length of the other side (the quotient) is unknown. The following steps and full-page diagram show how the rectangle model for division is related to the division algorithm.

> *Step 1:* First select the base-ten number pieces to represent 477.
>
> *Step 2:* Draw a line segment of 14 units to represent one dimension of the rectangle. Begin distributing the base-ten number pieces representing 477 to form a rectangle of width 14.
>
> *Step 3:* Three sections of width 10 can be incorporated into the rectangle. This takes 4 flats and 2 longs and leaves 5 longs and 7 units, which is not enough to complete another section of 10 (1 flat had to be traded for 10 longs to build this much).
>
> *Step 4:* Four sections of width 1 can be added onto the rectangle (1 long was traded for 10 units). This uses 5 longs and 6 units and leaves 1 unit remaining—not enough to make the rectangle any wider unless the remaining unit is cut into pieces.
>
> *Step 5:* The desired dimension of the rectangle (the quotient) is 34, and there is a remainder of 1.

Use your base-ten pieces to illustrate the paper-and-pencil division algorithm for each of the following quotients. Record your results by drawing a diagram for each quotient and matching parts of the unknown dimension to the corresponding digits in the division algorithm.

a. 144 ÷ 6

b. 134 ÷ 3

★ **c.** 587 ÷ 23

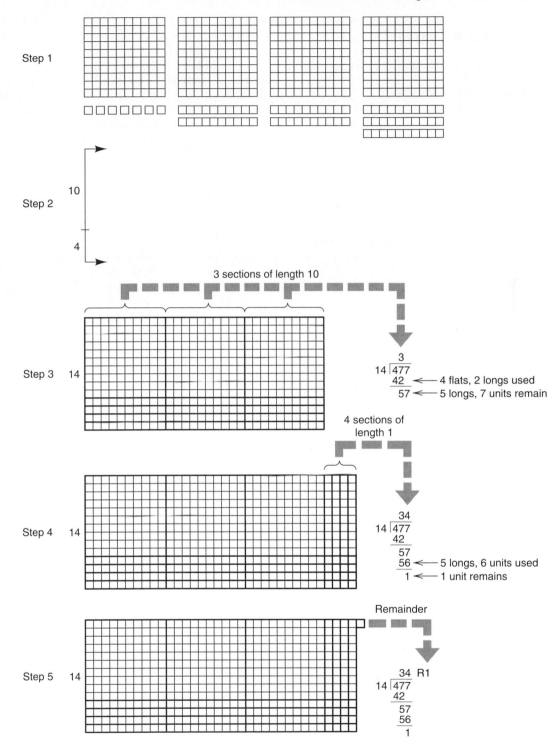

Step 1

Step 2

10

4

3 sections of length 10

Step 3   14

$$\begin{array}{r} 3 \\ 14\overline{)477} \\ \underline{42} \\ 57 \end{array}$$

← 4 flats, 2 longs used

← 5 longs, 7 units remain

4 sections of length 1

Step 4   14

$$\begin{array}{r} 34 \\ 14\overline{)477} \\ \underline{42} \\ 57 \\ \underline{56} \\ 1 \end{array}$$

← 5 longs, 6 units used

← 1 unit remains

Remainder

Step 5   14

$$\begin{array}{r} 34 \; R1 \\ 14\overline{)477} \\ \underline{42} \\ 57 \\ \underline{56} \\ 1 \end{array}$$

JUST FOR FUN

Here are several games and number tricks to try using a calculator.

ARABIAN NIGHTS MYSTERY

Select any three-digit number, such as 837, and enter it on your calculator twice to form a six-digit number (in this case, 837837). Then carry out the following steps: divide this number by 11, then divide the result by 7, and finally divide the result by 13. You may be surprised by the outcome. This trick has been called the Arabian nights mystery because it can be explained by using the number 1001, in reference to the book *Tales from the Thousand and One Nights*. Try this trick for some other three-digit numbers. Explain why it works.

KEYBOARD GAME (2 players)

The first player begins the game by entering a whole number on a calculator. The players then take turns subtracting single-digit numbers, with the following restriction: each player must subtract a nonzero digit, using a button adjacent to the one used by the preceding player. For example, if a player subtracts 6, the next player must subtract 9, 8, 5, 2, or 3. When a player's turn results in a number less than 0, that player loses the game.

MAGIC FORMULAS

Usually if someone asks you to select a number on which to perform some operations, you will choose an easy one. With the aid of a calculator, however, you do not have to be so careful about the number you select. For example, try a three- or four-digit number in the following formula.

- Select any number (remember this number, as it will be needed later), add 221, multiply by 2652, subtract 1326, divide by 663, subtract 870, divide by 4, and subtract the number you started with. Your result will be 3.

Most magic formulas such as the preceding one require that the original number be subtracted in the computation. There is no such requirement in the following formula. This trick, however, will work only on calculators with an eight-digit display and no "hidden digits."

- Select a three-digit number, divide by 9, divide by 10,000,000, multiply by 1,000,000, add 300, divide by 10,000,000, divide by 100, and multiply by 10,000,000. Your result will be 3.

PUZZLER

What is the minimum number of coins that you need to carry to pay the exact amount for any item costing from 1 to 99 cents?

IDEAS FOR THE ELEMENTARY CLASSROOM

SUGGESTED CLASSROOM ACTIVITY: VISUALIZING BASIC OPERATIONS

This activity encourages students to visualize and discuss whole number operations in nonsymbolic ways. It can be done with individuals, small groups, or the entire class, at all grade levels. Distribute about 24 tiles to each student. Write $24 \div 6$ on the chalkboard or overhead, and ask the students to make up a story about that expression, representing the story with their tiles. Encourage creativity and individuality as you walk around the classroom and acknowledge the representations. Then ask the students to share their stories and tile representations with the class. If the two representations below do not occur among the many representations, you might give them a story (to represent with the tile) so that both the *sharing* and *measurement* interpretations of division are represented.

Do similar activities for expressions such as 3×5, $7 + 6$, and $13 - 7$. You may be surprised by the many different interpretations.[2]

Readings for More Classroom Ideas

Bennett, A., E. Maier, and L. Ted Nelson, "Modeling Whole Numbers," in *Math and the Mind's Eye* (Unit III). Salem, OR: The Math Learning Center, Box 3226, 1988.

Bohan, Harry, and P. H. Shawaker. "Using Manipulatives Effectively: A Drive Down Rounding Road." *Arithmetic Teacher* 41 (January 1994): 246–248.

Burton, Grace M., et al. *Number Sense and Operations*, in the *Curriculum and Evaluation Standards for School Mathematics Addenda Series: Grades K–6*. Reston, VA: National Council of Teachers of Mathematics, 1993.

Englert, Gail, and R. Sinicrope. "Making Connections with Two-Digit Multiplication." *Arithmetic Teacher* 41 (April 1994): 446–448.

Graeber, Anna O. "Research into Practice: Misconceptions About Multiplication and Division." *Arithmetic Teacher* 40 (March 1993): 408–411.

Joslyn, Ruth E. "Using Concrete Models to Teach Large-Number Concepts." *Arithmetic Teacher* 38 (November 1990): 6–9.

[2]See A. Bennett, E. Maier, and L. Ted Nelson, "Basic Operations," in *Math and the Mind's Eye* (Unit II, Activity I), (Salem, OR: The Math Learning Center, Box 3226, 1988).

Rathmell, Edward C. and Larry Leutzinger. "Implementing the Standards: Number Representations and Relationships." *Arithmetic Teacher* 38 (March 1991): 20–23.

Reys, Barbara J., et al. *Developing Number Sense,* in the *Curriculum and Evaluation Standards for School Mathematics Addenda Series: Grades 5–8.* Reston, VA: National Council of Teachers of Mathematics, 1991.

Ross, Rita, and Ray Kurtz. "Making Manipulatives Work: A Strategy for Success." *Arithmetic Teacher* 40 (January 1993): 254–257.

Sutton, John T., and Tonya Urbatsch. "Transition Boards: A Good Idea Made Better." *Arithmetic Teacher* 38 (January 1991): 4–8.

Thompson, Frances. "Two-Digit Addition and Subtraction: What Works?" *Arithmetic Teacher* 38 (January 1991): 10–13.

Van Erp, Jos W. M. "The Power of Five: An Alternative Model." *Arithmetic Teacher* 38 (April 1991): 48–53.

Zepp, Raymond A. "Numbers and Codes in Ancient Peru: The Quipi." *Arithmetic Teacher* 39 (May 1992): 42–44.

CHAPTER 4

NUMBER

THEORY

Number theory offers many rich opportunities for explorations that are interesting, enjoyable, and useful.

. . . Challenging but accessible problems from number theory can be easily formulated and explored by students. For example, building rectangular arrays with a set of tile can stimulate questions about divisibility and prime, composite, square, even, and odd numbers. . . .[1]

ACTIVITY SET 4.1

MODELS FOR EVEN NUMBERS, ODD NUMBERS, FACTORS, AND PRIMES

Purpose To use models to provide visual images of basic concepts of number theory

Materials Colored tiles from the Manipulative Kit

Activity Some problems in number theory are simple enough for children to understand yet unsolvable by mathematicians. Maybe that is why this branch of mathematics has intrigued so many people, novices and professionals alike, for over 2000 years. For example, is it true that every *even number* greater than 4 can be expressed as the sum of two *odd prime numbers?* It is true for the first few even numbers:

$$6 = 3 + 3 \qquad 8 = 3 + 5 \qquad 10 = 5 + 5 \qquad 12 = 5 + 7 \qquad 14 = 7 + 7 \qquad 16 = 3 + 13$$

However, mathematicians have not been able to prove it is true for all even numbers greater than 4.

[1]*Curriculum and Evaluation Standards for School Mathematics* (Reston, VA: National Council of Teachers of Mathematics, 1989), 91–93.

The ideas of odd, even, factors, and primes are basic concepts of number theory. In this activity set, these ideas will be given geometric form to show that visual images can be associated with them.

Even and Odd Numbers

1. The nonzero whole numbers can be represented geometrically in many different ways. Here the first five consecutive numbers are represented as a sequence of tile figures. Extend the sequence by drawing the figures for the numbers 6, 7, and 13.

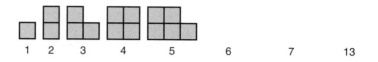

Describe, in your own words, how the figures for the even counting numbers differ from those for the odd counting numbers in the sequence above.

2. Here is a sequence for the first four *even numbers*.

a. Draw the figure for the seventh even number. What is the seventh even number?

Seventh even number _____

★ b. Describe in words what the figure for the 125th even number would look like. What is the 125th even number?

125th even number _____

c. Describe in words what the figure for the *n*th even number would look like. Write a mathematical expression for the *n*th even number.

nth even number _____

3. This sequence represents the first four *odd numbers.*

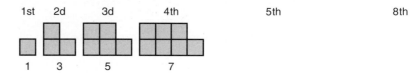

a. Draw the figures for the fifth and eighth odd numbers. What are the fifth and eighth odd numbers?

Fifth odd number _____

Eighth odd number _____

★ **b.** Describe in words how to draw the figure representing the 15th odd number. What is the 15th odd number?

15th odd number _____

c. Determine the 50th, 100th, and nth odd numbers by imagining what their figures would look like, based on the preceding sequence.

50th odd number _____   100th odd number _____ nth odd number _____

★ **d.** When the odd numbers, beginning with 1, are arranged in consecutive order, 7 is in the fourth position and 11 is in the sixth position. In what position is 79? 117? (Hint: Think about the figures for these numbers. You may wish to draw a rough sketch of the figures.)

79 is in the _____ position.   117 is in the _____ position.

4. With these models of odd and even numbers in mind, what can you say about the *oddness* or *evenness* of each of the following? Explain your answers, and draw a diagram to illustrate your explanation.

a. The sum of any two even numbers

★ **b.** The sum of any two odd numbers

c. The sum of any two consecutive whole numbers

d. The sum of any three consecutive whole numbers

★ e. The difference of any two odd numbers

f. The sum of any three odd numbers and two even numbers

5. The figures in the sequence for consecutive odd numbers can be rearranged as follows:

a. The L-shaped figures for the first five consecutive odd numbers can be pushed together to form a square. What does this tell you about the sum of the first five consecutive odd numbers?

★ **b.** Visualize the L-shaped figures for the first 10 consecutive odd numbers. What size square can be formed from these figures? What is the sum of the first 10 consecutive odd numbers?

c. Consider the sum of all odd numbers from 1 to 79.

$$1 + 3 + 5 + 7 + \cdots + 77 + 79$$

How many numbers are there? Determine the sum of the consecutive odd numbers from 1 to 79 by visualizing L-shaped figures forming a square.

Factors and Primes

6. All possible rectangular arrays that can be constructed with exactly 4 tiles, exactly 7 tiles, and exactly 12 tiles are diagrammed below. Use the tiles from your Manipulative Kit to form all possible rectangular arrays that can be constructed for the remaining numbers from 1 to 12 (remember a square is a rectangle). Record them in the spaces provided below.

Rectangles with 1 tile   Rectangles with 2 tiles   Rectangles with 3 tiles

Rectangles with 4 tiles   Rectangles with 5 tiles   Rectangles with 6 tiles

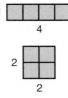

Rectangles with 7 tiles   Rectangles with 8 tiles   Rectangles with 9 tiles

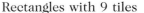

Rectangles with 10 tiles   Rectangles with 11 tiles   Rectangles with 12 tiles

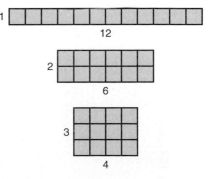

7. The dimensions of a rectangular array are factors of the number the array represents. For example, the number 12 has a 1×12 array, a 2×6 array, and a 3×4 array, and the factors of 12 are 1, 2, 3, 4, 6, and 12. Use your results from activity 6 to complete the following table by listing all the factors of each number and the total number of factors.

NUMBER	FACTORS	NUMBER OF FACTORS
1	_____	_____
2	_____	_____
3	_____	_____
4	1, 2, 4	3
5	_____	_____
6	_____	_____
7	1, 7	2
8	_____	_____
9	_____	_____
10	_____	_____
11	_____	_____
12	1, 2, 3, 4, 6, 12	6

8. Numbers with more than one rectangle, such as 12 and 4, are called *composite numbers*. Except for the number 1, all numbers that have exactly one rectangle are called *prime numbers*.

   a. Write a sentence or two to explain how you can describe prime and composite numbers in terms of *numbers of factors*.

★ **b.** How does the number 1 differ from the prime and composite numbers?

   c. Is there another number, like 1, that is neither prime nor composite? Explain why or why not in terms of rectangles.

   d. Some numbers are called *square numbers* or *perfect squares*. Look at the sketches in activity 6. Which numbers from 1 to 12 do you think could be called square numbers? State your reason.

★ e. Examine the rectangles representing numbers that have an odd number of factors. What conclusions can you draw about numbers that have an odd number of factors?

9. The numbers listed in your chart have 1, 2, 3, 4, or 6 factors.

   a. Identify a number that has exactly 5 factors. Are there other numbers with exactly 5 factors? Explain.

   b. Find two numbers which have more rectangles than the number 12. What are the factors of each of these numbers?

★ 10. The numbers 6, 10, and 15 each have exactly 4 factors. Looking at the rectangles for those numbers, determine what special characteristics the numbers with exactly 4 factors possess. List a few more numbers with exactly 4 factors, and explain how you could generate even more.

JUST FOR FUN

NUMBER CHART PRIMES AND MULTIPLES

A seventh-grade student, Keith, chose to do a math project based on identifying prime numbers with the sieve of Eratosthenes.[2] Keith's twist to the sieve added extra information. He used a number chart like the one here and put a triangle around 1 because it is neither prime nor composite. Then he circled 2 because it was prime and then put a black dot above each multiple of 2. Next he moved from 2 to the next undotted number, 3, circled 3 and put a blue dot to the right of each multiple of 3.

The chart below has been started using Keith's method. The multiples of 2 have a black dot above them. Circle 3 and put a blue dot to the right of each multiple of 3. Circle 5 and put a green dot beneath all multiples of 5. Circle 7 and put a red dot to the left of all multiples of 7. Finally, circle all the remaining numbers which have no colored dots in their squares.

1. How can we be sure that all the circled numbers are prime?
2. How can you use the chart to find all numbers which are multiples of 3 and 5?
3. Keith's chart actually included all numbers up to 1000. How many different colors did he use?

△1	②2	3	•4	5	•6	7	•8	9	•10
11	•12	13	•14	15	•16	17	•18	19	•20
21	•22	23	•24	25	•26	27	•28	29	•30
31	•32	33	•34	35	•36	37	•38	39	•40
41	•42	43	•44	45	•46	47	•48	49	•50
51	•52	53	•54	55	•56	57	•58	59	•60
61	•62	63	•64	65	•66	67	•68	69	•70
71	•72	73	•74	75	•76	77	•78	79	•80
81	•82	83	•84	85	•86	87	•88	89	•90
91	•92	93	•94	95	•96	97	•98	99	•100
101	•102	103	•104	105	•106	107	•108	109	•110
111	•112	113	•114	115	•116	117	•118	119	•120

△ neither prime nor composite

○ prime numbers

black dot   multiple of 2
blue dot   multiple of 3
green dot   multiple of 5
red dot   multiple of 7

[2]C. L. Bradford, "Keith's Secret Discovery of the Sieve of Eratosthenes," *Arithmetic Teacher* 21 (March 1974): 239–241.

PUZZLER

Change the coins from the arrangement shown in the top row to the one shown in the bottom row by moving one pair of coins at a time. On each move, you may slide a pair of adjacent coins to a new position in the row without interchanging them.

ACTIVITY SET 4.2

MODELS FOR GREATEST COMMON FACTOR AND LEAST COMMON MULTIPLE

Purpose To use a linear model to illustrate the concepts of greatest common factor and least common multiple and show how they are related

Materials No supplementary materials are needed.

Activity Greatest common factor (GCF) and least common multiple (LCM) are important concepts that occur frequently in mathematics. The GCF of two numbers is usually introduced by listing all the factors of two numbers, identifying the *common factors,* and then choosing the *greatest* of the common factors.

Factors of 12:   1, 2, 3, 4, ⑥, 12

Factors of 18:   1, 2, 3, ⑥, 9, 18

The LCM of two numbers if often introduced by listing multiples of each number, identifying *common multiples,* and choosing the *least* of the common multiples.

Multiples of 12:   12, 24, ㊱, 48, 60, 72, 84, 96, 108, 120, 132, 144, . . .

Multiples of 18:   18, ㊱, 54, 72, 90, 108, 126, 144, 162, 180, 198, . . .

In this activity set, the concepts of GCF and LCM will be visually represented by rods. The GCF will be viewed as the greatest common length into which two (or more) rods can be cut.

The LCM will be viewed as the shortest common length into which two (or more) rods will fit. This will be determined by placing copies of each rod end to end.

Greatest Common Factor

1. Here are rods of length 36 units and 54 units. Both rods can be cut evenly into pieces with a common length of 6 units.

a. There are five other ways to cut both rods evenly into pieces of common length. Mark those on the following five pairs of rods.

★ b. Because rods of length 36 and 54 can both be cut evenly into pieces of length 6, 6 is called a *common factor* of 36 and 54. List the other common factors of 36 and 54.

Common factors of 36 and 54: 6, _____ , _____ , _____ , _____ , _____

c. Circle the *greatest common factor*[3] of 36 and 54. The greatest common factor of 36 and 54 is abbreviated as GCF(36, 54).

2. Determine the greatest common factor of each pair of numbers below by indicating how you would cut the rods into common pieces of greatest length. Record your answer next to the diagram.

a. 36 / 24   GCF (36, 24) =

★ b. 18 / 25   GCF (18, 25) =

c. 42 / 28   GCF (42, 28) =

3. When two rods are cut into greatest common pieces, as in the activity above, the longer rod is always cut at a point coinciding with the length of the shorter rod. Explain why this happens. Draw a diagram to illustrate your explanation.

---

[3]Also commonly called the *greatest common divisor* or GCD.

4. a. Determine the greatest common factor of the numbers 20 and 12 by indicating how you would cut the two rods below into pieces of greatest common length.

b. The amount by which one rod exceeds the other is represented by the *difference rod*. Determine the GCF of the difference rod and the shorter rod using the diagram below.

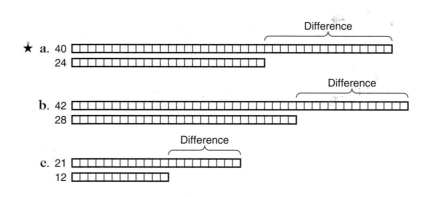

5. For each pair of rods shown below, determine the GCF of the shorter rod and the difference rod. Indicate how you would cut the rods on the diagrams below.

★ **a.** 40

24

Difference

b. 42

28

Difference

c. 21

12

Difference

6. Why do you think that the GCF of two numbers is equal to the GCF of their difference and the smaller number? Use a diagram with rods to explain.

7. The GCF of two numbers can be determined by computing the difference of the two numbers and then finding the GCF of the difference and the smaller of the two numbers. If the GCF of the smaller numbers is not apparent, this method of taking differences can be continued. For example,

$$GCF(78, 60) = GCF(18, 60) = GCF(18, 42) = GCF(18, 24)$$

$$= GCF(18, 6) = GCF(12, 6) = GCF(6, 6) = 6$$

and

$$\text{GCF}(198, 126) = \text{GCF}(72, 126) = \text{GCF}(72, 54) = \text{GCF}(18, 54)$$
$$= \text{GCF}(18, 36) = \text{GCF}(18, 18) = 18$$

Find the GCF of the following pairs of numbers.

a. 144, 27

★ b. 280, 168

c. 714, 420

★ d. 306, 187

Least Common Multiple

8. In the following diagram, the numbers 3 and 5 are represented by rods. When the rods of length 3 are arranged end to end alongside a similar arrangement of rods of length 5, the distances at which the ends evenly match are *common multiples* of 3 and 5 (15, 30, 45, etc.). The least distance at which they match, 15, is the *least common multiple* of 3 and 5. This least common multiple is written LCM(3, 5) = 15.

Find the LCM of each of the following pairs of numbers by drawing the minimum number of end-to-end rods of each length needed to make both rows the same length.

a. 8
   12

★ b. 14
     21

c. 5
   7

★ d. 8
     10

9. There is a relationship between the GCF and the LCM of two numbers. The first figure below shows the numbers 6 and 15; GCF(6, 15) = 3 is indicated by marks on the rods. The second figure shows that LCM(6, 15) = 30.

a. GCF(6, 15) = 3 and 3 divides the 6-unit rod into 2 parts and the 15-unit rod into 5 parts. Notice that 2 rods of length 15 and 5 rods of length 6 show that the LCM(6, 15) is 30. Use the rod diagrams in activity 8 to study the relationship between the GCD and LCM as you complete the following table.

	A	B	GCF (A, B)	LCM (A, B)
(1)	6	15	3	30
(2)	8	12	_____	_____
★ (3)	14	21	_____	_____
(4)	5	7	_____	_____
★ (5)	8	10	_____	_____

b. Based on your observations from part a, write a brief set of directions for finding the LCM of two numbers once you have determined the GCD.

10. For each of the following pairs of numbers, first compute the GCF of the pair and then use that information to compute the LCM.

★ a. 9, 15

GCF(9, 15) =

LCM(9, 15) =

b. 8, 18

GCF(8, 18) =

LCM(8, 18) =

★ **c.** 14, 35

GCF(14, 35) =

LCM(14, 35) =

d. 35, 42

GCF(35, 42) =

LCM(35, 42) =

· ·

JUST FOR FUN

STAR POLYGONS

Star polygons are often constructed to provide decorative and artistic patterns. The star polygon pictured here was formed from colored string and 16 equally spaced tacks on a piece of plywood. In the following activities, these patterns are analyzed by using the concepts of factor, multiple, greatest common factor, and least common multiple.[4]

p, after having hit all 14 points. The resulting figure is a star polygon.

In general, for whole numbers n and s, star (n, s) will denote a star polygon with n points and steps of s, provided that $s < n$. In the special cases where $s = 1$ or $s = n - 1$, the resulting figure will be a polygon.

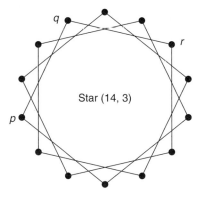

Star (14, 3)

Star polygons can be constructed by taking steps of a given size around a circle of points. Star (14, 3) was constructed by beginning at point p and taking a step of 3 spaces to point q. Three spaces from q is point r. Through this process we eventually come back to point

★ **1.** Sketch the following star polygons by beginning at point x and taking steps of s in a clockwise direction. Will the same star polygons be obtained if the steps are taken in a counterclockwise direction?

[4]A. B. Bennett, Jr., "Star Patterns," *Arithmetic Teacher* 25 (January 1978), 12–14.

Star (8, 3)   Star (9, 4)   Star (7, 2)   Star (7, 4)

★ **2.** Sketch the following pairs of star polygons. Make a conjecture about star *(n, s)* and star *(n, r)*, where *r + s = n*.

Star (12, 5)   Star (12, 7)   Star (10, 3)   Star (10, 7)

★ **3.** The star polygons in activities 1 and 2 can each be completed by beginning at any point and drawing one continuous path. In each of those examples, the path returns to the starting point after hitting all points. For star (15, 3), however, the path closes after hitting only 5 points. To complete this star, 3 different paths are needed. Determine the number of different paths for each of the following star polygons.

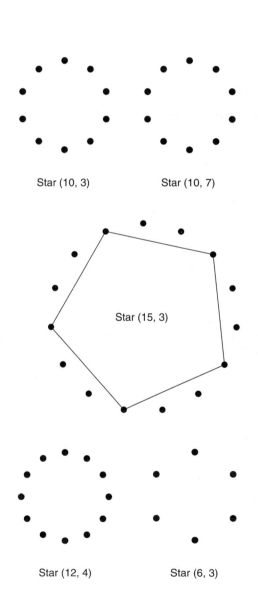

Star (15, 3)

Star (5, 1)   Star (10, 4)   Star (12, 4)   Star (6, 3)

★ **4.** What conditions must n and s satisfy in order for star (n, s) to be formed with 1 continuous path? Use your conjecture to sketch the 15-point star polygons that can be formed by 1 continuous path. There are 4 of these star polygons. Star $(15, 1)$, which is congruent to star $(15, 14)$, is one of them. Determine and sketch the remaining three star polygons, and write the number of steps for each.

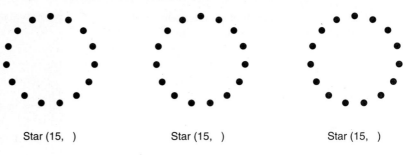

Star (15,)   Star (15,)   Star (15,)

★ **5.** Star $(14, 3)$ was constructed by beginning at point p and taking steps of 3 to points q, r, s, t, and so forth. After point t, the next step of 3 completes 1 *orbit* of the circle (once around the circle) and starts us on the second orbit. It takes 3 orbits before the path returns to its starting point. For the following star polygons, how many orbits are needed before a given path will return to its starting point?

Star (14, 3)

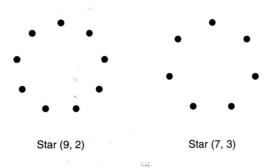

Star (9, 2)   Star (7, 3)   Star (14, 4)

6. Star $(7, 3)$ was drawn by starting at point 1 and connecting the points in the following order: 1, 4, 7, 3, 6, 2, 5, and 1. Three orbits are needed to complete this star. The number of orbits is just the number of times we need to go around the 7 points of the circle before the steps of 3 bring us back to the beginning point. That is, after taking steps of 3 for 21 spaces, we arrive back at the beginning point. The 21 spaces represent the least common multiple of 7 and 3.

Star (7, 3)

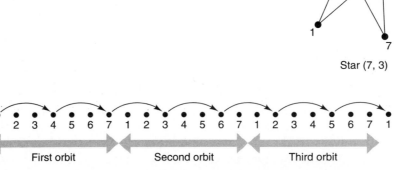

a. Explain how the concept of least common multiple can be used to determine the number of orbits for 1 path of star (15, 6). Check your answer.

★ **b.** Make a conjecture about the number of orbits needed to complete 1 path for star *(n, s)*.

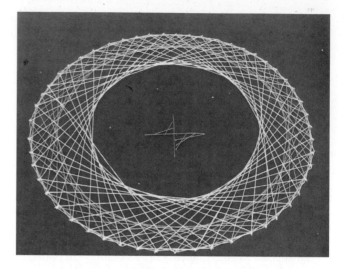

7. Create a star polygon. Any number of points may be used; they do not have to lie on a circle. Star polygons can be made by drawing with colored pencils (different colors for steps of different sizes) or by using colored thread or yarn. With a needle and thread, they can be stitched on posterboard. Several star polygons can be formed on the same set of points. Three star polygons have been stitched from 52 holes on the black posterboard pictured here. One star polygon is made from orange thread with steps of 2, another from green thread with steps of 10, and a third from yellow thread with steps of 15.

a. The star polygon with steps of 15 is the only one that can be constructed by 1 continuous path. Why?

★ **b.** How many orbits are needed to complete star (52, 15)?

· ·

PUZZLER

From a group of 10 people, can you form more committees of 2 or more committees of 8?

IDEAS FOR THE ELEMENTARY CLASSROOM

SUGGESTED CLASSROOM ACTIVITY: ODD-EVEN CLASS MODELS

Make several large demonstration (generic) odd and even cards, like those shown below, out of cardstock. Vary the lengths of the cards you make. These cards have no particular number value and can be used in a variety of ways as a physical model for odd and even numbers.

1. Students can use the cards to illustrate their answers to questions like "Is the sum of three odd numbers odd or even?" (See Activity Set 4.1, problem 4.)
2. Students may use the cards to make up questions of their own about odd and even numbers.

(continued)

(concluded)

3. You may use the cards as models for problem-solving situations you invent: "I'm thinking of two consecutive whole numbers whose sum is 77. What can you tell me about these numbers?"[5]

Even card

Odd card

[5]See A. Bennett, E. Maier, and L. Ted Nelson, "Odd and Even Numbers," in *Math and the Mind's Eye* (Unit II, Activity II), (Salem, OR: The Math Learning Center, Box 3226, 1988).

Readings for More Classroom Ideas

Beattie, Ian D. "Building Understanding with Blocks." *Arithmetic Teacher* 34 (October 1986): 5–11.

Bennett, A., E. Maier, and L. Ted Nelson. "Visualizing Number Concepts," in *Math and the Mind's Eye* (Unit II). Salem, OR: The Math Learning Center, Box 3226, 1988.

Cavanaugh, W. "The Spirograph and the Greatest Common Factor." *The Mathematics Teacher* 68 (February 1975): 162–163.

Fitzgerald, William M., and Jane Boyd. "Teacher to Teacher: A Number Line with Character." *Arithmetic Teacher* 41 (March 1994): 368–369.

Fitzgerald, William, Glenda Lappan, Elizabeth Phillips, and Mary Winter. *Factors and Multiples.* Middle Grades Mathematics Project. Menlo Park, CA: Addison-Wesley Publishing Company, 1986.

Newton, Clarie M., and S. Turkel. "Integrating Arithmetic and Geometry with Numbered Points on a Circle." *Arithmetic Teacher* 36 (January 1989): 28–31.

Robold, Alice I. "Patterns in Multiples." *Arithmetic Teacher* 29 (April 1982): 21–23.

Rockwell, C. "Another 'Sieve' for Prime Numbers." *Arithmetic Teacher* 20 (November 1973): 603–605.

Schaefer, Sister M. G. "Motivational Activities in Elementary Mathematics." *Arithmetic Teacher* 28 (May 1981): 17–18.

CHAPTER 5

INTEGERS AND FRACTIONS

Fraction symbols, such as $\frac{1}{4}$ and $\frac{3}{2}$, should be introduced only after children have developed the concepts and oral language necessary for symbols to be meaningful and should be carefully connected to both the models and oral language.[1]

ACTIVITY SET 5.1

MODELS FOR OPERATIONS WITH INTEGERS

Purpose To use black and red tiles to provide a model for adding, subtracting, multiplying, and dividing integers

Materials Black and red tiles from the Manipulative Kit

Activity The *integers* (sometimes called *positive and negative numbers* or *signed numbers*) are the numbers . . . $^-6$, $^-5$, $^-4$, $^-3$, $^-2$, $^-1$, 0, $^+1$, $^+2$, $^+3$, $^+4$, $^+5$, $^+6$. . . . Two thousand years ago, the Chinese dealt with positive and negative numbers by using black and red rods. We will use a similar model, black and red tiles, to illustrate addition, subtraction, multiplication, and division of integers. Black tiles will represent positive numbers and red tiles will represent negative numbers.

In this model every collection of red and black tiles has a *net value*. The *net value* of a collection is the number of red or black tiles remaining after all possible red and black tiles have been matched. An excess of red tiles will be designated by a negative integer, as in figure 1 below, and an excess of black tiles by a positive integer as in figure 2. The + and − signs are usually written as superscripts so as not to be confused with adding and subtracting.

[1]*Curriculum and Evaluation Standards for School Mathematics* (Reston, VA: National Council of Teachers of Mathematics, 1989), 58.

Net value ⁻3   Net value ⁺4

Using this model every integer can be represented in many ways. For example, the following three collections of tiles each have a net value of ⁻2 because when pairs of red and black are matched there is an excess of 2 red tiles in each collection.

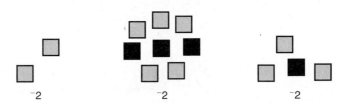

⁻2   ⁻2   ⁻2

If there are the same number of black tiles as there are red tiles in a collection, the collection has *net value 0*. In this case the positive integer for the black tiles and the negative integer for the red tiles are called *opposites* of each other.

1. Take a small handful of red and black tiles (from the Manipulative Kit) and drop them on a flat surface. Record the information about your collection in part a of the following table. Repeat the above directions three times and record the information in parts b, c, and d.

	TOTAL NUMBER OF TILES	NUMBER OF RED TILES	NUMBER OF BLACK TILES	NET VALUE
a.	_____	_____	_____	_____
b.	_____	_____	_____	_____
c.	_____	_____	_____	_____
d.	_____	_____	_____	_____

2. The following table contains partial results from collections of red and black tile that have been dropped. Use your red and black tiles to determine the missing table entries.

	TOTAL NUMBER OF TILES	NUMBER OF RED TILES	NUMBER OF BLACK TILES	NET VALUE
★ a.	_____	8	29	_____
b.	42	26	_____	_____
★ c.	_____	_____	14	8
d.	17	_____	_____	5
e.	20	_____	_____	⁻4
★ f.	_____	_____	11	⁻2

Addition

3. The following two collections represent the integers $^-3$ and $^+2$, respectively. Form each collection with your tiles. Combine the two collections to determine the sum, $^-3 + {}^+2$. What integer represents the sum of the two collections?

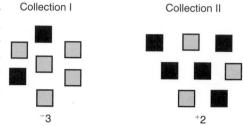

Collection I   Collection II

$^-3$ $^+2$

a. Represent $^-3$ with the fewest number of tiles. Do the same for $^+2$. Sketch these collections and show that, when combined, they represent the same sum as in the preceding figure.

b. Use your red and black tiles to determine these sums. Draw a sketch to indicate how you got your answer.

$^+7 + {}^-3 =$

$^-4 + {}^-3 =$

$^-8 + {}^+2 =$

★ c. Try to visualize black and red tiles as you determine these sums.

$^+50 + {}^-37 =$ $^-34 + {}^- 25 =$ $^-132 + {}^+70 =$

4. Write directions that will enable the reader to do the following. (You may wish to use the black and red tile terminology in your directions.)

a. Add any two negative integers.

★ **b.** Add a positive integer and a negative integer.

Subtraction

5. The collections A and B show one way to compute $^+5 - {}^+8$ with black and red tiles. It is not possible to take 8 black tiles from collection A, but collection A can be changed to collection B by adding 3 black tiles and 3 red tiles. Collection B still represents 5, but now 8 black tiles can be removed to determine that $^+5 - {}^+8 = {}^-3$.

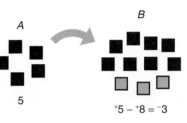

Use your tiles to form the following collections. Then change each collection to one that represents the same number but has enough tiles so that the appropriate number of tiles can be taken away. In each example, sketch the new collection. Use the results to complete the equations.

a. Change this collection so that 3 black tiles can be taken away.

$$^-4 - {}^+3 =$$

★ **b.** Change this collection so that 2 red tiles can be taken away.

$$^+5 - {}^-2 =$$

c. Change this collection so that 5 black tiles can be taken away.

$$^-3 - {}^+5 =$$

★ **6.** Explain how parts a, b, and c of activity 5 can be used to show that subtraction can be performed by adding opposites. That is, taking away a given number of one color is the same as adding the same number of the opposite color. Symbolically this is written $a - b = a + {}^-b$. (*Hint:* Reconstruct the sets in parts a, b, and c with your black and red tiles and watch what happens when you bring in extra tiles and then subtract.)

Multiplication[2]

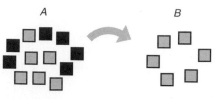

7. The red and black tiles can be used to illustrate a model for multiplication if we agree that in the product $n \times s$, n tells the number of times we *put in* (+) or *take out* (−) s red or black tiles. For example, $^-2 \times {}^+3$ means that 2 times we take out 3 black chips. This changes set A, which represents 0, to set B, which represents $^-6$. This shows that $^-2 \times {}^+3 = {}^-6$.

For each of the following activities, start with a collection of 8 red and 8 black tiles. Make the described changes to the collection. Sketch the resulting collection and record its value. Then write the complete number equation that has been illustrated.

a. Three times, put in 2 red tiles.

★ **b.** Two times, take out 4 red tiles.

c. Three times, take out 2 black tiles.

8. Use your tiles to show how you would illustrate $^-3 \times {}^-4$ with red and black tiles. Illustrate your results by drawing a sketch. Explain how you determined the number of red and black tiles you used in the initial collection.

Division

9. Review the measurement and sharing approaches to whole number division discussed in activity set 3.4.

---

[2]This model for multiplication can be described as the mail-delivery model. Bringing mail to you is a positive action and taking mail from you is a negative action. The mail contains bills for $1 each (debts) or checks for $1 each (assets). The mail carrier can bring (positive) or take away (negative), bills (negative) or checks (positive). Then, for example, $^-2 \times {}^+4$ signifies that 2 times the mail carrier takes away four $1 checks, and your net worth has decreased by $8.

a. Form a collection of 12 red tiles and use the sharing approach to determine the quotient $^-12 \div {}^+3$. Draw a sketch of your tiles to indicate how you obtained your answer.

b. Form a collection of 12 red tiles and use the measurement approach to determine the quotient $^-12 \div {}^-3$. Draw a sketch of your tiles to indicate how you obtained your result.

★ **c.** Explain why neither the sharing nor measurement approach can be used to illustrate $^+12 \div {}^-3$.

10. In whole number arithmetic we know that $6 \div 2 = 3$ because $2 \times 3 = 6$; that is, division can be defined in terms of multiplication. This same approach can be used for integer multiplication.

   a. Show that this approach gives the same answers as the methods in 9a and 9b above.

   b. What answer does it give for 9c?

   ★ **c.** Use any approach you wish to determine the following:

$$^+91 \div {}^-7 = \qquad\qquad ^-4 \div {}^-4 = \qquad\qquad ^-1001 \div {}^+11 =$$

$$^-221 \div {}^-17 = \qquad\qquad 0 \div {}^-9 =$$

JUST FOR FUN

The following four games for negative numbers require two dice, one white and one red. The white die represents positive numbers, and the red die represents negative numbers.

GAME 1 (Addition—2 to 4 players)

Each player begins the game with a marker on the zero point of the number line. On a turn, the player rolls the dice and adds the positive number from the white die to the negative number from the red die. This sum determines the amount of movement on the number line. If it is positive, the marker moves to the right, and if it is negative, the marker moves to the left. If the sum is zero, the player rolls again. The first player to reach either ⁻10 or 10 wins the game. If this game is played at

first by moving the marker separately for each die—to the right for the white die and to the left for the red die—it will quickly lead to the rule for adding positive and negative numbers.

GAME 2 (Addition and subtraction—2 to 3 players)

Each player selects one of the three cards shown below. On a player's turn, the dice are rolled and the two numbers are either added or subtracted. Suppose, for example, that you rolled 4 and ⁻6; you could add 4 + ⁻6 = ⁻2, subtract 4 − ⁻6 = 10, or subtract ⁻6 − 4 = ⁻10. The answer is then marked on the player's card. The first player to complete row, column, or diagonal wins the game.

GAME 1

GAME 2

⁻9	⁻11	⁻1	8	10
12	3	⁻10	⁻2	⁻6
8	⁻12	⁻7	⁻4	⁻5
2	6	11	7	1
⁻3	0	5	9	4

Card 1

5	12	10	⁻1	⁻9
⁻10	⁻3	7	11	⁻8
⁻4	2	4	⁻6	⁻2
9	⁻7	⁻5	⁻11	1
8	6	3	0	⁻12

Card 2

⁻1	⁻7	9	4	⁻6
8	⁻5	11	⁻12	6
⁻11	1	⁻2	7	⁻9
⁻3	10	12	⁻4	3
2	⁻8	5	0	⁻10

Card 3

GAME 3 (Multiplication and inequality—2 to 4 players)

On a turn, the player rolls the dice and multiplies the positive number from the white die by the negative number from the red die. This operation is repeated a second time, and the player selects the greater of the two products. In this example, each player has had four turns. The greater product in each case has been circled. Player B is ahead at this point with the greater score: a total of ⁻12. After 10 rounds, the player with the greater total wins the game.

Chance Option: If a player obtains two undesirable numbers, such as ⁻25 and ⁻15, he or she may use the *chance option,* which involves rolling the dice a third time. If the third product is greater than the other two—say, ⁻12—the player may select this number. If the third product is less than or equal to either of the other two—say, ⁻18—then the smallest of the three numbers (⁻25 in this example) must be kept as the player's score.

GAME 4 (All four basic operations—1 to 4 players)

Roll the dice four times, and record the four negative numbers from the red die and the four positive numbers from the white die. Using each number no more than once, write these eight numbers in the blanks of the equations under Round 1 so that you complete as many equations as possible. Repeat this activity for Round 2 and Round 3. You receive 1 point for each equation. If you complete all four equations for a given round, you receive 4 points plus 2 bonus points. The total number of points for the three rounds is your score.

GAME 1

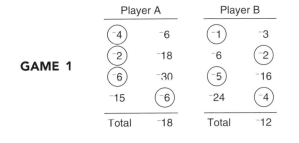

	Player A		Player B	
	⊛⁻4	⁻6	⊛⁻1	⁻3
	⊛⁻2	⁻18	⁻6	⊛⁻2
	⊛⁻6	⁻30	⊛⁻5	⁻16
	⁻15	⊛⁻6	⁻24	⊛⁻4
	Total	⁻18	Total	⁻12

GAME 2

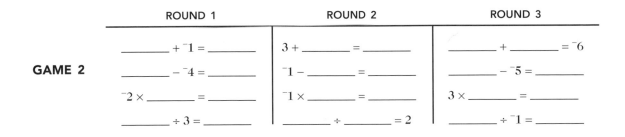

ROUND 1	ROUND 2	ROUND 3
_____ + ⁻1 = _____	3 + _____ = _____	_____ + _____ = ⁻6
_____ − ⁻4 = _____	⁻1 − _____ = _____	_____ − ⁻5 = _____
⁻2 × _____ = _____	⁻1 × _____ = _____	3 × _____ = _____
_____ ÷ 3 = _____	_____ ÷ _____ = 2	_____ ÷ ⁻1 = _____

ACTIVITY SET 5.2

FRACTION MODELS FOR EQUALITY AND INEQUALITY

Purpose To use Fraction Bars to provide a visual model for the *part-to-whole* and *division* concepts of fractions, fraction equality and inequality, and fraction rounding and estimation[3]

Materials Fraction Bars from the Manipulative Kit

Activity The set of Fraction Bars consists of 32 bars divided into 2, 3, 4, 6, or 12 equal parts. The bars are colored (halves—green, thirds—yellow, fourths—blue, sixths—red, and twelfths—orange) so that the user can easily distinguish bars with different numbers of parts. Various fractions are named by shading parts of the bars. For example, the bar to the left represents $\frac{5}{6}$ (five-sixths). The top number in the fraction, the *numerator,* tells the number of shaded parts, and the bottom number, the *denominator,* tells the number of equal parts into which the bar is divided. This model illustrates the *part-to-whole* concept of fractions. It emphasizes the *unit* and models fractions in relation to this unit. The *division* concept of fractions is introduced in activity 10.

A Fraction Bar with all of its parts shaded is called a *whole* bar and equals 1. A bar with no parts shaded is called a *zero bar* and equals zero.

$$\frac{3}{3} = 1 \qquad\qquad \frac{0}{4} = 0$$

1. The fractions for the bars in the figure to the left are equal because both bars have the same amount of shading. In the set of 32 Fraction Bars, there are three bars whose fractions equal $\frac{2}{3}$. Sort your set of bars into piles so that the bars with the same shaded amount are in the same pile.

★ **a.** There are five bars whose fractions are equal to $\frac{0}{4}$. How many bars represent the other fractions listed here?

FRACTION	NUMBER OF BARS WITH EQUAL FRACTIONS
$\frac{0}{4}$	5
$\frac{1}{2}$	_____
$\frac{2}{3}$	_____
$\frac{6}{6}$	_____
$\frac{1}{4}$	_____

[3]Fraction Bars is a registered trademark of Scott Resources, Inc.

b. Complete this table by writing in the sixths, fourths, thirds, and halves that are equal to the twelfths. (Note: Many of the squares will be blank.)

Twelfths	$\frac{0}{12}$	$\frac{1}{12}$	$\frac{2}{12}$	$\frac{3}{12}$	$\frac{4}{12}$	$\frac{5}{12}$	$\frac{6}{12}$	$\frac{7}{12}$	$\frac{8}{12}$	$\frac{9}{12}$	$\frac{10}{12}$	$\frac{11}{12}$	$\frac{12}{12}$
Sixths													
Fourths													
Thirds													
Halves													

2. The $\frac{1}{3}$ bar has more shading than the $\frac{1}{4}$ bar, so $\frac{1}{3}$ is greater than $\frac{1}{4}$. This is written $\frac{1}{3} > \frac{1}{4}$ (or $\frac{1}{4} < \frac{1}{3}$).

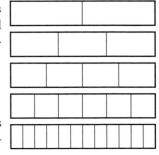

★ **a.** Select the following Fraction Bars from your set of bars:

$$\frac{5}{6}, \frac{1}{4}, \frac{11}{12}, \frac{2}{3}, \frac{1}{6}, \frac{5}{12}, \frac{3}{4}, \frac{1}{3}, \frac{7}{12}, \frac{1}{2}, \text{ and } \frac{1}{12}$$

Place these bars in increasing order from the smallest shaded amount to the largest shaded amount and complete the following inequalities.

$$— < \frac{1}{6} < — < — < — < \frac{1}{2} < — < — < — < — < \frac{11}{12}$$

b. Each of the preceding fractions has a common denominator of 12. Rewrite these inequalities using only fractions with a denominator of 12.

$$— < \frac{2}{12} < — < — < — < — < — < — < — < — < \frac{11}{12}$$

3. By placing the five different types of Fraction Bars in a column, we can visualize many equalities and inequalities. For example, by comparing the vertical lines of these bars, we can see that

$$\frac{1}{2} = \frac{6}{12} \qquad \frac{2}{3} < \frac{3}{4} \qquad \frac{5}{6} = \frac{10}{12}$$

a. List 10 different equalities of pairs of fractions that can be illustrated by comparing the vertical lines of these bars.

★ **b.** List 10 different inequalities of pairs of fractions that can be illustrated by these bars.

4. Many inequalities for fractions can be determined mentally by visualizing the bars representing the fractions. For example, we can determine that $\frac{1}{5}$ is less than $\frac{1}{4}$, because each part of a bar with 5 equal parts is smaller than each part of a bar with 4 equal parts.

Mentally determine the correct inequality sign to put between each pair of fractions. Explain your reasoning in terms of Fraction Bars.

    a. $\dfrac{1}{3}$ $\dfrac{1}{10}$

 ★ **b.** $\dfrac{5}{11}$ $\dfrac{4}{6}$

    c. $\dfrac{2}{3}$ $\dfrac{9}{10}$

 ★ **d.** $\dfrac{1}{50}$ $\dfrac{1}{30}$

5. Rounding fractions to the nearest whole number can be facilitated by sketching or visualizing Fraction Bars. For example, on the bars representing $1\frac{2}{7}$, the shaded amount is closer to 1 whole bar than to 2 whole bars. So to the nearest whole number, $1\frac{2}{7}$ rounds to 1.

On the other hand, on the bars representing $1\frac{4}{7}$, the shaded amount is closer to 2 whole bars than to 1 whole bar. So to the nearest whole number, $1\frac{4}{7}$ rounds to 2.

Round the following fractions to the nearest whole number. Draw a Fraction Bar sketch to justify your answer.

Fraction	Diagram	Nearest whole number

★ **a.** $4\dfrac{3}{7}$ _____

b. $\dfrac{1}{5}$ _____

★ **c.** $\dfrac{13}{16}$ _____

d. $2\dfrac{7}{9}$ _____

6. Each part of this $\frac{3}{4}$ bar has been split into 2 equal parts. There are now 8 parts, and 6 of these are shaded. Because this splitting has neither increased nor decreased the total shaded amount of the bar, both $\frac{3}{4}$ and $\frac{6}{8}$ are fractions for the same amount.

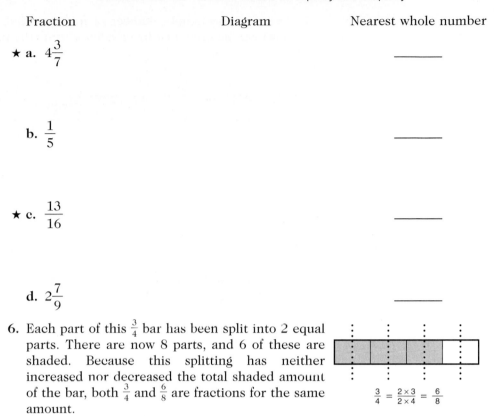

$$\frac{3}{4} = \frac{2 \times 3}{2 \times 4} = \frac{6}{8}$$

★ **a.** Split each part of these bars into 2 equal parts, and complete the equations.

$$\frac{4}{9} = \qquad \frac{3}{10} = \qquad \frac{1}{5} =$$

★ **b.** Split each part of these bars into 3 equal parts, and complete the equations.

$$\frac{6}{7} = \qquad \frac{5}{8} = \qquad \frac{1}{6} =$$

★ **c.** Split each part of these bars into 4 equal parts, and complete the equations.

$$\frac{0}{3} = \qquad \frac{3}{4} = \qquad \frac{1}{2} =$$

d. Suppose that each part of the Fraction Bar for $\frac{x}{y}$ is split into 3 equal parts. How many of the parts will be shaded? How many parts will there be in all? Write the fraction for this bar.

7. There are an infinite number of fractions that are equal to $\frac{2}{3}$. These fractions can be generated by equally splitting the parts of a $\frac{2}{3}$ bar.

$$\frac{2}{3} = \frac{2 \times 2}{2 \times 3} = \frac{4}{6} \qquad \frac{2}{3} = \frac{3 \times 2}{3 \times 3} = \frac{6}{9} \qquad \frac{2}{3} = \frac{4 \times 2}{4 \times 3} = \frac{8}{12}$$

a. If each part of a $\frac{2}{3}$ bar is split into 5 equal parts, what fraction does the bar represent?

★ **b.** If each part of a $\frac{2}{3}$ bar is split into 17 equal parts, what fraction does the bar represent?

c. What effect does splitting each part of any Fraction Bar into 17 equal parts have on the numerator and denominator of the fraction for the bar?

★ **d.** Split each of the following bars to illustrate the given equality.

$$\frac{5}{6} = \frac{10}{12} \qquad\qquad \frac{5}{6} = \frac{15}{18} \qquad\qquad \frac{5}{6} = \frac{20}{24}$$

8. The parts of a $\frac{2}{3}$ bar are bigger than the parts of a $\frac{3}{4}$ bar. If each part of the $\frac{2}{3}$ bar is split into 4 equal parts and each part of the $\frac{3}{4}$ bar is split into 3 equal parts, both bars will then have 12 parts of equal size. The new fractions for these bars will have a common denominator of 12.

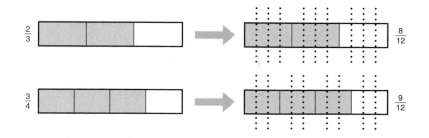

For each of the following pairs of bars, split the parts so that all the new parts are the same size. The corresponding fractions will have the same denominator. Complete the equations.

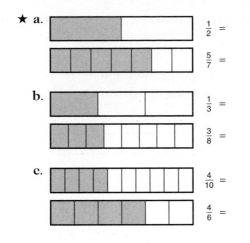

★ a. $\frac{1}{2} =$

     $\frac{5}{7} =$

b. $\frac{1}{3} =$

     $\frac{3}{8} =$

c. $\frac{4}{10} =$

     $\frac{4}{6} =$

9.   Imagine that you have a $\frac{3}{5}$ bar and $\frac{5}{7}$ bar (or draw a sketch to represent them).

   a. When both bars are split so that all parts have the same size, the two fractions will have the same denominators. Complete these equations so that both fractions have the same denominator.

$$\frac{3}{5} = \qquad\qquad \frac{5}{7} =$$

   b. Which is greater, $\frac{3}{5}$ or $\frac{5}{7}$?

     Replace the fractions in each of the following pairs with fractions having the same denominator. Circle the greater fraction in each pair (or state that they are equal).

   c. $\dfrac{1}{3} =$ ★ d. $\dfrac{7}{9} =$ e. $\dfrac{4}{6} =$ ★ f. $\dfrac{11}{15} =$

     $\dfrac{2}{7} =$ $\dfrac{8}{10} =$ $\dfrac{6}{9} =$ $\dfrac{8}{11} =$

10.   The *division* concept of fractions relates quotients of whole numbers to fractions. For example, 3 whole bars are placed end to end to represent the number 3. If this 3 bar is divided into 4 equal parts, each part will be $\frac{3}{4}$ of a whole bar. This shows that $3 \div 4 = \frac{3}{4}$.

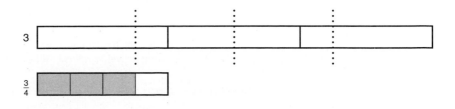

Illustrate each quotient by dividing the given bar into equal parts. Then complete the equation by writing a fraction or mixed number.[4]

a. $3 \div 2 =$

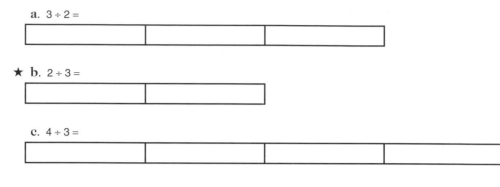

★ **b.** $2 \div 3 =$

c. $4 \div 3 =$

JUST FOR FUN

These two fraction games provide extra practice in comparing fractions. In FRIO[5] you compare unequal fractions, and in Fraction Bingo you search for equal fractions.

FRIO (2 to 4 players)

Each player is dealt five bars in a row face up. These bars should be left in the order in which they are dealt. The remaining bars are spread face down. Each player, in turn, takes a bar that is face down and uses it to replace any one of the five bars. The object of the game is to get five bars in

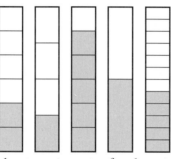

order from the *smallest* shaded amount to the *largest* or from the largest to the *smallest*. In this example the five bars will be in order if the $\frac{2}{6}$ bar is replaced by a whole bar and the $\frac{1}{4}$ bar is replaced by an $\frac{11}{12}$ bar. The first player to get five fraction bars in decreasing or increasing order wins the game.

FRACTION BINGO (2 to 4 players)

Each player selects a fraction bingo mat from those shown below. The deck of 32 bars is spread face down. Each player, in turn, takes a bar and circles the fraction or fractions on his or her mat that equal the fraction from the bar. The first player to circle four fractions in any row, column, or diagonal is the winner.

Strategy: If the bars are colored green, yellow, blue, red, and orange for halves, thirds, fourths, sixths, and twelfths, respectively, you can increase your chances of winning by selecting bars of the appropriate color.

Mat 1

$\frac{4}{6}$	$\frac{1}{6}$	$\frac{0}{4}$	$\frac{11}{12}$
$\frac{5}{12}$	$\frac{1}{4}$	$\frac{5}{6}$	$\frac{3}{6}$
$\frac{3}{4}$	$\frac{1}{12}$	$\frac{1}{3}$	$\frac{11}{12}$
$\frac{6}{12}$	$\frac{4}{4}$	$\frac{9}{12}$	$\frac{10}{12}$

Mat 2

$\frac{1}{3}$	$\frac{1}{4}$	$\frac{1}{6}$	$\frac{0}{3}$
$\frac{7}{12}$	$\frac{0}{6}$	$\frac{1}{12}$	$\frac{4}{6}$
$\frac{2}{3}$.	$\frac{3}{4}$	$\frac{5}{6}$	$\frac{5}{12}$
$\frac{11}{12}$	$\frac{2}{2}$	$\frac{3}{12}$	$\frac{1}{2}$

Mat 3

$\frac{2}{3}$	$\frac{1}{4}$	$\frac{2}{6}$	$\frac{6}{12}$
$\frac{5}{6}$	$\frac{0}{3}$	$\frac{5}{12}$	$\frac{1}{6}$
$\frac{7}{12}$	$\frac{4}{4}$	$\frac{1}{2}$	$\frac{11}{12}$
$\frac{3}{4}$	$\frac{8}{12}$	$\frac{1}{12}$	$\frac{1}{3}$

Mat 4

$\frac{1}{4}$	$\frac{1}{6}$	$\frac{7}{12}$	$\frac{1}{2}$
$\frac{0}{3}$	$\frac{5}{12}$	$\frac{2}{3}$	$\frac{4}{4}$
$\frac{1}{12}$	$\frac{5}{6}$	$\frac{11}{12}$	$\frac{2}{12}$
$\frac{6}{6}$	$\frac{3}{4}$	$\frac{0}{12}$	$\frac{1}{3}$

PUZZLER

At a certain college, $\frac{1}{4}$ of the first-year women students are from homes where both parents are professionals. Of these, $\frac{3}{5}$ are interested in the same profession as one of their parents. The latter group is composed of 18 students. How many first-year women students attend the college?[6]

[4]If long strips of paper are available, the big bars such as the 2 bar (the length of 2 whole bars) and the 3 bar (the length of 3 whole bars) can be cut to actual length. These strips can then be folded to carry out the activities.

[5]R. Drizigacker, "FRIO, or FRactions In Order," *Arithmetic Teacher* 13 (December 1966), 684–685.

[6]From the "April Calendar" of *The Mathematics Teacher* 81 (April 1988), 278–279.

ACTIVITY SET 5.3

COMPUTING WITH FRACTION BARS

Purpose To use Fraction Bars to perform the basic operations of addition, subtraction, multiplication, and division in a visual and intuitive manner

Materials Fraction Bars from the Manipulative Kit

Activity Piaget has charted the cognitive development of preadolescents, and his research indicates that even at the age of 12, most children deal only with symbols that are closely tied to their per-ceptions. For example, the symbolic representa-

$$\frac{1}{6} + \frac{2}{3} = \frac{5}{6}$$

tion $\frac{1}{6} + \frac{2}{3} = \frac{5}{6}$ has meaning for most elementary school children only if they can relate it directly to concrete or pictorial representations.[7]

The following table documents the lack of conceptual understanding of frac-tions and fraction addition exhibited by 13-year-olds when they were asked to estimate the answer to $\frac{12}{13} + \frac{7}{8}$.[8] Over 50 percent of the students responded with the incorrect answers 19 and 21. Why do you think so many students arrived at those incorrect answers?

RESPONSES	PERCENT RESPONDING, AGE 13
○ 1	7
● 2	24
○ 19	28
○ 21	27
○ I don't know	14

Students may learn fraction skills at a rote manipulation level, but when their memory fails or they encounter a nonstandard application, they have no conceptual basis to fall back on.

In this activity set, Fraction Bars will be used to develop visual images of fraction operations. These images can be called forth as needed for computa-tions, estimations, and problem solving.

Addition and Subtraction

1. *Addition and Subtraction:* Write the missing fractions and the sum or dif-ference of the fractions for each pair of bars. Determine your answers by visual inspection of bars, and then check your results by computation.

[7]M. J. Driscoll, "The Role of Manipulatives in Elementary School Mathematics," *Research within Reach: Elementary School Mathematics* (St. Louis, MO.: Cemrel Inc., 1983), 1.
[8]T. P. Carpenter, H. Kepner, M. K. Corbitt, M. M. Lindquist, and R. E. Reys, "Results and Implications of the Second NAEP Mathematics Assessment: Elementary School," *Arithmetic Teacher* 27 (April 1980), 10–12, 44–47.

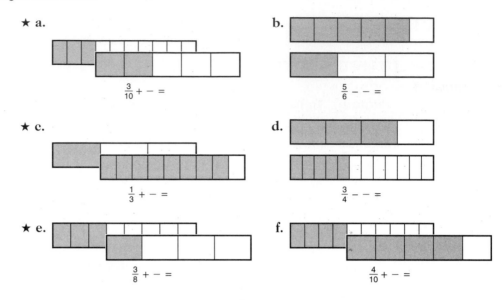

★ a.
$\frac{3}{10} + \underline{} - \underline{} =$

b.
$\frac{5}{6} - \underline{} - \underline{} =$

★ c.
$\frac{1}{3} + \underline{} - \underline{} =$

d.
$\frac{3}{4} - \underline{} - \underline{} =$

★ e.
$\frac{3}{8} + \underline{} - \underline{} =$

f.
$\frac{4}{10} + \underline{} - \underline{} =$

2. Turn your set of bars face down and select any four pairs. Complete the following equations for the sum and difference of each pair of fractions. (Subtract the smaller from the larger if the fractions are unequal.)

_____ + _____ = _____   _____ − _____ = _____

_____ + _____ = _____   _____ − _____ = _____

_____ + _____ = _____   _____ − _____ = _____

_____ + _____ = _____   _____ − _____ = _____

3. *Obtaining Common Denominators:* If each part of the $\frac{2}{3}$ bar is split into 4 equal parts and each part of the $\frac{1}{4}$ bar is split into 3 equal parts, both bars will have 12 parts of the same size. These new bars show that $\frac{2}{3} + \frac{1}{4} = \frac{11}{12}$ and $\frac{2}{3} - \frac{1}{4} = \frac{5}{12}$.

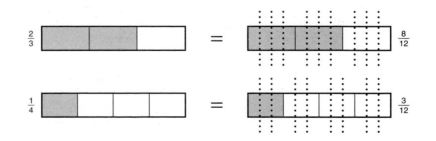

Split the parts of the following Fraction Bars so that each pair of bars has the same number of parts of the same size.

Use the bars from parts a, b, and c above to compute the following sums and differences.

★ d. $\dfrac{5}{6} + \dfrac{1}{4} =$ e. $\dfrac{3}{5} + \dfrac{2}{3} =$ f. $\dfrac{2}{9} + \dfrac{3}{6} =$

★ g. $\dfrac{5}{6} - \dfrac{1}{4} =$ h. $\dfrac{2}{3} - \dfrac{3}{5} =$ i. $\dfrac{3}{6} - \dfrac{2}{9} =$

4. Sketch Fraction Bars for each pair of fractions, and then split the parts of the bars to carry out the operation. Use your diagrams to explain how you reached your conclusions.

★ a. $\dfrac{5}{9} + \dfrac{1}{3}$

b. $\dfrac{1}{4} + \dfrac{3}{5}$

★ c. $\dfrac{2}{5} - \dfrac{1}{3}$

d. $\dfrac{1}{2} - \dfrac{2}{7}$

Multiplication

5. You can determine $\frac{1}{3} \times \frac{1}{6}$ by splitting the shaded part of a $\frac{1}{6}$ bar into 3 equal parts. One of these smaller parts is $\frac{1}{18}$ of a bar, because there are 18 of these parts in a whole bar.

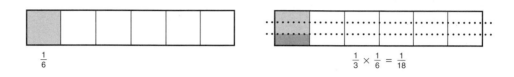

$$\frac{1}{6} \qquad \qquad \frac{1}{3} \times \frac{1}{6} = \frac{1}{18}$$

To multiply $\frac{5}{6}$ times $\frac{2}{4}$, split the shaded part of the $\frac{2}{4}$ bar into 6 equal sections with horizontal lines. Five of these shaded sections equal $\frac{10}{24}$ of the whole bar, because there are 24 small parts in a whole bar.

$$\frac{5}{6} \times \frac{2}{4} = \frac{10}{24}$$

★ **a.** Split the shaded amount of each bar into 2 equal parts. Use this result to complete the given equations.

$$\frac{1}{2} \times \frac{1}{3} = \qquad \frac{1}{2} \times \frac{4}{5} = \qquad \frac{1}{2} \times \frac{6}{8} =$$

★ **b.** Split the shaded amount of each bar into 3 equal parts, and complete the equations.

$$\frac{1}{3} \times \frac{1}{4} = \qquad \frac{2}{3} \times \frac{1}{6} = \qquad \frac{2}{3} \times \frac{9}{10} =$$

★ **c.** Split the shaded amount of each bar into 4 equal parts, and complete the equations.

$$\frac{1}{4} \times \frac{1}{2} = \qquad \frac{3}{4} \times \frac{1}{5} = \qquad \frac{3}{4} \times \frac{8}{9} =$$

6. Sketch a Fraction Bar for $\frac{4}{5}$ and visually determine the product $\frac{2}{3} \times \frac{4}{5}$. Write a description of the procedure you used.

Division

7. Using the *measurement* approach to division (see activity set 3.4), we can write $\frac{1}{2} \div \frac{1}{6} = 3$, because the shaded portion of the $\frac{1}{6}$ bar can be measured off exactly 3 times on the shaded part of the $\frac{1}{2}$ bar.

Similarly, $\frac{5}{6} \div \frac{1}{3} = 2\frac{1}{2}$, because the shaded portion of the $\frac{1}{3}$ bar can be measured off $2\frac{1}{2}$ times on the shaded part of the $\frac{5}{6}$ bar.

Use your Fraction Bars to determine the following quotients.

a. $\dfrac{3}{4} \div \dfrac{1}{12} =$ ★ **b.** $\dfrac{10}{12} \div \dfrac{1}{6} =$

c. $\dfrac{7}{12} \div \dfrac{1}{6} =$ ★ **d.** $1 \div \dfrac{2}{3} =$

e. $\dfrac{3}{2} \div \dfrac{3}{4} =$

Sketch Fraction Bars to determine the following quotients. Use your sketch to explain your reasoning.

★ **f.** $\dfrac{7}{8} \div \dfrac{1}{4} =$

g. $\dfrac{7}{10} \div \dfrac{1}{5} =$

Estimation

8. It is often helpful to draw a sketch or visualize a fraction model when you are trying to estimate with fractions. For example, to estimate the quotient $1\frac{5}{7} \div \frac{1}{8}$, you can compare Fraction Bars representing $1\frac{5}{7}$ to bars representing eighths. There are 8 eighths in 1 whole bar and about 6 eighths in the $\frac{5}{7}$ bar. So, $\frac{1}{8}$ can be measured off about 14 times, and $1\frac{5}{7} \div \frac{1}{8} \approx 14$.

$$1\frac{5}{7} \div \frac{1}{8} \approx 14$$

Use a visual approach to estimate the following fraction operations. Draw Fraction Bar sketches and explain how you arrived at your estimation.

a. $1\frac{3}{4} \div \frac{1}{3}$

★ b. $\frac{5}{8} - \frac{1}{6}$

c. $\frac{4}{5} + \frac{1}{2}$

★ d. $\frac{2}{3} \times \frac{5}{6}$

All Four Operations

9. ★ a. The following 10 fractions are from the Fraction Bars:

$$\frac{1}{6}, \frac{2}{4}, \frac{5}{12}, \frac{2}{6}, \frac{0}{3}, \frac{3}{4}, \frac{3}{12}, \frac{2}{3}, \frac{1}{2}, \frac{1}{4}$$

Using each fraction only once, try placing these fractions in the 10 blanks to form four equations.

$$\underline{} + \underline{} = \underline{} \qquad\qquad 3 \times \underline{} = \underline{}$$

$$\underline{} - \underline{} = \underline{} \qquad\qquad \underline{} \div \underline{} = 2$$

b. Spread your bars face down and select any 10 of them. Using the fraction from each bar only once, complete as many of these four equations as possible. If you cannot form all four equations, continue to select bars, one at a time, until all the equations can be completed.

Fractions selected: _____, _____, _____, _____, _____,

_____, _____, _____, _____, _____

$$\underline{} + \underline{} = \underline{} \qquad\qquad 3 \times \underline{} = \underline{}$$

$$\underline{} - \underline{} = \underline{} \qquad\qquad \underline{} \div \underline{} = 2$$

c. Solitaire: The activity in part b can be played like a solitaire game. See how many turns it takes you to complete the four equations by selecting only 10 bars on each turn.

JUST FOR FUN

These three games challenge you to perform operations on fractions.

FRACTION BAR BLACKJACK (Addition—2 to 4 players)

Spread the bars face down. The object is to select one or more bars so that the fraction or the sum of fractions is as close to 1 as possible, but not greater than 1. The first player selects bars one at a time, trying to get close to 1 without going over. (A player may wish to take only 1 bar.) Player 1 finishes his or her turn by saying "I'm holding." After every player in turn has finished, the players show their bars. The player who is closest to a sum of 1, but not over, wins the round.

Examples: Player 1 has a sum greater than 1 and is over. Player 2 has a greater sum than player 3 and wins the round.

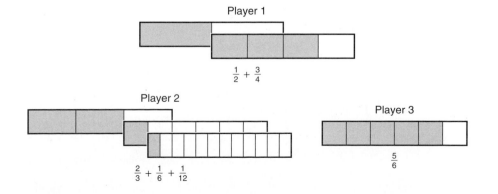

Player 1

$\frac{1}{2} + \frac{3}{4}$

Player 2

$\frac{2}{3} + \frac{1}{6} + \frac{1}{12}$

Player 3

$\frac{5}{6}$

SOLITAIRE (Subtraction)

Spread the Fraction Bars face down. Turn over two bars and compare their shaded amounts. If the difference between the two fractions is less than $\frac{1}{2}$, you win the two bars. If not, you lose the bars. See how many bars you can win by playing through the deck. Will you win the top pair of bars shown here? the bottom pair?

GREATEST QUOTIENT (Division—2 to 4 players)

Remove the zero bars from your set of 32 bars and spread the remaining bars face down. Each player takes two bars. The object of the game is to get the greatest possible quotient by dividing one of the fractions by the other. The greatest *whole* number of times that one fraction divides into the other is the player's score. Each player has the option of taking another bar to improve his or her score or passing. If the player selects another bar, he or she must first discard one bar. The first player to score 21 points wins the game.

Examples: The whole number part of the quotient can be determined by comparing the shaded amounts of the bars. The score for the top two bars is 4, because the shaded amount of the $\frac{2}{3}$ bar is 4 times greater than the shaded amount of the $\frac{1}{6}$ bar. The score for the bottom two bars is 1, because the quotient is greater than 1 but less than 2.

IDEAS FOR THE ELEMENTARY CLASSROOM

SUGGESTED CLASSROOM ACTIVITY: INTEGER BALLOON

An intuitive understanding of a helium balloon is an effective model for beginning positive and negative number concepts. Students can make a balloon model (we'll call it UPORDOWN) like the one that follows (with extra balloons and sandbags that can be attached or taken off) and place it near a vertical scale. It is also convenient to have a model for the overhead so that students can demonstrate their actions. Suppose UPORDOWN is in equilibrium with 10 balloons and 10 sandbags. When 1 balloon is attached, it goes up 1 level; when 2 sandbags are added, it goes down 2 levels; and so forth. Ask the students to demonstrate answers to questions like the following: What happens to UPORDOWN when 3 balloons are detached? 4 sandbags are taken off?

Students can use UPORDOWN to demonstrate sequences of operations as in "adding 4 sandbags and 3 balloons moves the big balloon 1 level down"; "adding 2 balloons and taking away 3 sandbags moves the big balloon 5 levels up." Depending on the backgrounds of your students, these examples might be summarized as

$$4S + 3B = 1 \text{ down} \qquad 2B - 3S = 5 \text{ up}$$

or, with + for B and "up" and minus for S and "down,"

$$^-4 + {}^+3 = {}^-1 \qquad {}^+2 - {}^-3 = {}^+5$$

PUZZLER

Starting with a blank sheet of $8\frac{1}{2}$-by-11-inch paper, you can determine a length of $2\frac{1}{2}$ inches in one fold.

Then by folding the paper in half, you can determine a length of 3 inches. (Note: There are other ways to obtain a length of 3 inches.)

Circle all the remaining lengths in this list that you can obtain by folding the paper.

1    $1\frac{1}{2}$ 2 $\textcircled{2\frac{1}{2}}$ $\textcircled{3}$ $3\frac{1}{2}$ 4 $4\frac{1}{2}$ 5 $5\frac{1}{2}$ 6 $6\frac{1}{2}$
7    $7\frac{1}{2}$ 8 $8\frac{1}{2}$ 9 $9\frac{1}{2}$ 10 $10\frac{1}{2}$ 11

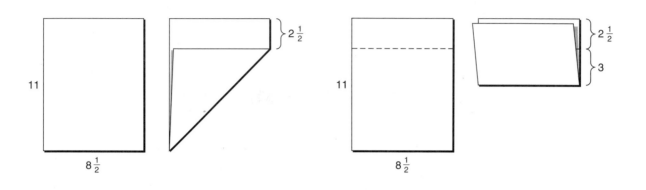

Readings for More Classroom Ideas

Bennett, A., and P. Davidson. *Fraction Bars Step-by-Step Teacher's Guide.* Fort Collins, CO: Scott Resources, Inc., 1982.

Bennett, A., E. Maier, and L. Ted Nelson. "Modeling Rationals" and "Modeling Integers," in *Math and the Mind's Eye* (Units IV and VI). Salem, OR: The Math Learning Center, Box 3226, 1988.

Caldwell, Janet H. "Communicating About Fractions with Pattern Blocks." *Teaching Children Mathematics* 2 (November 1995): 156–161.

Cramer, Kathleen, and Nadine Bezuk. "Multiplication of Fractions: Teaching for Understanding." *Arithmetic Teacher* 39 (November 1991): 34–37.

Curcio, Frances R., Francine Sicklick, and Susan B. Turkel. "Divide and Conquer: Unit Strips to the Rescue." *Arithmetic Teacher* 35 (December 1987): 6–12.

Dirkes, M. Ann. "Draw to Understand." *Arithmetic Teacher* 39 (December 1991): 26–29.

Edge, Douglas, "Fractions and Panes." *Arithmetic Teacher* 34 (April 1987): 13–17.

Foreman, Linda, and Albert Bennett. "Linear Model for Fractions," in *Visual Mathematics* (Lessons 40–42). Salem, OR: The Math Learning Center, Box 3226, 1995.

Maher, C., R. Davis, and A. Alston. "Teachers Paying Attention to Students' Thinking." *Arithmetic Teacher* 39 (May 1992): 34–37.

Ott, J., D. Snook, and D. Gibson. "Understanding Partitive Division of Fractions." *Arithmetic Teacher* 39 (October 1991): 7–11.

Pothier, Yvonne, and Daiyo Sawada. "Partitioning: An Approach to Fractions." *Arithmetic Teacher* 38 (December 1990): 12–17.

Schultz, James E. "Area Models—Spanning the Mathematics of Grades 3–9." *Arithmetic Teacher* 39 (October 1991): 42–46.

Van de Walle, John, and C. S. Thompson. "Let's Do It: Fractions with Fraction Strips." *Arithmetic Teacher* 32 (December 1984): 4–9.

Zaweojewski, Judith S. "Ideas: Fractions as Areas." *Arithmetic Teacher* 34 (December 1986): 18–25.

CHAPTER 6

DECIMALS: RATIONAL AND IRRATIONAL

The approach to decimals should be similar to work with fractions, namely placing strong and continued emphasis on models and oral language and then connecting this work with symbols. . . . Exploring ideas of tenths and hundredths with models can include preliminary work with equivalent decimals.[1]

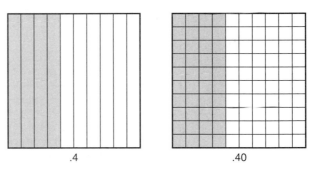

.4   .40

ACTIVITY SET 6.1

MODELS FOR DECIMALS

Purpose To use Decimal Squares[2] as a visual model for the part-to-whole concept of decimals and for illustrating decimal equality, inequality, place value, and estimation

Materials Decimal Squares are on Material Cards 23–26.

Activity The results of the second mathematics assessment of the National Assessment of Educational Progress (NAEP) have implications for the use of models in the teaching of decimal concepts.

[1]*Curriculum and Evaluation Standards for School Mathematics* (Reston, VA: National Council of Teachers of Mathematics, 1989), 59.
[2]Decimal Squares is a registered trademark of Scott Resources, Inc.

In analyzing the computational errors made on the decimal exercises it is evident that much of the difficulty lies in a lack of conceptual understanding. . . . It is important that decimals be thought of as numbers and the ability to relate them to models should assist in understanding.[3]

The Decimal Squares model for decimals is an extension of the number piece model that was used for whole numbers in Chapter 3. The base-ten number piece model started with a unit and the pieces increased in size by a factor of 10 (10 units equal 1 long, 10 longs equal 1 flat, etc.). The Decimal Squares model starts with the unit, but the number pieces decrease in size by a factor of 10, as shown here. The number pieces representing decimals are individually too small to be handled, so they are indicated on the unit number piece by shading.

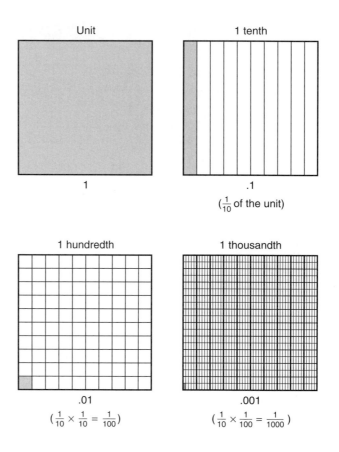

The decimals 3 tenths, 37 hundredths, and 379 thousandths can be illustrated as follows:

[3]T. P. Carpenter, M. K. Corbitt, H. S. Kepner, M. M. Lindquist, and R. E. Reys, "Decimals: Results and Implications from National Assessment," *Arithmetic Teacher* 28 (April 1981), 34–37.

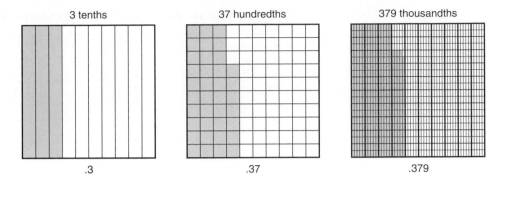

3 tenths   37 hundredths   379 thousandths

.3   .37   .379

Part to Whole

1. Shade each square below so that the decimal tells how much of the square is shaded.

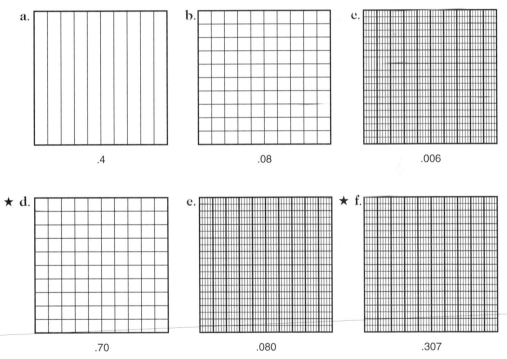

a.   b.   c.

.4   .08   .006

★ d.   e.   ★ f.

.70   .080   .307

2. Below each square write the decimal that represents the shaded amount.

a.   ★ b.   c.

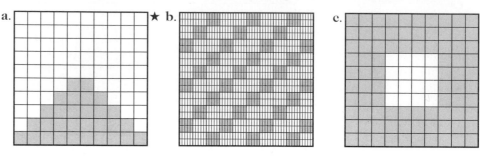

_____   _____   _____

Write the decimal that represents each of the following squares:

d. 9 shaded parts out of 10   _____

e. 13 shaded parts out of 100   _____

★ **f.** 9 shaded parts out of 100   _____

g. 8 shaded parts out of 1000   _____

★ **h.** 90 shaded parts out of 1000   _____

Equality

3. The decimals for the following squares are equal because each square is the same size and has the same amount of shading. That is, 4 parts out of 10 is equal to 40 parts out of 100, and 40 parts out of 100 is equal to 400 parts out of 1000.

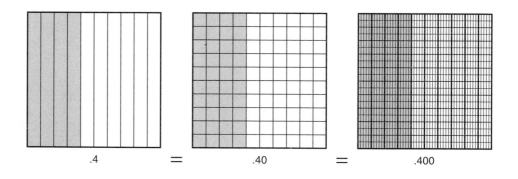

.4   =   .40   =   .400

Fill in the boxes below each square to complete the statement and the equation.

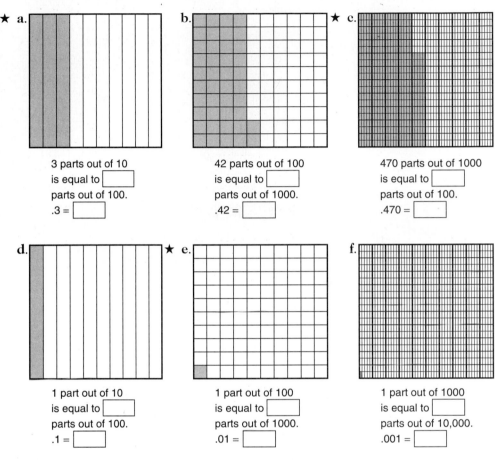

★ a.

3 parts out of 10
is equal to [   ]
parts out of 100.
.3 = [   ]

b.

42 parts out of 100
is equal to [   ]
parts out of 1000.
.42 = [   ]

★ c.

470 parts out of 1000
is equal to [   ]
parts out of 100.
.470 = [   ]

d.

1 part out of 10
is equal to [   ]
parts out of 100.
.1 = [   ]

★ e.

1 part out of 100
is equal to [   ]
parts out of 1000.
.01 = [   ]

f.

1 part out of 1000
is equal to [   ]
parts out of 10,000.
.001 = [   ]

Place Value

4. The decimal .435 is represented by the shaded parts in both squares below. Figure a represents .435 the way we say its decimal name, "four hundred thirty-five thousandths," because 435 parts out of 1000 are shaded. In figure b the encircled parts of the square show that .435 can also be thought of as 4 tenths, 3 hundredths, and 5 thousandths and that each digit has *place value* as recorded in the table.

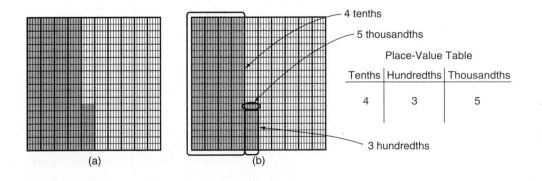

4 tenths

5 thousandths

Place-Value Table

Tenths	Hundredths	Thousandths
4	3	5

3 hundredths

(a)   (b)

For each of the squares, circle the parts that show the decimal in place-value form. Write the digits for each decimal in the place-value table below the square.

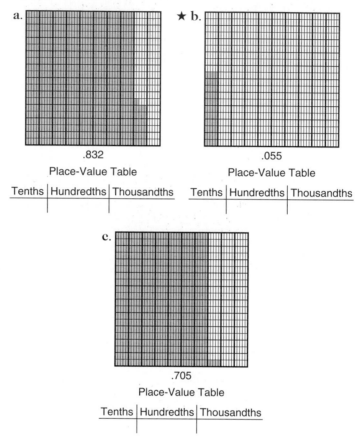

a.

.832

Place-Value Table

Tenths	Hundredths	Thousandths

★ b.

.055

Place-Value Table

Tenths	Hundredths	Thousandths

c.

.705

Place-Value Table

Tenths	Hundredths	Thousandths

★ d. Explain why it is never necessary to use a digit greater than 9 in any column of a place-value table representing a decimal number.

5. When each part of a Decimal Square for hundredths is partitioned into 10 equal parts, there are 1000 parts. One of these parts is 1 thousandth of the whole square and represents the decimal .001.

.001 →

    a. Suppose each part of a Decimal Square for thousandths is partitioned into 10 equal parts. What fraction of the whole square is 1 of these parts? What is the decimal for 1 of these small parts, and what is the name of the decimal?

★ b. Suppose each part of a Decimal Square for thousandths is partitioned into 100 equal parts. What fraction of the whole square is 1 of these parts? What is the decimal for 1 of these small parts, and what is the name of the decimal?

Inequality

6. The Decimal Squares for .62 and .610 show that .62 is greater than .610, because its square has the greater shaded amount. We can also determine that .62 > .610 by thinking in terms of place value. The digit 6 in .62 and .610 tells us that 6 tenths of both squares are shaded. That is, 6 full columns of both squares are shaded. Looking at the next column, we see that the square for .62 has 2 hundredths (or 20 thousandths) shaded, whereas the square for .610 has 1 hundredth (or 10 thousandths) shaded. So .62 > .610.

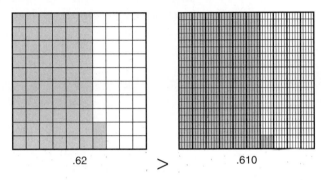

.62   >   .610

Determine an inequality for each pair of decimals, and explain the reason for the inequality by describing their Decimal Squares. For example, .4 > .27 because the square for .4 has 4 full columns shaded and the square for .27 has less than 3 full columns shaded.

a. .7   .43

★ **b.** .042   .04

c. .3   .285

d. Write the following decimals as equivalent decimals, with three decimal places. Circle the greatest and underline the least.

.3   .27   .298

★ **e.** Write the following decimals as equivalent decimals, with four decimal places. Circle the greatest and underline the least.

.042   .0047   .04

7. The following question is from a 1979 mathematics assessment test that was given to students entering universities.

Question: Which of the following numbers is the smallest?

a. .07   **b.** 1.003   **c.** .08   **d.** .075   **e.** .3

Less than 30 percent of 7100 students answered this question correctly.[4] Explain how to determine the correct answer by describing Decimal Squares for these decimals.

Approximation

8. **a.** Using a Decimal Square for tenths, determine how many complete parts should be shaded to best approximate $\frac{1}{3}$ of the whole square. Shade these parts. Beneath the square, record the decimal that represents the shaded part.

b. Shade complete parts of each of these two Decimal Squares to best approximate $\frac{1}{3}$ of a whole square. Beneath each square, record the decimal that represents the shaded portion of the square.

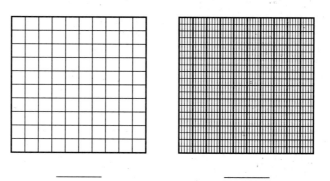

★ **c.** Shade complete parts of each of these Decimal Squares to best approximate $\frac{1}{6}$ of a whole square. Write the decimal that represents the shaded part of each square.

[4]A. Grossman, "Decimal Notation: An Important Research Finding," *Arithmetic Teacher* 30 (May 1983), 32–33.

JUST FOR FUN

In Decimal Bingo you practice identifying equal decimals. The Decimal Place-Value Game provides more insight on place values.

DECIMAL BINGO (2 to 4 players)

Each player selects one of the following four bingo mats with decimals. The deck of Decimal Squares should be spread face down. Each player in turn takes a square and circles the decimal or decimals on the bingo mat that equal the decimal for the square. The winner is the first player to circle four decimals in any row, column, or diagonal.

.30	.400	.1	.70
.7	.55	.3	.8
.10	.40	.85	.95
.8	.300	.05	.550

Mat 1

.60	.50	.3	.10
.1	.75	.600	.5
.450	.30	.15	.525
.500	.45	.425	.750

Mat 2

.70	.2	.50	.40
.5	.4	.450	.65
.20	.700	.375	.675
.400	.45	.475	.650

Mat 3

.75	.300	.60	.4
.600	.9	.30	.350
.40	.750	.325	.25
.35	.6	.575	.90

Mat 4

DECIMAL PLACE-VALUE GAME (2 to 4 players)

Players each draw a place-value table like the one next to the dice. Each player in turn rolls two dice until he or she obtains a sum less than 10. The player then records this number in one of the three columns in his or her place-value table. Only one number is written in one column on each turn, and the number cannot be moved to another column after it has been written down. After each player has had three turns, the player with the greatest three-place decimal is the winner. The first player to win five rounds wins the game.[5]

Variation: Use a place-value table with four columns, and roll the dice to obtain the digits in a four-place decimal.

Place-Value Table

Tenths	Hundredths	Thousandths

[5]Another way to generate numbers for this game is to write each digit from 0 to 9 on a separate card and then draw one card at random from this deck.

ACTIVITY SET 6.2

OPERATIONS WITH DECIMAL SQUARES

Purpose To use Decimal Squares to illustrate decimal addition, subtraction, multiplication, and division

Materials Decimal Squares are on Material Cards 23–26.

Activity It is almost impossible to compute on a calculator without getting decimal numbers. Because of our technology and the frequent occurrence of decimals, it has been suggested that decimal concepts be taught earlier in the elementary school curriculum.

> Calculators create whole new opportunities for ordering the curriculum and for integrating mathematics into science. No longer need teachers be constrained by the artificial restriction to numbers that children know how to employ in the paper-and-pencil algorithms of arithmetic. Decimals can be introduced much earlier since they arise naturally on the calculator. Real measurements from science experiments can be used in mathematics lessons because the calculator will be able to add or multiply the data even if the children have not yet learned how. They may learn first what addition and multiplication mean and when to use them, and only later how to perform these operations manually in all possible cases.[6]

Early introduction of the decimal concepts of addition, subtraction, multiplication, and division in the elementary school curriculum makes it imperative that children have good physical and visual models that embody these concepts. The goal is to develop concepts and a decimal number sense rather than paper-and-pencil manipulative skills. For example, a child may not know the traditional moving-the-decimal-point algorithm of computing .35 ÷ .05 but may "see" that the answer is 7 by using the Decimal Squares model—and then verify this result by using a calculator.

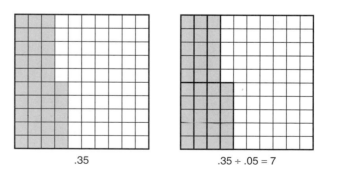

.35   .35 ÷ .05 = 7

[6]National Research Council, *Everybody Counts: A Report to the Nation on the Future of Mathematics Education* (Washington, DC: The National Academy Press, 1989), 47–48.

Addition

1. Addition of decimals can be illustrated by determining the total shaded amount of two or more squares. Fill in the missing number, and compute the sum by counting the total number of shaded parts.

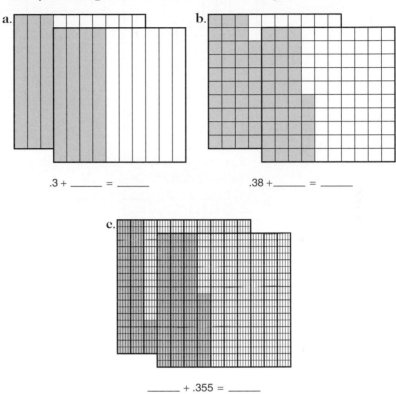

a. .3 + _____ = _____

b. .38 + _____ = _____

c. _____ + .355 = _____

2. Shade each square to represent the decimal written beneath it. Add the decimals by determining the total shaded amount of the two squares. Explain how you arrived at your answer.

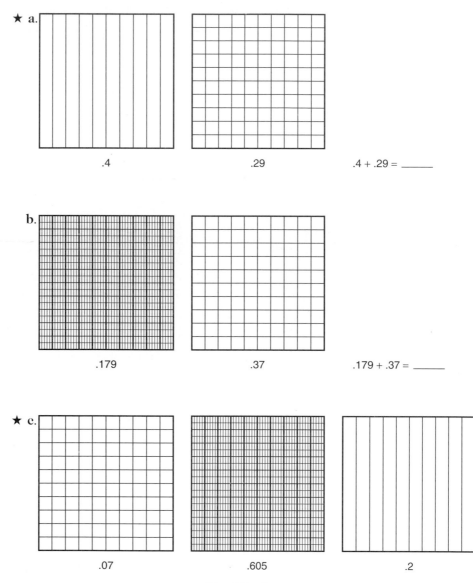

★ a.

.4   .29   .4 + .29 = _____

b.

.179   .37   .179 + .37 = _____

★ c.

.07   .605   .2

.07 + .605 + .2 = _____

Subtraction

3. Subtraction of decimals can be illustrated with Decimal Squares by circling the amount to be taken away—*take-away concept for subtraction*—and counting the number of shaded parts that remain.

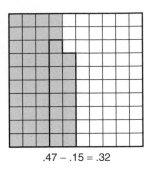

.47 − .15 = .32

For each of the following, circle the amount to be taken away and complete the equation.

a.   b.   c.

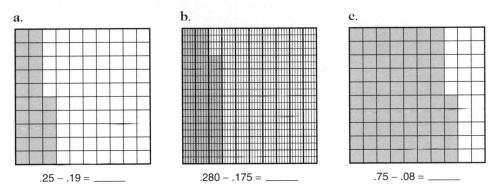

.25 − .19 = _____   .280 − .175 = _____   .75 − .08 = _____

4. Shade each square to represent the decimal written beneath it. Determine the differences by *comparing* the shaded parts of the squares. In part a, for example, you may find the difference by determining what must be added to .07 to get .5. Briefly explain how you arrived at each answer.

★ a.

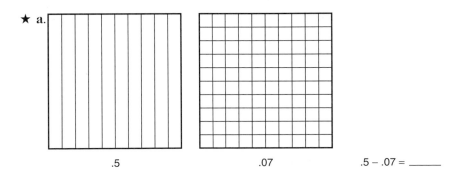

.5   .07   .5 − .07 = _____

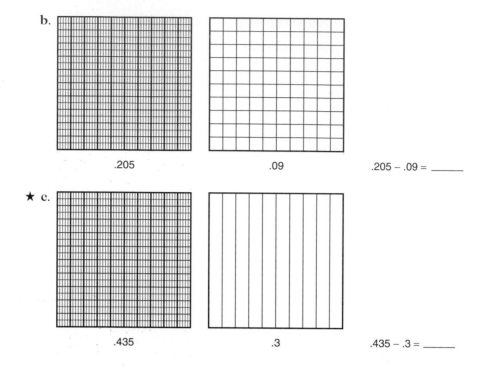

b.

.205   .09   .205 − .09 = _____

★ c.

.435   .3   .435 − .3 = _____

Multiplication

5. Here is the decimal square for .45. If there were 3 of these Decimal Squares, there would be a total of 3 × 45 = 135 shaded parts. Since there are 100 parts in each whole square, the total shaded amount would be 1 whole square and 35 parts out of 100.

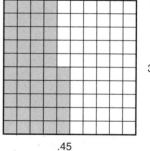

3 × .45 = 1.35

.45

In a similar manner, compute the following products and explain your answers in terms of the shaded parts of squares.

a. 6 × .83 = _____

★ b. 4 × .725 = _____

c. 10 × .72 = _____

★ d. Explain, in terms of Decimal Squares, why multiplication by 10 results in a decimal number with the same digits but with the decimal point in a different place.

6. The product .3 × .2 means "take 3 tenths of 2 tenths." To do this, we split the shaded amount of the .2 square into 10 equal parts and take 3 of them. The result is 6 hundredths. This shows that .3 × .2 = .06.

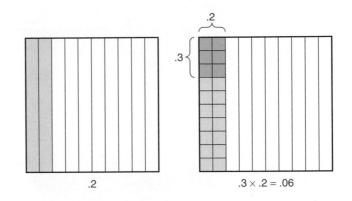

The shaded portion of the first figure below represents the decimal 1.2. When the shaded area representing 1.2 is split into 10 equal parts and 3 are taken, as in the second figure, the result is 3 tenths and 6 hundredths, or 36 hundredths.

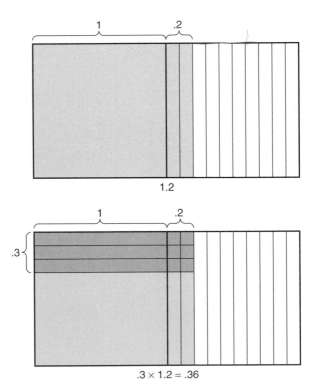

The product 1.3×1.2 can be thought of as 1×1.2 added to $.3 \times 1.2$ and represented as shown below. The shaded portion represents 1 unit, 5 tenths, and 6 hundredths. So $1.3 \times 1.2 = 1.56$.

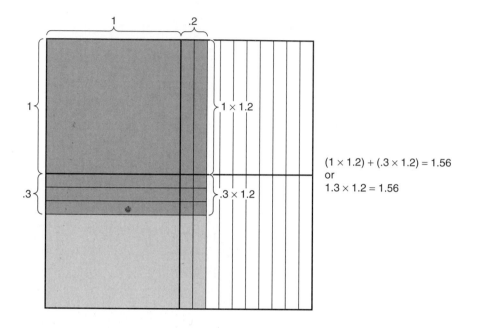

$(1 \times 1.2) + (.3 \times 1.2) = 1.56$
or
$1.3 \times 1.2 = 1.56$

In a similar manner, sketch a Decimal Square diagram to illustrate each of the following. Determine the product from the diagram and explain your reasoning.

a. $.4 \times .3$

b. $.4 \times 1.3$

★ c. 1.4×1.3

d. 2.4×1.3

Division

7. The *sharing method of division* can be used to illustrate the division of a decimal by a whole number. In the following square, the shaded portion representing .60 has been divided into 3 equal parts to illustrate .60 ÷ 3. Since each of these parts has 20 shaded parts, .60 divided by 3 is .20.

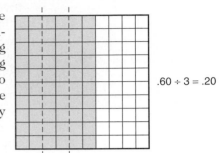

.60 ÷ 3 = .20

Divide each Decimal Square into parts, and use the result to determine the quotient.

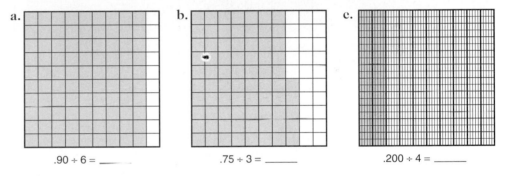

a. .90 ÷ 6 = _____

b. .75 ÷ 3 = _____

c. .200 ÷ 4 = _____

8. Use the following Decimal Squares to determine the indicated quotients. Record each quotient beneath the square, and shade that amount on the Decimal Square.

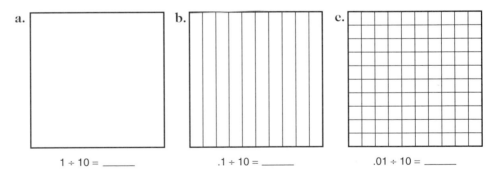

a. 1 ÷ 10 = _____

b. .1 ÷ 10 = _____

c. .01 ÷ 10 = _____

★ 9. In view of the preceding results, explain why dividing a decimal number, such as 2.87, by 10 results in a decimal with the same digits but the decimal point moved one place to the left.

10. The *measurement concept of division* involves repeatedly measuring off or subtracting one amount from another. It can be seen in the following square that 15 of the shaded parts can be measured off from 75 parts 5 times.

Draw lines on the following Decimal Squares to indicate how the measurement concept of division can be used to obtain the indicated quotient.

$.75 \div .15 = 5$

a.

$.8 \div .2 =$ _____

*b.

$.70 \div .05 =$ _____

c.

$.600 \div .3 =$ _____

★ **d.** On the Second National Assessment of Educational Progress, students were asked to estimate $250 \div .5$. Only 39 percent of the 17-year-olds correctly estimated this quotient; 47 percent ignored the decimal point, giving an answer of 50.[7] Use the measurement concept of division to explain why $250 \div .5 = 500$.

All Four Operations

11. Use the Decimal Squares from Material Cards 23–26 for parts b and c of this activity.

    a. The following 10 decimals represent Decimal Squares:

      .3   .75   .8   .650   .15   .2   .35   .45   .400   .350

    Complete these equations by placing the 10 decimals in the boxes.

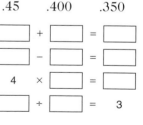

    b. Spread the Decimal Squares face down and select 10 of them. List your 10 decimals. Using each of your decimals only once, complete as many of the four equations as possible. If you cannot complete all four equations, continue to select Decimal Squares one at a time (recording each decimal) until you can complete all the equations.

[7]National Assessment of Educational Progress, "Math Achievement Is Plus and Minus," *NAEP Newsletter* 12 (5) (October 1979), 2.

10 decimals selected: _____, _____, _____, _____, _____,

_____, _____, _____, _____, _____

c. **Solitaire:** The activity in part b can be played like a solitaire game. See how many turns it takes you to complete the four equations by selecting only 10 Decimal Squares on each turn.

☐ + ☐ = ☐

☐ − ☐ = ☐

3 × ☐ = ☐

☐ ÷ ☐ = 2

. . . .

JUST FOR FUN

Build skills in performing operations on decimals with these games—addition in the first game, division in the second, and subtraction in the third.

DECIMAL SQUARES BLACKJACK (2 to 4 players)

The dealer shuffles the deck of Decimal Squares and deals one square face down to each player. The dealer also gets one square. The object of the game is to use one or more squares to get a decimal or a sum of two or more decimals that is less than or equal to 1, without going over. To get an additional square from the dealer, a player says "Hit me." When a player wants no more additional squares, he or she says "I'm holding." After every player has said "I'm holding," the players show their squares. The player whose sum is closest to 1, but not greater than 1, wins 1 point. The winner is the first player to win 5 points.

GREATEST QUOTIENT (2 to 4 players)

Spread the Decimal Squares face down. Each players chooses two squares and computes the quotient of one decimal divided by the other. The object is to get the greatest quotient. The player with the greatest quotient wins all the squares used in that round, including any discarded squares. If there is a tie, the squares are placed aside and the winner of the next round gets them. Play continues until the deck has been played through and no more rounds are possible. The winner is the player who has won the most squares.

Chance Option: A player can attempt to increase a quotient by choosing a new square. However, before choosing a new square, the player must discard one of the previously chosen squares.

GREATEST DIFFERENCE (2 to 4 players)

This game is similar to the greatest quotient game except that the player with the greatest difference wins the round.

ACTIVITY SET 6.3

A MODEL FOR INTRODUCING PERCENT

Purpose To use base-ten number pieces to introduce the concept of percent and to illustrate and solve various percent problems

Materials Base-ten pieces from the Manipulative Kit

Activity Percent is a common and widely used mathematical concept. From television to newspapers to shopping, the word *percent* enters our life almost daily, as noted in the following passage.

> Percentages are everywhere—in the food we eat ([a serving of] cornflakes contains 25% of our recommended daily allowance of vitamin A), in the clothes we wear (35% cotton), in our favorite television programs (watched by 55% of the television audience), and in the money we earn (27% tax bracket) and spend ($5\frac{1}{2}$% sales tax). In modern society, people who do not understand percentages will have difficulty reading articles and advertisements that appear in newspapers, determining if they are being cheated by financial institutions or retail establishments, or knowing if they are being misled by politicians.[8]

When something is divided into 100 equal parts, one part is called *one percent* and written 1%. The 10 by 10 grids from the base-ten number pieces are divided into 100 equal parts so the smallest square is 1 percent and the whole grid is 100 percent. These number pieces will be used to explore the concept of percent and solve various percent problems.

100%   10%   1%

The classical three cases of percent are visualized using this model.

Percent and whole:	25% of 150 = ?
Part and whole:	?% of 150 = 90
Percent and part:	6% of ? = 24

At the end of this activity set, Fraction Bars are split into approximately 100 parts to provide percent and decimal estimations for fractions.

---

1. If the 10 by 10 grid represents 100%, determine what percent is represented by each of the following collections of number pieces.

[8]James H. Wiebe, "Manipulating Percentages," *The Mathematics Teacher* (January 1986), 23–26.

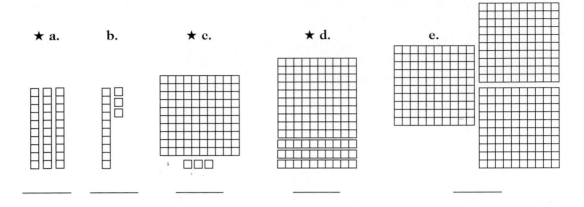

★ a.   b.   ★ c.   ★ d.   e.

_____   _____   _____   _____   _____

2. If the 10 by 10 grid represents 100%, use your pieces to form a collection to represent each of the percentages below. Draw a sketch to record your answers.

★ **a.** 23%   **b.** 98%   ★ **c.** 105%

d. 123%   **e.** 202%   ★ **f.** $\frac{1}{2}$%

Value 300

3. Suppose that a value of 300 is assigned to the 10 by 10 grid and that this value is spread evenly among all the small squares.

★ **a.** Describe an easy method for performing a mental calculation to find the value of this collection.

Using mental calculations determine the value of each of the following collections:

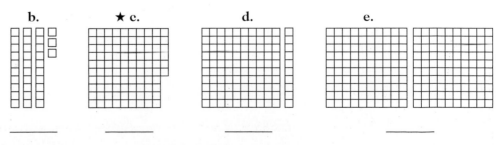

b.   ★ **c.**   **d.**   **e.**

_____   _____   _____   _____

Value 150

4. Suppose that the 10 by 10 grid is assigned a value of 150 and that this value is spread evenly among all the small squares.

★ a. Form a collection of pieces that represents 25% of the 10 by 10 grid. Determine the value of this collection without doing paper-and-pencil computations. Explain your method.

Repeat part a by forming collections of pieces representing the following percentages and determining each of their values using mental computations. Explain your thinking in each case.

b. 75%

★ c. 7%

Value 450

d. 111%

e. 210%

5. Assign a value of 450 to the 10 by 10 grid.

★ a. Form a collection of pieces that has a value of 270. Determine what percent of the 10 by 10 grid the value 270 represents. Record a sketch of your collection and the percent it represents.

Repeat the directions of part a for collections having the following values:

b. 108   ★ c. 441

d. 585   e. 909

6.★ a. Form a collection of pieces that represents 6% of a 10 by 10 grid. If this collection has a value of 24, what is the value of the 10 by 10 grid? Draw a sketch and explain your thinking.

Repeat the directions of part a when

b. 40% has a value of 30 ★ **c.** 55% has a value of 132

d. 125% has a value of 180.

Some Percent Statements

7. Many statements that deal with percent can be represented with the number piece model. Consider the statement "Last year the charity benefit raised $6720, which was 120% of its goal." 120% can be represented with these number pieces.

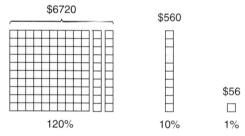

There are several observations that can be made by looking at the model:

(1) Because 120% has a value of $6720, one can see from the model that each long has a value of $560 ($6720 ÷ 12) or that each small square has a value of $56 (6720 ÷ 120).

(2) Last year's goal (100%) must have been $5600 (10 × $560 or 100 × $56).

(3) The goal was exceeded by $1120 ($6720 − $5600).

Model each of the following statements with your number pieces. Make a sketch of your model, record at least one *percent* observation, and explain how you arrived at it.

★ **a.** 65% of the firm's 320 employees were women.

★ **b.** 280 of the school's 800 students were absent.

c. I bought this sweater for $126 at the store's 30% off sale.

d. This year the charity benefit had a goal of $7000 and it raised 135% of its goal.

e. In a certain county, 57 of the schools have a student-to-teacher ratio that is greater than the recommendations for accreditation. The 57 schools are 38% of the number of schools in the county.

f. A new company entered the New York Stock Exchange in July and by December the price of each share of stock had risen (increased) 223% to $32.50 a share.

Fractions as Percents

8. Fractions with denominators that are factors of 100 can be readily expressed as percents. For example, if each part of a $\frac{3}{4}$ bar is split into 25 equal parts, the bar will have 75 parts shaded out of 100 equal parts. So $\frac{3}{4}$ equals 75%, or the decimal .75.

$$\frac{3}{4} = 75\% = .75$$

Imagine splitting each of the following bars into 100 equal parts. Indicate above each part of a bar the number of new parts after splitting, and then determine the percent and decimal equivalents for each fraction.

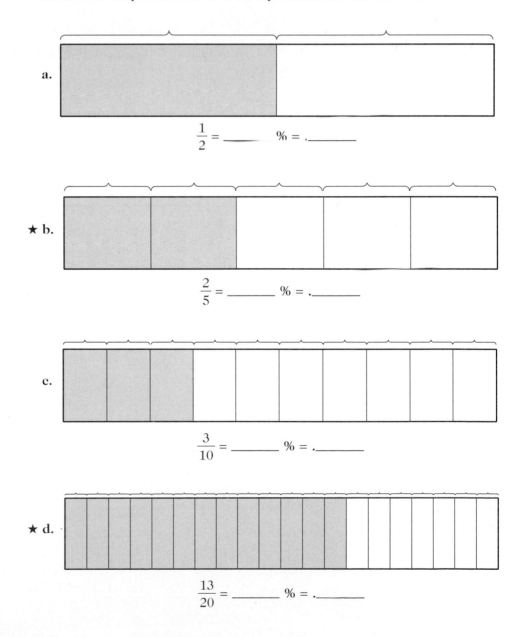

a.

$$\frac{1}{2} = \underline{\hspace{2cm}}\% = .\underline{\hspace{2cm}}$$

★ b.

$$\frac{2}{5} = \underline{\hspace{2cm}}\% = .\underline{\hspace{2cm}}$$

c.

$$\frac{3}{10} = \underline{\hspace{2cm}}\% = .\underline{\hspace{2cm}}$$

★ d.

$$\frac{13}{20} = \underline{\hspace{2cm}}\% = .\underline{\hspace{2cm}}$$

Fractions as Approximate Percents

9. To obtain an approximate percent for the fraction $\frac{1}{7}$, visualize a $\frac{1}{7}$ fraction bar. This bar has 1 part shaded out of 7 parts. If each part of the bar is split into 14 equal parts, the result will be 14 shaded parts out of 98 parts.

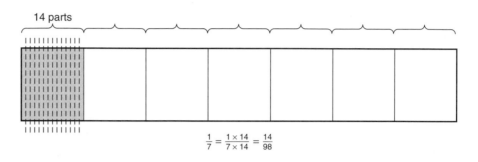

$$\frac{1}{7} = \frac{1 \times 14}{7 \times 14} = \frac{14}{98}$$

If each part of the $\frac{1}{7}$ bar is split in 15 equal parts, there will be 15 shaded parts out of 105 parts.

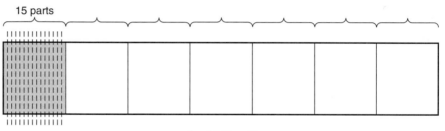

$$\frac{1}{7} = \frac{1 \times 15}{7 \times 15} = \frac{15}{105}$$

Because 105 is not as close to 100 as 98 is, we can say that $\frac{1}{7}$ is approximately 14%. Since 14% is $\frac{14}{100}$, the decimal .14 is also an approximation for $\frac{1}{7}$.

Determine a percent and decimal approximation for each of the following fractions by splitting the corresponding fraction bar into approximately 100 parts (or visualizing the splitting). Explain how you arrived at your percent for each fraction by indicating the number of parts due to splitting.

a. $\frac{1}{3} \approx$ _____% = ._____

★ b. $\dfrac{5}{6} \approx$ _____% = ._____

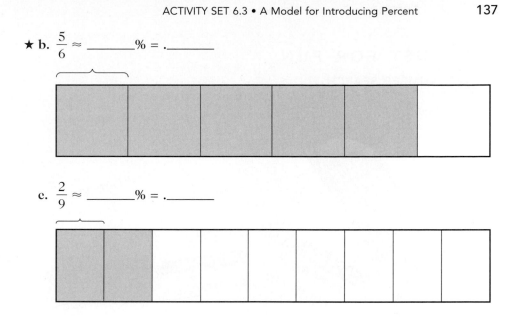

c. $\dfrac{2}{9} \approx$ _____% = ._____

JUST FOR FUN

NUMBER SEARCH

Find equal pairs of decimals, percents, and fractions. See if you can find 20 such pairs.

Which rectangle has the greater percent of its area shaded?

ACTIVITY SET 6.4

IRRATIONAL NUMBERS ON THE GEOBOARD

Purpose   To use geoboards and/or dot paper to represent figures whose sides and perimeters have lengths that are irrational numbers

Materials   A geoboard and rubber bands (optional). There is a template for making a rectangular geoboard on Material Card 27.

Activity   When we used the rod model for greatest common factors (Activity Set 4.2), we saw that any two rods with whole number lengths could be cut evenly into rods of equal common length. In some cases the lengths of the rods may be relatively prime, like 3 and 8, but the rods can still be cut evenly into pieces with common length 1.

If two rods do not have whole number lengths but do have rational number lengths, can they still be cut evenly into rods of equal common length? Again the answer is yes. Suppose, for example, the rods have lengths $3\frac{1}{3}$ and $5\frac{1}{2}$. Because these numbers are equal to $3\frac{2}{6}$ and $5\frac{3}{6}$, the rods can both be cut evenly into pieces of length $\frac{1}{6}$.

Does it then follow that any two lengths can be evenly cut into pieces of equal common length? About 2300 years ago, mathematicians would have answered yes. They thought that any two lengths are *commensurable*—that is, have a common unit of measure. This unit might be very small, such as a millionth or a billionth of an inch, but surely there would always be such a length. When the Greek mathematician Hippasus (470 B.C.) discovered that the side and the diagonal of a square are *incommensurable*—that is, do not have a common unit of measure—he caused such a crisis in mathematics that, reportedly, he was taken to sea and never returned. His discovery ultimately led to new types of numbers, called *irrational numbers,* which are represented by infinite nonrepeating decimals.

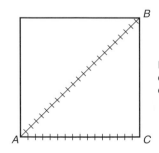

In a square, diagonal $\overline{AB}$ and side $\overline{AC}$ cannot be cut into pieces of equal common length.

1. Region *X* represents 1 unit of area on the geoboard. Region *Y* can be subdivided into 6 unit squares and 4 halves so that it has an area of 8 square units. If this figure is formed on the geoboard, it may be helpful to use rubber bands to subdivide it into unit squares and halves. Region *Z* is half of a rectangle of area 6 square units, so *Z* has an area of 3 square units.

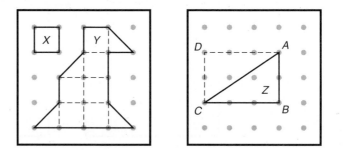

Determine the area of each of the following geoboard regions. Record the areas inside the figures.

2. One way to determine the area of square W is to enclose it inside the larger square that has an area of 9 square units and then subtract the area of the triangular corners. Each of the triangular corners has an area of 1 square unit. So the area of square W is $9 - 4 = 5$ square units.

Here are seven other squares that can be constructed on the geoboard. Determine the area of each square. Record the areas inside the squares.

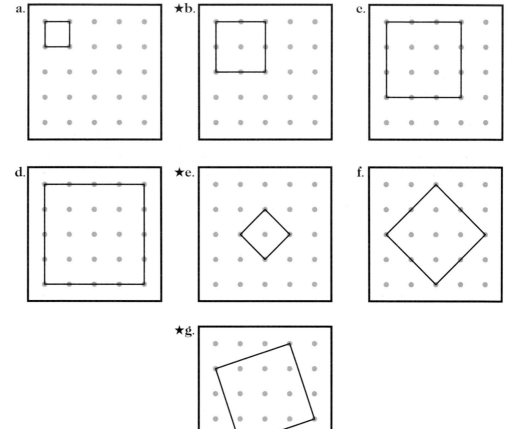

3. For any square, the length of a side times itself gives the area of the square.

Side length × side length = area

Square *W* in activity 2 has an area of 5 square units. The length of a side of square *W* is $\sqrt{5}$ because by definition $\sqrt{5}$ is *the number that, when multiplied times itself, gives* 5. That is, $\sqrt{5} \times \sqrt{5} = 5$. One of the squares in activity 2 has an area of 9, and the length of a side is $\sqrt{9}$. Notice that $\sqrt{9} = 3$ because $3 \times 3 = 9$.

Finish recording the areas (from least to greatest) and the corresponding side lengths for the eight squares in activity 2.

Area of square: _____   _____   _____   5   _____   9   _____   _____

Length of side: _____   _____   _____ $\sqrt{5}$ _____   3   _____   _____

★ 4. Determine the lengths of the three line segments in the next figure by first drawing a square on each segment and finding the area of the square. The corners of a sheet of paper can be used to draw the sides and locate the corners of the square. The corners of each square will be on dots. (The dotted lines form a square on segment a.)

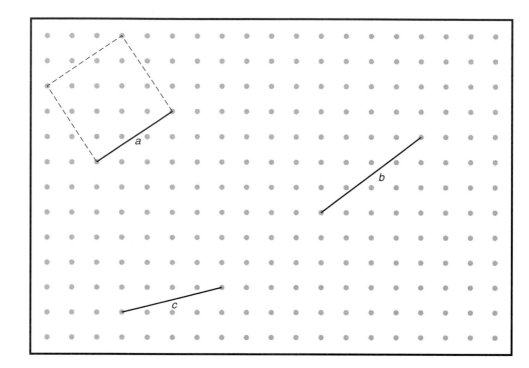

5. **Calculator Activity:** If n is a positive integer and not a perfect square (that is, n is not 0, 1, 4, 9, 16, 25, 36, . . .), then $\sqrt{n}$ is an *irrational number.* For example, $\sqrt{5}$ is an irrational number. When written as decimals, irrational numbers have infinite and nonrepeating decimal expansions.

   a. Use the $\sqrt{}$ key on your calculator to obtain an approximate value for $\sqrt{5}$. Record the decimal from your calculator display.

   b. Multiply the calculator's decimal for $\sqrt{5}$ times itself and record the result. Did you get 5? If not, why do you think you didn't?

   c. Explain the advantages of labeling the length of a segment with a symbol like $\sqrt{5}$ rather than writing out the digits for $\sqrt{5}$ that appear on a calculator display.

6. Each of the following figures has three squares surrounding a right triangle (a right triangle has one angle of 90°). For each figure, determine the area of each square and complete the table.

	SQUARE A	SQUARE B	SQUARE C
a. Figure 1	_____	_____	_____
★ b. Figure 2	_____	_____	_____
c. Figure 3	_____	_____	_____
★ d. Figure 4	_____	_____	_____

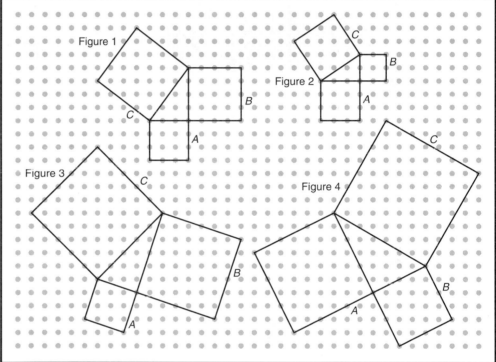

7. For every right triangle, the same relationship holds between the area of the square on the longest side (the hypotenuse) and the area of the squares on the other two sides (the legs).

   a. Use the data from activity 6 to make a conjecture, in writing, about this relationship.

   b. Use this relationship to find the area of the square on the hypotenuse for each of the following figures. Record your results in the table, and then use them to determine the length of the hypotenuse.

	AREA OF SQUARE ON HYPOTENUSE	LENGTH OF HYPOTENUSE
(1) Figure 1	_____	_____
★ **(2)** Figure 2	_____	_____
(3) Figure 3	_____	_____
★ **(4)** Figure 4	_____	_____

 JUST FOR FUN

GOLDEN RECTANGLES

Some rectangles are more aesthetically pleasing than others. One in particular, the *golden rectangle,* has been the favorite of architects, sculptors, and artists for over 2000 years. The Greeks of the fifth century B.C. were fond of this rectangle. The front of the Parthenon in Athens fits into a golden rectangle.

In the nineteenth century, the German psychologist Gustav Fechner found that most people unconsciously favor the golden rectangle. Which one of the following rectangles do you feel has the most pleasing dimensions?

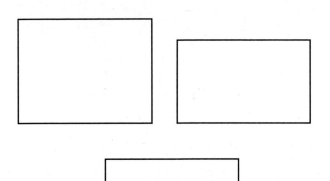

The length of a golden rectangle divided by its width is an irrational number that, when rounded to three decimal places, is 1.618. Measure the preceding rectangles to determine which is closest to a golden rectangle. Measure some other rectangles, such as greeting cards, credit cards, business cards, index cards, pictures, and mirrors, to see if you can find a golden rectangle. (A ratio of 1.6 is close enough.) Check the ratio of the length of the front of the Parthenon to its width.

A golden rectangle can be constructed from a square such as *ABCD* by placing a compass on the mid-point of side $\overline{AB}$ and swinging an arc *DF*. Then *FBCE* is a golden rectangle.

Make a golden rectangle, and check the ratio of its sides. If the sides of the square have length 2, then $BF = 1 + \sqrt{5}$. Use your calculator to determine $(1 + \sqrt{5}) \div 2$ (the ratio of the sides of the rectangle) to three decimal places. Cut out your rectangle and fold it in half along its longer side. Is the result another golden rectangle?

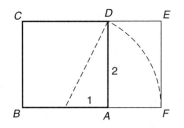

The ratio of the sides of a golden rectangle is called the *golden mean* or *golden ratio*.[9] It is surprising that this number (approximately 1.618) is also associated with the Fibonacci numbers: 1, 1, 2, 3, 5, 8, 13, ... The ratios of successive terms in this sequence ($\frac{1}{1}, \frac{2}{1}, \frac{3}{2}, \frac{5}{3}, \frac{8}{5}, . . .$) get closer and closer to the golden ratio. The ratio $\frac{8}{5}$, for example, is 1.6. Use your calculator to determine how far you must go in the Fibonacci sequence before the ratio of numbers is approximately 1.618.

• •

PUZZLER

These nine plants are in a square fenced garden. Construct two more square fences so that *each* plant is contained inside its own fence.

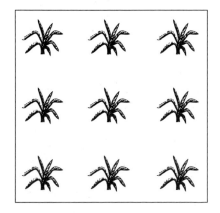

[9]Several occurrences of the golden ratio are described in C. F. Linn, *The Golden Mean* (New York: Doubleday, 1974).

IDEAS FOR THE ELEMENTARY CLASSROOM
SUGGESTED CLASSROOM ACTIVITY: BASE PIECE DECIMAL MODEL

Another physical model for decimals can be made by using the base-ten pieces from the Manipulative Kit. If the largest of the three base-ten pieces in the kit is designated as 1 (the unit), then the two smaller pieces represent .1 ($\frac{1}{10}$) and .01 ($\frac{1}{100}$). So, for example, the decimal 2.37 is represented by the collection shown in the following figure. The students can discuss why a decimal point is needed when the numeral is written. Also, decimals can be added and subtracted by regrouping number pieces.

For classroom demonstration, a number piece representing 10 can be made by taping 10 units in a strip (or cutting a piece of cardstock 10 cm by 100 cm). A number piece representing 100 could be made with a square piece of paper or cardstock measuring 1 m on each edge. This model provides a nice way to visualize the relative sizes of numbers.[10]

Readings for More Classroom Ideas

Bennett, A., E. Maier, and L. Ted Nelson. "A Conceptual Model for Solving Percent Problems." *Mathematics Teaching in the Middle School* 1 (April 1994): 20–25.

Bennett, A., E. Maier, and L. Ted Nelson. "Modeling Percentages and Ratios," in *Math and the Mind's Eye* (Unit VII). Salem, OR: The Math Learning Center, Box 3226, 1991.

Bennett, A., E. Maier, and L. Ted Nelson. "Modeling Rationals," in *Math and the Mind's Eye* (Unit IV). Salem, OR: The Math Learning Center, Box 3226, 1988.

Caldwell, Janet H. "Communicating About Fractions with Pattern Blocks." *Teaching Children Mathematics* 2 (November 1995): 156–161.

Carraher, Terezinha N., and A. D. Schliemann. "Research into Practice: Using Money to Teach About the Decimal System." *Arithmetic Teacher* 36 (December 1988): 42–43.

Curcio, Frances R., et al. *Understanding Rational Numbers and Proportions,* in the *Curriculum and Evaluation Standards for School Mathematics Addenda Series: Grades 5–8.* Reston, VA: National Council of Teachers of Mathematics, 1994.

Fennell, Francis. "The Newspaper: A Source for Applications in Mathematics." *Arithmetic Teacher* 30 (October 1982): 22–26.

Haubner, Mary Ann. "Percents: Developing Meaning Through Models." *Arithmetic Teacher* 40 (December 1992): 232–234.

Quintero, Ana H. "Helping Children Understand Ratios." *Arithmetic Teacher* 34 (May 1987): 17–21.

---

[10]For more information about this model for decimals, see A. Bennett, E. Maier, and L. Ted Nelson, "Modeling Rationals" (Unit IV, Activities 6–9), *Math and the Mind's Eye* (Salem, Ore.: The Math Learning Center, Box 3226, 1988).

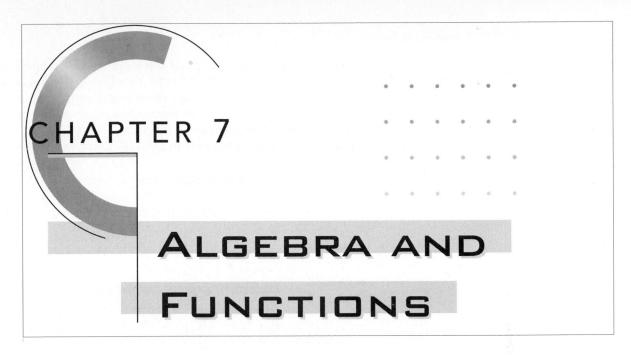

CHAPTER 7

ALGEBRA AND FUNCTIONS

It is essential that in grades 5–8 students explore algebraic concepts in an informal way to build a foundation for the subsequent formal study of algebra. . . . Activities in grades 5–8 should build on students' K–4 experiences with patterns. They should continue to emphasize concrete situations that allow students to investigate patterns in number sequences, make predictions, and formulate verbal rules to describe patterns.[1]

ACTIVITY SET 7.1

SOLVING STORY PROBLEMS WITH ALGEBRA PIECES

Purpose   To use algebra pieces as a visual model for representing and solving algebra story problems

Materials   Algebra pieces are on Material Card 28.

Activity   The Greek algebra of the Pythagoreans (ca. 540 B.C.) and Euclid (ca. 300 B.C.) was not symbolic, as we think of algebra, but geometric. An arbitrary number was expressed as a line segment. To express the sum of two arbitrary numbers, the Greeks joined the two segments end to end. The product of two numbers was the area of a rectangle with the two segments as sides.

Two numbers   Sum of two numbers   Product of two numbers

[1]*Curriculum and Evaluation Standards for School Mathematics* (Reston, VA: National Council of Teachers of Mathematics, 1989), 102.

Unit   Algebra piece

In this activity set, we will represent and solve algebra story problems using a geometric model similar to that of the Greeks. Our concrete geometric model will consist of two types of pieces: an algebra piece and a unit. The algebra piece will be used to represent an arbitrary line segment or number. It can represent any real number. Each unit will represent a length of 1 unit.

The algebra pieces can be placed together to form different expressions.

An arbitrary number

Twice a number

3 more than a number

2 more than 3 times a number

The product of a number times itself

1. Form the rectangle shown here with your algebra pieces.

★ **a.** Describe, in a sentence, the relationship between the length and the width of this rectangle.

★ **b.** If the perimeter of this rectangle is 54 units, explain how you can determine the length and the width of the rectangle using only your algebra-piece model.

★ **c.** Use your algebra pieces to alter the rectangle so that its length is 3 more units than twice its width. Draw a sketch of your new rectangle.

d. If this new rectangle has a perimeter of 54 units, explain how you can determine its length and its width using only your algebra-piece model.

2. If an algebra piece represents a positive integer, then two consecutive positive integers are represented by the algebra pieces in figure a. Figure b illustrates the sum of the two consecutive integers.

(a)   (b)

a. Represent four consecutive positive integers with your algebra pieces. Sketch them here.

b. Use your model to determine which four consecutive integers have a sum of 58. Explain your solution by referring to your algebra-piece model for the sum of four consecutive positive integers.

★ **3.** Use your algebra pieces to represent the sides of the triangle described as follows:

The second side of the triangle is twice the length of the first side. The third side of the triangle is 6 units longer than the second side.

a. Draw a sketch of your algebra-piece model.

b. Use your model to determine the length of each side of the triangle if the perimeter of the triangle is 66 units. Using your model, explain how you arrived at your conclusion.

4. A box contains $2.25 in nickels and dimes. There are 3 times as many nickels as dimes. If 1 algebra piece represents the *number of dimes* in the box, explain why the algebra pieces shown here represent the total number of nickels and dimes.

a. Suppose each dime is replaced by its value in nickels so that there are only nickels in the box. Explain why the total number of coins is now represented by the following number pieces.

b. The total amount of money in the box is $2.25. Explain how to use this information to determine the number of coins represented by each algebra piece in the last diagram.

c. How can you use the above information to determine the original number of dimes and nickels in the box?

Activities 5–11: Use your algebra pieces to represent the information in each story problem. Sketch your algebra-piece model for each problem. Using your algebra pieces, explain how you arrived at each conclusion.

★ **5.** Two pieces of rope differ in length by 7 meters. End to end, their total length is 75 meters. How long is each piece? (*Hint:* Let an algebra piece represent the length of the shorter rope, and let the unit piece be 1 meter.)

6. There are 3 boys on the school playground for every girl on the playground. Altogether there are 76 children. How many are boys? (*Hint:* Let 1 algebra piece represent the number of girls on the playground.)

★ **7.** Andrea has a collection of nickels, and Greg has a collection of dimes. Andrea has 4 times as many nickels as Greg has dimes. Andrea has 80 cents more than Greg. How much money does Greg have? (*Hint:* Let 1 algebra piece represent the number of dimes Greg has.)

8. The length of a rectangle is 5 feet less than twice its width. Determine the length and the width if the perimeter is 56 feet. (*Hint:* The figure at the left represents "5 less.")

9. Three-fifths of the students in a class are women. If the number of men in the class were doubled and the number of women were increased by 9, there would be an equal number of men and women. How many students are there? (*Hint:* Represent the women by 3 algebra pieces and the men by 2 algebra pieces.)

★ **10.** The sum of two numbers is 64. The second number is 5 less than twice the first number. What are the two numbers? (*Hint:* Let 1 algebra piece represent the first number, construct the second number, and add.)

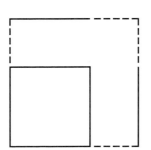

11. This algebra-piece sketch represents two overlapping squares. By how much does the length of a side of the smaller square differ from the length of a side of the larger square?

    a. On the diagram, shade the area that represents the difference between the squares.

    b. Use the algebra-piece sketch of the two squares to solve the following problem. Explain how you arrived at your conclusion.

    Two numbers differ by 5, and their squares differ by 125. What are the two numbers? (*Hint:* How must the difference of 125 be distributed in the L-shaped section of the sketch?)

PUZZLER

Marcea bought a sleeping bag, and the sales tax amounted to $14.20. If she had purchased the bag across the state line where the sales tax is 1% lower, the tax would have amounted to $12.78. What was the before-tax price of the bag?

JUST FOR FUN

ALGEBRAIC EXPRESSIONS GAME[2] (2 teams)

In this game, players match algebraic expressions to word descriptions. Copies of algebraic expression cards appear on Material Card 29. There are two decks of 12 cards, one for each team. Each student has an expression card similar to the samples below.

Play: The two teams play simultaneously. On team A, the game begins with player 1 saying, "I have $n + 1$. Who has two less than a number?" Then player 2 (on the same team), who has the card with $n - 2$, says, "I have $n - 2$. Who has one more than two times a number?" The game continues in this manner.

On team B, player 1 is the player with the $n + 2$ card, and player 2 is the player with an algebraic expression matching the word description on player 1's card.

Each deck of 12 cards is circular. That is, the last card in the deck calls the first card. Therefore, all the cards in the deck should be used. If there are fewer than 12 students on a team, some students can use more than one card. If there are more than 12 students on a team, two students can share a card, or more cards can be made.

Objective: The two teams compete against each other to complete the cycle of cards in the shortest amount of time.

Variation: The game can be changed so that word descriptions are matched to algebraic expressions. Two sample cards are shown here. In this case player 1 says, "I have two more than three times a number. Who has $4x - 1$?" Player 2 says, "I have one less than four times a number. Who has $3x + 5$?" Make a deck of these cards and play this version of the game.

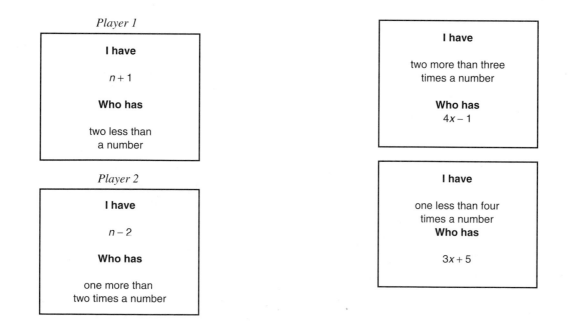

[2]T. Giambrone, "I HAVE . . . WHO HAS. . . ?" *The Mathematics Teacher* 73 (October 1980), 504–506.

ACTIVITY SET 7.2

GEOMETRIC MODELS FOR ALGEBRAIC EXPRESSIONS

Purpose To express products of algebraic terms geometrically

Materials Base-ten pieces from the Manipulative Kit

Activity In the preceding activity you saw that the ancient Greek mathematicians thought of numbers as line segments. The sum of two arbitrary numbers was represented by joining the two segments end to end and the product of two numbers was represented as the area of a rectangle with the two segments as sides. In this activity the geometric method employed by the Greeks is used to model sums and products of variables. Two arbitrary numbers x and y are represented by line segments and their sum, $x + y$, is represented by placing the line segments for x and y end to end as shown here.

$$x \qquad y \qquad x+y$$

Products, such as x times x or x times y, are represented as the *areas* of rectangles (or squares) with segments x and y as their sides, as in the following figures:

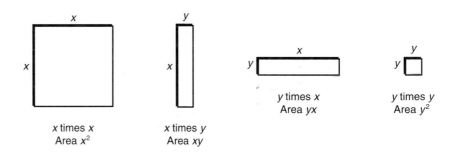

x times x
Area x^2

x times y
Area xy

y times x
Area yx

y times y
Area y^2

For this activity set, turn your base-ten pieces over to the blank side. In the first three activities the flat represents x^2, the long represents xy or yx, and the unit represents y^2. With the pieces identified this way we will refer to them as *algebra pieces*.

1. The product $(x + y)$ times $(x + y)$ is illustrated by this square, whose sides have length $x + y$. Build this figure with your area algebra pieces.

   a. On the diagram above, one of the four parts is labeled with the algebraic term representing its area. Label the remaining three parts with the algebraic terms representing their area.

   ★ **b.** Use your square and the fact that $xy = yx$ to write the following product as the sum of three algebraic terms.

$$(x + y)(x + y) =$$

2. Here are four algebra-piece diagrams for algebraic products. In each diagram label the areas of the parts and then write the product as the sum of algebraic terms.

★ **a.** $(3y)(3y) =$

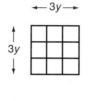

b. $(x + 2y)(x + 2y) =$

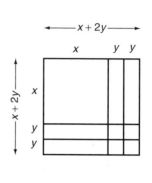

★ **c.** $x(x + y) =$

d. $y(x + y) =$

3. Build a model with algebra pieces to represent each product. Sketch the model and label the dimensions and the areas of each part. Use the model to determine the product.

★ **a.** $y(2x + y)$

b. $x(x + 2y)$

c. $(x + 3y)^2$

d. $(2x + 3y)(2x + 2y)$

In the remaining activities we will let one line segment have arbitrary length and call it *x*, but the other segment will have length 1. For example, below are lengths *x*, 1, and sums $x + 1$ and $x + 2$.

| *x* | 1 | *x* + 1 | *x* + 2 |

The algebra pieces will then have the following values.

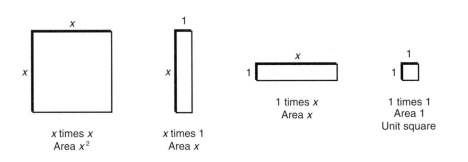

x times *x*
Area x^2

x times 1
Area *x*

1 times *x*
Area *x*

1 times 1
Area 1
Unit square

4. One large square, 5 rectangles, and 6 unit squares can be used to form a rectangle as shown here.

Which of the following collections of algebra pieces can be used to form a rectangle? Sketch the rectangle if it can be formed.

a. 1 square
3 rectangles
2 units

★ **b.** 1 square
3 rectangles
3 units

★ **c.** 1 square
7 rectangles
12 units

d. 1 square
5 rectangles
4 units

e. 1 square
7 rectangles
10 units

f. 2 squares
6 rectangles
4 units

g. 2 squares
9 rectangles
4 units

h. 2 squares
5 rectangles
3 units

i. 3 squares
5 rectangles
2 units

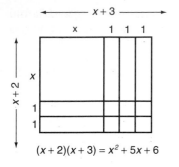

$(x + 2)(x + 3) = x^2 + 5x + 6$

5. There are two ways to express the area of the figure here. First, it has a width of $x + 2$ and a length of $x + 3$, so its area is the product of these two factors: $(x + 2)(x + 3)$. Second, it has an area composed of 1 large square, 5 rectangles, and 6 unit squares, so its area is $x^2 + 5x + 6$. Therefore we can write $(x + 2)(x + 3) = x^2 + 5x + 6$.

For each of the algebra piece diagrams below, record the dimensions and the equation which expresses the area in two ways, as shown in the example.

★ **a.**   **b.**   ★ **c.**

d.   **e.**   **f.**

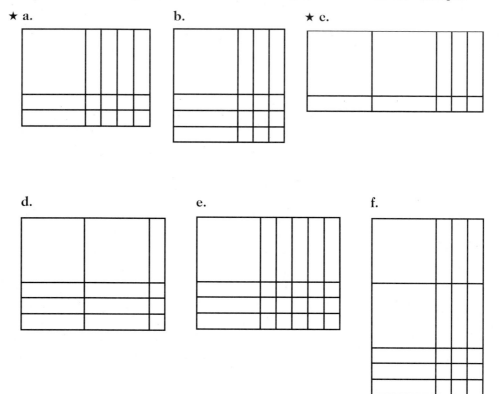

6. Given an algebraic expression like $2x^2 + 4x + 2$, we can think of it in terms of algebra pieces as two squares of area x^2, 4 rectangles of area x, and 2 unit squares. Since these pieces can be formed into a rectangle, as shown here, we can write the algebraic expression as the product of its length and its width: $2x^2 + 4x + 2 = (2x + 2)(x + 1)$.

Express each of the following algebraic expressions in terms of your algebra pieces. If a rectangle can be formed with the pieces, determine its dimensions and write the factors of the algebraic expression.

★ **a.** $x^2 + 7x + 10$ **b.** $3x^2 + 5x + 2$ **c.** $x^2 + 6x + 9$

★ **d.** $x^2 + x + 1$ **e.** $2x^2 + 5x + 3$ **f.** $3x^2 + 7x + 4$

g. $2x^2 + 7x + 6$ **h.** $x^2 + 4x + 4$ **i.** $4x^2 + 7x + 3$

. . . .

JUST FOR FUN

Both of these games use coordinate grids from Material Card 7.

COORDINATE GUESSING (2 players or teams)

The object of this game is to determine the coordinates of the opponent's target. Each player uses a pair of rectangular grids such as the ones shown here (Material Card 7). Each player draws three targets on one grid and records guesses as to the opponent's targets on the other grid. A target consists of three adjacent intersection points of the grid (in rows, columns, or diagonals) whose coordinates are whole numbers.

The players should not be able to see each other's grids. They take turns guessing three points at a time by giving the coordinates of each point. When a guessed point is on a target, the opponent must acknowledge this immediately. The game ends when one player has identified all three of the opponents' targets.

Variation: To speed up the game, you may wish to agree to inform your opponent whenever a guess is within 1 unit (horizontally or vertically) of a target.

Three targets

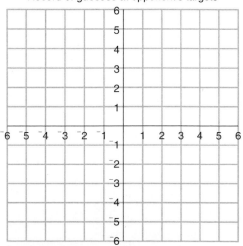

Record of guesses at opponent's targets

HIDE-A-REGION (2 players or teams)

This game is similar to Coordinate Guessing, but players search for the opponent's rectangle. Each player uses a pair of rectangular grids (Material Card 7). The game begins with the players agreeing on the area for the rectangles. Each player then sketches a rectangle on one grid, with the coordinates of the vertices being integers. (The players should not see each other's grids.) The players take turns guessing points by giving coordinates. Only one guess is allowed on each turn. Each player must tell whether the opponent's guess is an exterior, interior, vertex, or boundary point. Both players keep a record of their opponent's guesses and their own guesses. The first player to locate all four vertices of the opponent's rectangle is the winner.

Rectangle of area 12

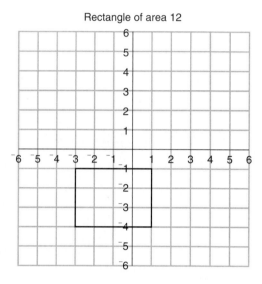

Record of guesses to locate opponent's rectangle

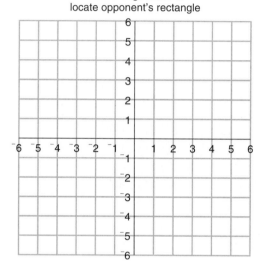

Variation: The players may agree to switch the shape of the region but keep all other rules the same.

For example, instead of a rectangle, the region could be a right triangle, triangle, or parallelogram.

- -

PUZZLER

In the first diagram, a block is standing on end on the table and an identical block is on its side on the floor. The distance between the highest parts of both blocks is 32 inches.

In the second diagram, the blocks are in reversed position and the distance between them is 28 inches.

How tall is the table?

IDEAS FOR THE ELEMENTARY CLASSROOM

SUGGESTED CLASSROOM ACTIVITY: PATTERN BLOCK PERIMETERS

Students of all ages can visualize and extend patterns. The first three terms of four pattern block sequences of varying difficulty are represented here.

1. Depending on the students' level, they may be able to use their pieces to build the next three terms of a sequence.

2. Build the 10th term of a sequence without building all the terms between.

3. Describe in words what the 20th term looks like without building it.

4. Determine the perimeter of each of the pattern block pieces using the length of the side of the square as 1 unit. (All perimeters are whole numbers.)

5. When students understand perimeter, ask them to determine the perimeter of each figure in the sequence and predict the perimeter of the 10th or 20th pattern based on the visualization of those terms.

6. (For students ready to generalize) Discover methods for predicting the perimeter of the 100th or nth figure in the sequence.[3]

PUZZLER

You and your friend each have some pennies. If you give your friend 1 penny, then you and your friend will have the same number of pennies. If your friend gives you 1 penny, then you will have twice as many pennies as your friend. How many pennies do each of you have?

Readings for More Classroom Ideas

Arcidiacono, Michael J., and E. Maier. "Picturing Algebra," in *Math and the Mind's Eye* (Unit IX). Salem, OR: The Math Learning Center, Box 3226, 1993.

Berman, Barbara, and F. Friederwitzer. "Algebra Can Be Elementary . . . When It's Concrete." *Arithmetic Teacher* 36 (April 1989): 21–24.

Cramer, Kathleen, and Thomas Post. "Making Connections: A Case for Proportionality." *Arithmetic Teacher* 40 (February 1993): 342–346.

Edwards, Ronald. *Algebra Magic Tricks.* Pacific Grove, CA: Critical Thinking Press and Software, 1992.

[3]See A. Bennett, E. Maier, and L. Ted Nelson, "Seeing Mathematical Relationships," in *Math and the Mind's Eye* (Unit I) (Salem, OR: The Math Learning Center, Box 3226, 1988).

Hirsch, Christian R. "Finding Factors Physically." *Mathematics Teacher* 75 (May 1982): 388–393.

Howden, Hilde. "Implementing the Standards: Patterns, Relationships, and Functions." *Arithmetic Teacher* 37 (November 1989): 17–24.

Kinach, Barbara. "Solving Linear Equations Physically." *Mathematics Teacher* 78 (September 1985): 437–447.

Loewen, A. C. "Lima Beans, Paper Cups, and Algebra." *Arithmetic Teacher* 38 (April 1991): 34–37.

Maier, Eugene, and M. Shaughnessy. "Graphing Algebraic Relationships," in *Math and the Mind's Eye* (Unit XI). Salem, OR: The Math Learning Center, Box 3226, 1996.

Metz, James R. "Slope as Speed." *Mathematics Teacher* 81 (April 1988): 285–289.

Schultz, James. "Implementing the Standards: Teaching Informal Algebra." *Arithmetic Teacher* 38 (May 1991): 34–37.

Smith, Robert F. "Let's Do It: Coordinate Geometry for Third Graders." *Arithmetic Teacher* 33 (April 1986): 6–11.

CHAPTER 8

STATISTICS

In grades K–4, students begin to explore basic ideas of statistics by gathering data appropriate to their grade level, organizing them in charts or graphs, and reading information from displays of data. These concepts should be expanded in the middle grades. . . . Instruction in statistics should focus on the active involvement of students in the entire process: formulating key questions; collecting and organizing data; representing the data using graphs, tables, frequency distributions, and summary statistics; analyzing the data; making conjectures; and communicating information in a convincing way.[1]

ACTIVITY SET 8.1

RANDOMNESS, SAMPLING, AND SIMULATION IN STATISTICS

Purpose To clarify the idea of a random event and apply that idea to sampling and simulation in statistics

Materials Green and red tiles from the Manipulative Kit, the table of random digits from Material Card 8, and containers such as boxes and bags for selecting samples

© 1965 United Feature Syndicate, Inc.

[1]*Curriculum and Evaluation Standards for School Mathematics* (Reston, VA: National Council of Teachers of Mathematics, 1989), 105.

Activity   One of the main objectives of statistics is to make decisions or predictions about a population (students in schools, voters in a country, lightbulbs, fish, and so forth) based on information taken from a sample of the population. A poorly chosen sample will not truly reflect the nature of the population. An important requirement is that the sample be randomly chosen. *Randomly chosen* means that every member of the population is equally likely to be selected.

Once a sample has been chosen, it is useful to determine a single number that describes the data. An *average* is one type of value or measure that represents a whole set of data. There are three averages commonly used to describe a set of numbers: mean, median, and mode. Let's use these averages to describe the following set of numbers:

$$2, 3, 4, 6, 8, 11, 12, 12, 12, 18$$

The *mean,* which is commonly referred to as the average, is the sum of the values divided by the total number of values. The sum of the 10 numbers is 88, so the mean is 8.8 ($88 \div 10$). The *median* is the middle value when all the values are arranged in order. The median for these values is 9.5, which is halfway between the two middle values 8 and 11. The *mode* is the value that occurs most frequently—in this case, the mode is 12.

Simulations are processes that help answer questions about a real problem; they are experiments that closely resemble the real situation. These experiments usually involve random samples.

In this activity set, we will explore the notion of random numbers, experimentally select random samples, and use the idea of randomness to simulate a real situation.

1. **Random Digits:** Three methods for generating a list of random digits are described below.

   a. **Container Selection Method:** One way to obtain random digits is to write each digit, 0 through 9, on a chip; place all 10 chips in a container; shake the container to thoroughly mix the chips; and then draw one chip, without looking, from the container. If every chip in the container has an equal chance of being selected, then the one you draw will be a *random digit.* By replacing that chip and repeating the process many times, you can form a list of random digits. Write the digits on chips or slips of paper, put them in a container, and draw them out to generate a list of 100 random digits. Record five digits on each of the 20 blanks below.

_____	_____	_____	_____
_____	_____	_____	_____
_____	_____	_____	_____
_____	_____	_____	_____
_____	_____	_____	_____

b. Calculator Method: Here is a method for generating a list of random digits using a calculator.

Example

(1) Choose an arbitrary five-digit number: 72194
(2) Square that number: $(72194)^2 = 52\underline{11973}636$
(3) Select 5 middle digits of the result, and square that number: $(11973)^2 = 143\underline{35272}9$
(4) Repeat the process: $(33527)^2 = 11\underline{24059}729$

Each string of middle digits—11973, 33527, and 24059—is a group of random digits. Select your own arbitrary five-digit number and generate 100 random digits using the calculator process. Record five digits on each of the blanks below.

_____	_____	_____	_____
_____	_____	_____	_____
_____	_____	_____	_____
_____	_____	_____	_____
_____	_____	_____	_____

c. "Top-of-the-Head" Method: Can a list of random digits be produced by writing numbers down as quickly as possible, as they pop into your head? Try this method of generating 100 digits. Record the digits below in groups of five.

_____	_____	_____	_____
_____	_____	_____	_____
_____	_____	_____	_____
_____	_____	_____	_____
_____	_____	_____	_____

2. For each list of digits that you generated in activity 1, determine, by tallying, the number of times (frequency) each digit occurred in that list.

Container Selection Method			Calculator Method			Top-of-the-Head Method		
DIGIT	TALLY	FREQUENCY	DIGIT	TALLY	FREQUENCY	DIGIT	TALLY	FREQUENCY
0	_____	_____	0	_____	_____	0	_____	_____
1	_____	_____	1	_____	_____	1	_____	_____
2	_____	_____	2	_____	_____	2	_____	_____
3	_____	_____	3	_____	_____	3	_____	_____
4	_____	_____	4	_____	_____	4	_____	_____
5	_____	_____	5	_____	_____	5	_____	_____
6	_____	_____	6	_____	_____	6	_____	_____
7	_____	_____	7	_____	_____	7	_____	_____
8	_____	_____	8	_____	_____	8	_____	_____
9	_____	_____	9	_____	_____	9	_____	_____
	Total	100		Total	100		Total	100

a. If you had to determine some commonsense ways to judge whether or not a sequence of digits was indeed random, what are some factors you would consider?

b. If each digit in your list has a frequency from 7 to 13, then you can have confidence that you have a random sequence of digits.[2] Compare the three methods of generating random digits. How would you rate the top-of-the-head method? Was the top-of-the-head method biased in favor of any particular digit?

3. Sampling and Predictions: The objective of sampling is to make predictions about a large population. Samples are usually relatively small. For example, some national television ratings are based on a sample of only 1100 people. The following activity is designed to show how a sample can represent the given population.

Have a classmate put any one of the following three populations of tiles in a container, without your knowing the numbers of red and green tiles. *Don't look at the contents of the container until you have completed all parts of this activity.*

[2]Such limits as these (7 and 13) for determining if a distribution is uniform can be obtained from a statistical test called the chi-square test.

POPULATION 1	**POPULATION 2**	**POPULATION 3**
25 red tiles	20 red tiles	10 red tiles
5 green tiles	10 green tiles	20 green tiles

Draw a tile and check off its color in the following table. Return the tile to the container and repeat this activity. After every five draws, make a prediction as to which population you think is in the container. Continue the experiment until you have selected 25 times.

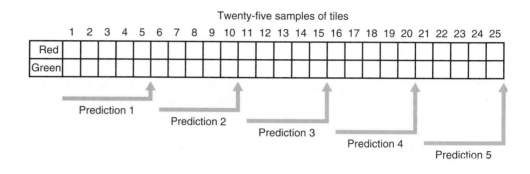

Twenty-five samples of tiles

a. Compute the percentage of red tiles in each of the following groups.

　　First 5　　　　First 10　　　　First 15　　　　First 20　　　　All 25

b. As the size of the sample increases, the likelihood that it represents the population becomes greater. Based on your sample of 25 tiles, predict which of the three given populations you have sampled. Would you have selected the same population if your sample size had been only the first 5 tiles? The first 10? Now look at the contents of the container to check your prediction.

4. **Stratified Sampling:** Following are the income and regional living area for 18 households. Write the information for each household on a separate piece of paper, and place the pieces of paper in a container.

Lake Property	Lake Property	Lake Property	Suburban	Suburban	Suburban	Suburban	Suburban	Suburban
$210,000	$180,000	$140,000	$70,000	$60,000	$44,000	$40,000	$35,000	$26,000
City	City	City	City	City	City	City	City	City
$40,000	$35,000	$24,000	$22,000	$20,000	$20,000	$18,000	$17,000	$15,000

a. The average of all 18 incomes is $56,444.44. Select 6 pieces of paper at random from the container. Compute the average (mean) income of your sample and record it here. By how much does it differ from the average of all 18 incomes?

★ **b.** There are many different samples of 6 incomes that you could have selected. Suppose, for example, your sample contained the 6 greatest incomes. What would be the average of these 6 incomes? What would be the average of the 6 smallest incomes?

c. The average of the 6 greatest incomes and the average of the 6 smallest incomes differ significantly from the average of all 18 incomes. By using a technique called *stratified sampling,* you can avoid getting an unrepresentative sample. Separate the total population of 18 incomes by living area into 3 different containers. Notice that the lake property, suburban, and city salaries represent $\frac{1}{6}$, $\frac{1}{3}$, and $\frac{1}{2}$ of the population, respectively. To obtain a proportional *stratified sample* of 6 incomes, select 1 lake property income ($\frac{1}{6}$ of 6), 2 suburban incomes ($\frac{1}{3}$ of 6), and 3 city incomes ($\frac{1}{2}$ of 6) from their individual containers. Compute the average of these 6 incomes. By how much does it differ from the average of all 18 incomes?

★ **d.** If the stratified sampling procedure in part c is used, what is the greatest possible average that can be obtained for 6 incomes?

What is the smallest possible average that can be obtained?

Compare these averages to those in part b and discuss the advantages of stratified sampling.

5. Simulation: People with type O blood are called universal donors because their blood can be used in transfusions to people with different blood types. About 45 percent of the population has type O blood. If blood donors arrive at the blood bank with random blood types, how many donors, on the average, would it take to obtain five donors with type O blood? Make a conjecture.

a. There are 100 two-digit numbers from 00 to 99 and the numbers from 00 to 44 represent 45 percent of them. Without looking, put your pencil point on the page of random digits on Material Card 8. Beginning with the digit closest to the pencil point, list consecutive pairs of digits from the table of random digits until your list includes exactly five two-digit numbers from 00 to 44. If any pair of digits represents a donor, how many donors would have to arrive at the blood bank to obtain five donors with type O blood?

b. The procedure you followed in part a is a *simulation*—a way to answer a problem by running an experiment which resembles the problem. Assuming that blood donors who go to the blood bank have random blood types and that 45 percent have type O, your experiment simulated the number of donors needed to obtain five donors with type O blood. Run the same experiment a total of 10 times and record your results here.

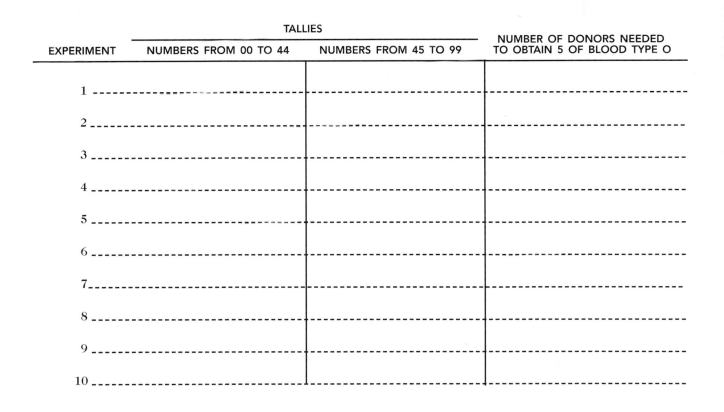

EXPERIMENT	TALLIES NUMBERS FROM 00 TO 44	NUMBERS FROM 45 TO 99	NUMBER OF DONORS NEEDED TO OBTAIN 5 OF BLOOD TYPE O
1			
2			
3			
4			
5			
6			
7			
8			
9			
10			

c. The mean of the numbers of donors in the 10 experiments is the *average number* for these experiments. Based on your experimental results, what is the average number of donors the blood bank would have to receive to obtain five donors with type O blood?

JUST FOR FUN

SIMULATED RACING GAME (2 players)

In this race, one player flips a coin and the other rolls a die. At the start of play, each player rolls the die, and the high roller gets to use the die in the game. The race track is 12 steps long, and the racers move simultaneously. That is, the coin is flipped and the die is rolled at the same time. The coin tosser can move 1 step for heads and 2 steps for tails. The die roller can move the number of steps that comes up on the die. The race continues until 1 person lands on the last step. However, *the winner must land on the last step by exact count.* It is possible for this race to end in a tie. Find a person to race against and complete several races using a die and a coin.

1. Does this appear to be a fair race? That is, do the wins seem to be evenly distributed between the die roller and the coin tosser? You may wish to have a larger sample of completed races on which to base your conclusions. Use the table of random numbers on Material Card 8 to simulate die rolling and coin flipping as follows:

- *Coin flipping*—Put your pencil down on an arbitrary point in the table. If the closest digit is even, call the outcome heads; if it is odd, call the outcome tails. For the succeeding flip, move to the next digit in the table and do the same. Repeat this process until the game is complete.
- *Die tossing*—Put your pencil down on an arbitrary point in the table. If the closest digit is a 1, 2, 3, 4, 5, or 6, let it represent your first roll of the die. If that digit is a 0, 7, 8, or 9, move to the next digit in the table that is not a 0, 7, 8, or 9 and let it represent your roll. For the succeeding roll, move to the next digit in the table and do the same. Repeat this process until the game is complete.

2. What happens when the length of the race (number of steps) is shortened? For example, will a two-step race be won more frequently by one player than the other? Try races of different lengths. Can you draw some conclusion about the fairness of the race and its length?

	START	1	2	3	4	5	6	7	8	9	10	11	FINISH
Coin flipper	X	__	__	__	__	__	__	__	__	__	__	__	__
Die roller	X	__	__	__	__	__	__	__	__	__	__	__	__

PUZZLER

Assume the probability of a baby being a boy is $\frac{1}{2}$. Which of the following sequences of births is more likely to occur in a six-child family?

GBBGBG   or   GGGGBG

---

[3]An excellent source for simulation activities is M. Gnanadesikan, R. Scheaffer, and J. Swift, *The Art and Techniques of Simulation* (Palo Alto, CA: Dale Seymour Publications, 1987).

ACTIVITY SET 8.2

SCATTER PLOTS: LOOKING FOR RELATIONSHIPS

Purpose To look for associations or trends between two sets of data

Materials A tape measure or ruler and string

Activity Scatter plots provide a visual means of looking for a relationship between two variables. As an example, one middle school student with two very tall parents wanted to see if, in general, taller people married taller people. She randomly selected students in her school and recorded the heights of their parents. Then for each set of parents she placed a point on the following graph which pairs the father's height with the mother's. From this scatter plot she hoped to reach some conclusions. Do you think there is any association in parental heights based on her scatter plot?

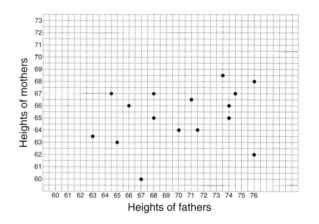

This activity set will review scatter plots and trend lines and then you will collect your own data and look for associations and trends.

---

1. Use the scatter plot above to answer the following questions.

   ★ **a.** What is the height of the shortest mother? The tallest mother?

   b. What are the heights of the shortest and tallest fathers?

   c. What is the difference in height between the shortest and tallest mother? The shortest and tallest father?

   ★ **d.** For how many couples was the woman taller than the man?

2. One method for determining an association on a scatter plot is to draw a single straight line that approximates the location of the points. One such line is called a *median-fit line*. A median-fit line can be drawn after a few simple steps. First, the points of the scatter plot are separated into three approxi-

mately equal groups, as shown in figure 1. If possible, the two outer sections (1st and 3d) should have the same number of points.

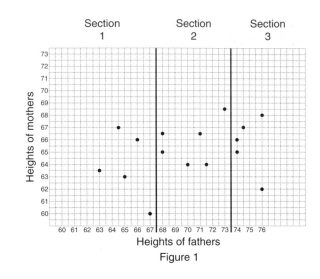

Figure 1

a. In figure 2 a vertical median line (dotted) has been drawn in sections 1 and 2 of the scatter plot. Since there are an odd number of points in section 1, the line passes through the middle point (3d point from the left and 3d from the right). Since there are an even number of points in section 2, the median line is midway between the middle points. Draw the vertical median line in section 3.

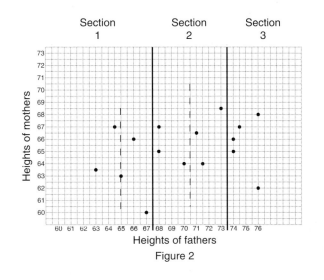

Figure 2

★ b. In figure 3 a horizontal median line (dotted) has been drawn in section 1. It passes through the middle (or median) point as the points are viewed from top to bottom. Draw the horizontal median lines in the other two sections.

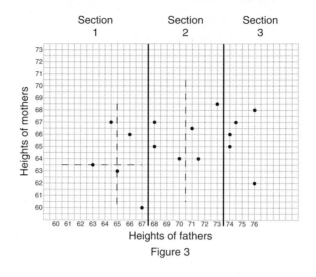

Figure 3

c. Place a straightedge through the two points where the vertical and horizontal median lines intersect in the sections 1 and 3. Then slide the straightedge one-third of the distance between it and the point where the medians intersect in section 2 and draw the median-fit line.

d. The median-fit line reflects the association between the two variables, height of mother and height of father. Write a summary of the conclusions you can draw by looking at the median-fit line.

e. Suppose that the median-fit line had looked like one of the following. What would you have concluded about the parental height relationships for each of these cases?

3. To construct your own scatter plot, collect the following information from a sample of at least 20 people: height, arm span, and wrist circumference. Arm span means the distance from the tip of one index finger to the other when the arms are outstretched in opposite directions and parallel to the floor. To measure the circumference of the wrist use a tape measure or wrap a string about the wrist and then measure the string with a ruler.

Data Record

	1	2	3	4	5	6	7	8	9	10	11	12	13	14	15	16	17	18	19	20
Height																				
Arm span																				
Wrist																				

On grid I below, form a scatter plot that compares heights and arm spans. Put a scale on the horizontal axis for heights and a scale on the vertical axis for arm spans. The range of each scale will depend on the range of the measures you obtained. Draw a median-fit line for the scatter plot. Then write a summary of your observations and conclusions which includes your judgment of the strength of the association between the two measurements (based on how well you think the median-fit line approximates the data).

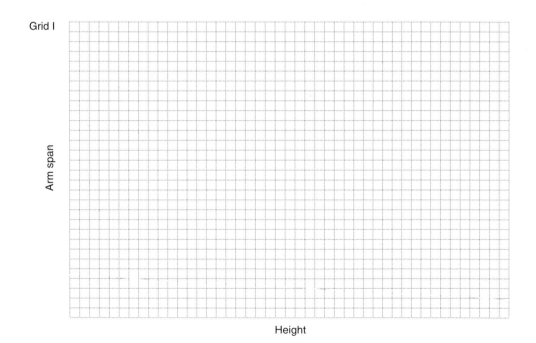

Grid I

Arm span

Height

On grid II repeat the process but put the wrist measurements on the vertical axis. Write your summary.

Note: If a graphing calculator is available a test of the strength of the median-fit line as a "fit" to the points of the scatter plot can be found by entering the data points and checking the correlation coefficient. The closer the correlation coefficient is to +1 or −1, the better the fit.

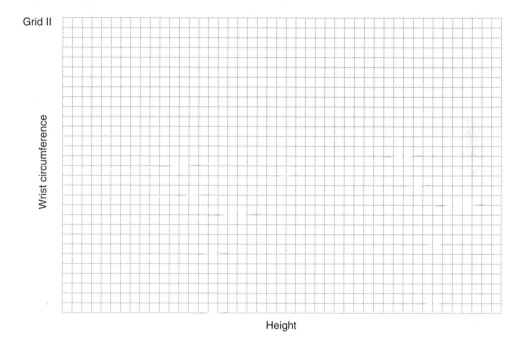

Grid II

Wrist circumference

Height

JUST FOR FUN

PAGE GUESSING

Does performance improve with practice? In this activity you will see if you can improve your page location performance with practice.

Find a book with several hundred pages and note the total number of pages it contains. Arbitrarily pick a page number in that book and record it as your target page. Before opening the book, estimate where you think that target page is located and then try to open the book as close to that page as possible. In the fol-

lowing table record the page number opened to and the number of pages you were off target (the difference between the target number and the page you opened). Close the book and try again. After five trials, graph your results on the grid provided below. Then, plot what you think the next few points on the graph would be if you were to continue. Continue your experiment a few more times to check your predictions. Repeat with another book to see if you improve with practice.

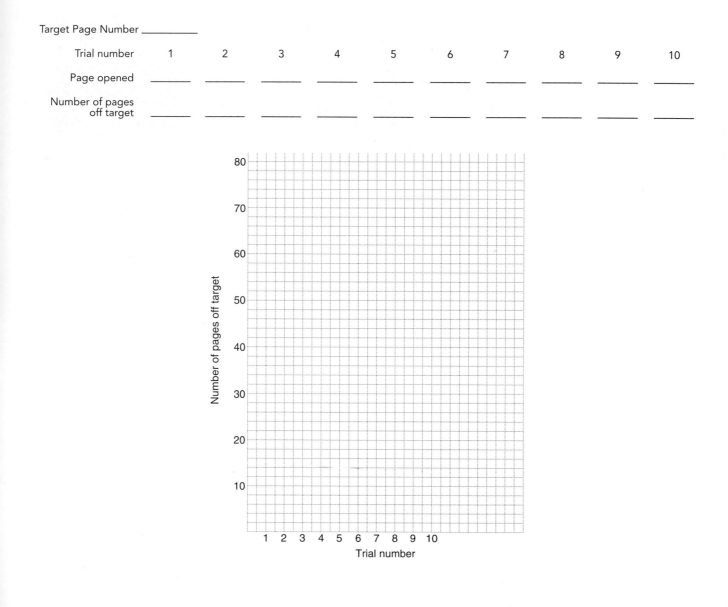

Target Page Number _____

Trial number	1	2	3	4	5	6	7	8	9	10
Page opened	_____	_____	_____	_____	_____	_____	_____	_____	_____	_____
Number of pages off target	_____	_____	_____	_____	_____	_____	_____	_____	_____	_____

ACTIVITY SET 8.3

STATISTICAL DISTRIBUTIONS: OBSERVATIONS AND APPLICATIONS

Purpose To construct and apply frequency distributions

Materials The table of random digits on Material Card 8

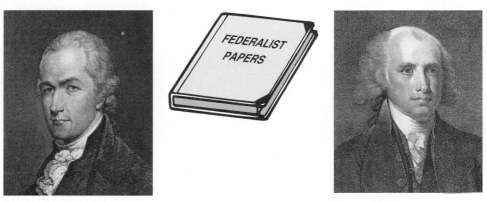

Alexander Hamilton *James Madison*

Activity Once measurements from a population sample have been collected, they are arranged by grouping similar measurements together in a table, chart, or graph. A *frequency distribution* is a tabulation of values by categories or intervals. An interesting illustration of the use of frequency distributions was in the resolution of the controversy over authorship of the *Federalist Papers*.[4] This is a collection of 85 political papers written in the eighteenth century by Alexander Hamilton, John Jay, and James Madison. There is general agreement on the authorship of all but 12 of these papers. In order to determine who should be given credit for the 12 disputed papers, frequency distributions were compiled for certain filler words such as *by, to, of,* and *on.*

Forty-eight of Hamilton's papers were analyzed to see how many times he used the word *by* in every 1000 words. In 18 out of 48 papers, he used *by* an average of 7 times. This is indicated by the longest bar of the top distribution in figure a. In others of his papers he used *by* at different rates, as indicated by the other bars of that distribution. A distribution of Madison's usage of *by* in 50 of his papers is shown in the middle distribution of figure a. Notice that Madison's distribution looks like the distribution of *by* in the disputed papers shown in the bottom of figure a. A similar analysis for the word *to* is shown in figure b. These and similar distributions for other filler words support the contention that Madison was the author of the disputed papers.

[4]F. Mosteller et al., *Statistics: A Guide to the Unknown* (New York: Holden-Day, 1972), 164–175.

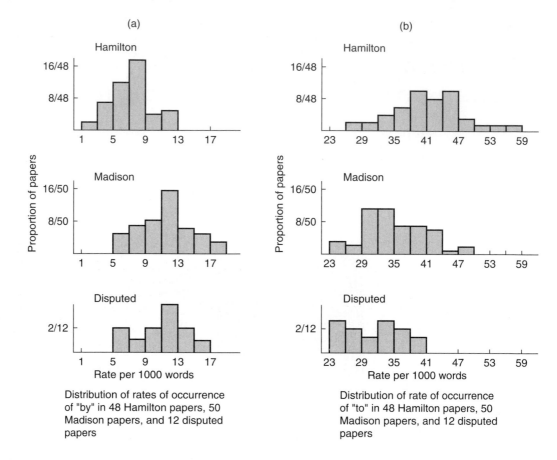

(a)

Hamilton

Madison

Disputed

Rate per 1000 words

Distribution of rates of occurrence of "by" in 48 Hamilton papers, 50 Madison papers, and 12 disputed papers

(b)

Hamilton

Madison

Disputed

Rate per 1000 words

Distribution of rate of occurrence of "to" in 48 Hamilton papers, 50 Madison papers, and 12 disputed papers

Several types of frequency distributions commonly occur. If each category or interval of the distribution has approximately the same number of values, the distribution is called a *uniform distribution*. For example, the following bar graph shows the frequency distribution for the outcomes of rolling a die 3000 times. The frequency of each outcome varies between approximately 480 and 520.

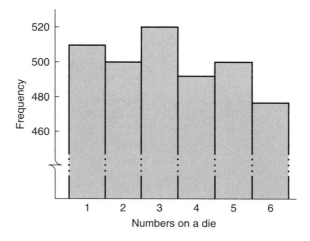

One of the most useful distributions in statistics is the *normal distribution.* This distribution often occurs in the physical, social, and biological sciences. The graph of a normal distribution is the familiar bell-shaped curve. This curve is symmetric about the mean, with a gradual decrease at both ends. The heights of a large sample of adult men will be *normally distributed,* as shown in the following graph.

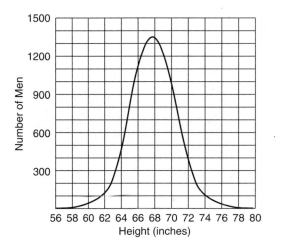

1. When four coins are tossed, there are six ways to get exactly two heads. Think of the coins as being a penny, nickel, dime, and quarter. The penny and dime may be heads and the nickel and quarter tails; the penny and nickel heads and the dime and quarter tails; and so forth. Fill in the remaining four ways of getting exactly two heads. Then fill in all other possible ways the coins can come up.

| H | H | T | T | | | | |
| H | T | H | T | | | | |

This graph shows the number of different outcomes for tosses of four coins at a time. The frequency of 6 above 2 heads corresponds to the six different combinations of two heads. There are frequencies of 1 above 0 heads and 4 heads, because these two events can occur only if the tosses result in all tails or all heads. This distribution looks like a normal curve. As the number of coins being tossed increases, the distribution of outcomes theoretically gets close to a normal curve.

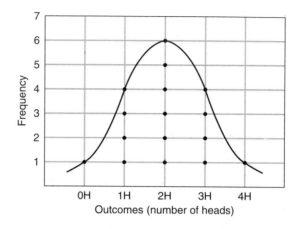

a. Use the table of random digits on Material Card 8 to simulate the tossing of six coins. Pick an arbitrary starting point in the table and, counting even digits as heads and odd digits as tails, record the number of heads in each block of six digits. Simulate 64 tosses of six coins, and record the number of heads for each toss in the table below. Each blank in the table will contain a digit from 0 to 6, depending on the number of heads counted in the toss.

1	2	3	4	5	6	7	8	9	10	11	12	13
14	15	16	17	18	19	20	21	22	23	24	25	26
27	28	29	30	31	32	33	34	35	36	37	38	39
40	41	42	43	44	45	46	47	48	49	50	51	52
53	54	55	56	57	58	59	60	61	62	63	64	

b. Plot the frequency of each outcome on this grid. For example, the number of times you got two heads should be plotted above 2H on the graph. Theoretically, about 78 percent of the outcomes should be 2, 3, or 4 heads. What percent of your outcomes are 2, 3, or 4 heads?

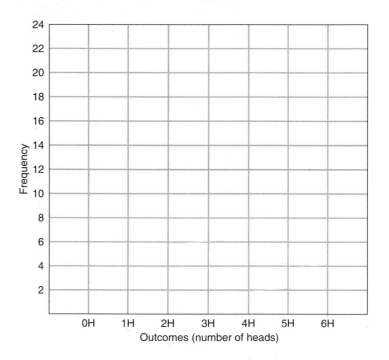

★ **c.** Suppose that an outcome of heads represents the birth of a girl and an outcome of tails represents that of a boy. In addition, suppose that each of the coin tosses in part a represents a family that is planning to have six children. Explain how you would use the data to predict approximately what percent of those families will have *at least* three girls.

2. When measurement such as weight, range of eyesight, or IQ are compiled for a large number of people, they are usually normally distributed. The following list contains the pulse rates of 60 students. Use these data to complete the bar graph below. Do the pulse rates appear to you to be close to a normal distribution?

Pulse rates (beats per minute)/Frequency

Pulse	53	56	57	58	61	62	63	64	65	66	67	68	69	70	71	72	73	74	75	76	77	78	79	80	81	82	84	86	89	91	92
Freq.	1	2	1	1	1	3	1	1	3	1	2	2	2	6	1	4	3	4	2	3	1	1	2	3	1	1	2	2	1	1	1

★ **a.** One property of a normal distribution is that 68 percent of the measurements are within 1 standard deviation on either side of the mean and 95 percent are within 2 standard deviations on either side of the mean, as illustrated below. The set of pulse rates has a mean of 72 and a standard deviation of 8.7. Does the distribution of pulse rates satisfy this property? Record your findings.

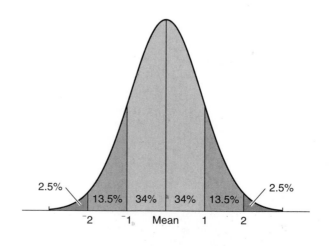

b. Even smaller numbers of measurements may tend to be normally distributed. Draw a bar graph of your classmates' pulse rates taken over a 10-second interval. One property of approximately normal curves is that the mean, median, and mode are approximately equal. Determine the mean, median, and mode for the pulse rates of your class. Are they approximately equal?

3. Some people are not aware of the uneven distribution of letters which occurs in words. One such person may have been Christofer Sholes, the inventor of the typewriter. He gave the left hand 56 percent of all the strokes, and he gave the two most agile fingers on the right hand two of the least often used letters of the alphabet, j and k. This table shows the frequencies, in terms of percentages of occurrence, of letters in large samples.

E	12.3%	S	6.6%	U	3.1%	B	1.6%	J	0.1%
T	9.6%	R	6.0%	P	2.3%	G	1.6%	Z	0.1%
A	8.1%	H	5.1%	F	2.3%	V	0.9%		
O	7.9%	L	4.0%	M	2.2%	K	0.5%		
N	7.2%	D	3.7%	W	2.0%	Q	0.2%		
I	7.2%	C	3.2%	Y	1.9%	X	0.2%		

★ **a.** There are 350 letters in the preceding paragraph. Count the number of times that e, s, c, w, and k occur and compute their percentages. Compare your answer with the percentages that have been computed for large samples.

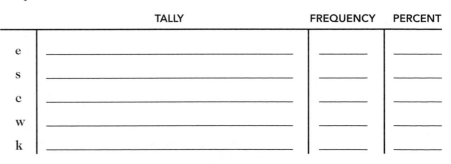

	TALLY	FREQUENCY	PERCENT
e			
s			
c			
w			
k			

b. The most frequently occurring letter in the English language is *e*. In 1939 a 267-page novel entitled *Gadsby* was released by the Wetzel Publishing Company. The novel was known not for its literary merit, but rather for one distinctive feature: Not 1 of its 50,000 words contained the letter *e*. Try to compose a sentence of at least ten words that does not use the letter *e*.

★ **c.** In Morse code, letters are represented by dots and dashes so that they can be sent by electrical impulses. A dot consumes 1 time unit, a dash consumes 3 time units, and 1 time unit is needed for each space between symbols. In 1938 Samuel Morse assigned the symbols with the shortest time intervals to the letters that occurred most frequently, according to his sample of 12,000 words from a Philadelphia newspaper. Although Morse's code assignment is more efficient than it would have been if he had assigned letters haphazardly, it can still be improved. Devise a new and more efficient assignment of Morse's code symbols for the nine letters in this table. How many fewer time units do you require for these nine letters than Samuel Morse did?

CODE SYMBOL	NUMBER OF TIME UNITS	LETTERS	REASSIGNED CODE SYMBOL
•	1	e	_____
—	3	t	_____
• —	5	a	_____
— — —	11	o	_____
— •	5	n	_____
• •	3	i	_____
• • •	5	s	_____
• — •	7	r	_____
• • • •	7	h	_____

4. It is surprising to learn that the leading digits of numbers *do not occur with the same frequency*—that is, are not evenly distributed.[5] Find an opponent and try this experiment. Choose a book that contains tables of numbers, such as areas or populations of cities or lengths of rivers. Let your opponent pick the table. (Or, use the following table.) For each number in the table beginning with a 1, 2, 3, or 4, you win; for each number beginning with a 5, 6, 7, 8, or 9, your opponent wins. Even though you are winning on fewer leading digits, you should come out ahead in the long run.

---

[5]An explanation of this phenomenon can be found in W. Weaver, *Lady Luck* (New York: Doubleday, 1963), 270–277.

U.S. Population — Places of 5,000 or More

Place	1970	Place	1970
Haddon Heights	9,365	Palmyra	6,969
Haledon	6,767	Paramus	26,381
Hammonton	11,464	Park Ridge	8,709
Hanover Twp.	10,700	Passaic	55,124
Harrison	11,811	Paterson	144,824
Hasbrouck Heights	13,651	Paulsboro	8,084
Hawthorne	19,173	Pennsauken Twp.	36,394
Hazlet Twp.	22,239	Penns Grove	5,727
Highland Park	14,385	Pennsville	11,014
Hightstown	5,431	Pequannok Twp.	14,350
Hillsdale	11,768	Perth Amboy	38,798
Hillside Twp.	21,636	Phillipsburg	17,849
Hoboken	45,380	Pine Hill	5,132
Hopatcong	9,052	Piscataway Twp.	36,418
Hopewell Twp. (Mercer)	10,030	Pitman	10,257
Irvington	59,743	Plainfield	46,862
Jackson Twp.	18,276	Pleasantville	13,778
Jersey City	260,350	Point Pleasant	15,968
Keansburg	9,720	Pompton Lakes	11,397
Kearny	37,585	Princeton	12,331
Kendall Park	7,412	Princeton North	5,488
Kenilworth	9,165	Prospect Park	5,176
Keyport	7,205	Rahway	29,114
Kinnelon	7,600	Ramblewood	5,556
Lake Hiawatha	11,389	Ramsey	12,571
Lake Mohawk	6,262	Randolph Twp.	13,296
Lake Parsippany	7,488	Raritan	6,691
Lakewood	17,874	Red Bank	12,847
Laurence Harbor	6,715	Ridgefield	11,308
Laconia	8,847	Ridgefield Park	13,990
Lincoln Park	9,034	Ridgewood	27,547
Linden	41,409	Ringwood	10,393
Lindenwold 1973	16,265	River Edge	12,850
Linwood	6,159	Riverside Twp.	8,591
Little Falls Twp.	11,727	Rochelle Park Twp.	6,380
Little Ferry	9,064	Rockaway	6,383
Little Silver	6,010	Roselle	22,585
Livingston Twp.	30,127	Roselle Park	14,227
Lodi	25,163	Rumson	7,421
Long Branch	31,774	Runnemede	10,475
Lyndhurst Twp.	22,729	Rutherford	20,802
Madison	16,710	Saddle Brook Twp.	15,975
Magnolia	5,893	Salem	7,648
Mahwah Twp.	10,800	Sayreville	32,508
Manville	13,029	Scotch Plains Twp.	22,279
Maple Shade Twp.	16,464	Secaucus	13,228
Maplewood Twp.	24,932	Somerdale	6,510
Margate City	10,576	Somers Point	7,919
Marlboro Twp.	12,273	Somerville	13,652
Marlton	10,180	South Amboy	9,338
Matawan	9,136	South Orange	16,971
Maywood	11,087	South Plainfield	21,142
McGuire	10,933	South River	15,428
Mercerville-Hamilton Sq.	24,465	Sparta Twp.	10,819
Metuchen	16,031	Spotswood	7,891
Middlesex	15,038	Springfield Twp.	15,740

★ **a.** The populations in the preceding table are four-, five-, and six-digit numbers. The least number is 5132, and the greatest number is 260,350. In the table below, all numbers from 5132 to 260,350 have been separated into four intervals. Check the intervals that contain winning numbers for you. There are 4868 numbers in the first interval. Determine the number of numbers in each of the other intervals.

INTERVAL	WIN OR LOSE	NUMBER OF NUMBERS
5132 to 9,999	_____	4868
10,000 to 49,999	_____	_____
50,000 to 99,999	_____	_____
100,000 to 260,350	_____	_____

b. You can see from part a that the intervals in which you win contain more numbers than do the intervals in which your opponent wins. According to these numbers, about how many times greater is your chance of winning?

★ **c.** There are 112 populations in the preceding table. How many of these populations will make you a winner? How many will make your opponent a winner?

d. Carry out the investigation in parts a–c for a table of numbers chosen from another book.

• •

JUST FOR FUN

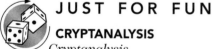

CRYPTANALYSIS

Cryptanalysis is the analysis and deciphering of cryptograms, codes, and other secret writings. Successful cryptanalysis has been important in gaining many military victories and in preventing crime and espionage. One of the earliest cryptographic systems known was used by Julius Caesar and is called the Caesar cipher. Enciphering a message using this system involves replacing each letter of the alphabet by the let-

ter that is 3 letters beyond it: A is replaced by D, B by E, C by F, and so forth. Use the Caesar cipher to decipher the statement on this scroll.

It is not known why Caesar selected 3 as the number of places to shift the alphabet. Any whole number greater than 1 can be used.

One way of improving cryptograms is to eliminate word lengths. The following message is written in groups of 5 letters. It was enciphered by shifting each letter of the alphabet the same number of letters to the right.

OITQT   MWAPW   EMLUM   VWNAK   QMVKM   BPIBE   MQOPQ   VOIVL   UMIAC

ZQVOI   VMEWZ   BPEPQ   TMVME   BWVKW   VDQVK   MLITI   ZOMXZ   WXWZB

QWVWN   BPMUB   PIBEM   QOPQV   OIVLU   MIACZ   QVOIZ   MBPMW   VTGQV

DMABQ   OIBQW   VABPI   BIZME   WZBPE   PQTMK   PIZTM   AAQVO   MZ

One method of determining the amount of shift is to make a frequency distribution of the letters in the message and compare it to a frequency distribution of letters in common use. The following bar graph shows the percentage of occurrence of each letter (rounded to the nearest whole number) in a large sample of unencrypted words. There are some important patterns. Among the high-frequency letters, we see that three (A, E, and I) are 4 letters apart; two (N and O) are next to each other; and three (R, S, and T) are side by side. Among the low-frequency letters, two (J and K) occur as a pair, and six (U, V, W, X, Y, and Z) are side by side.

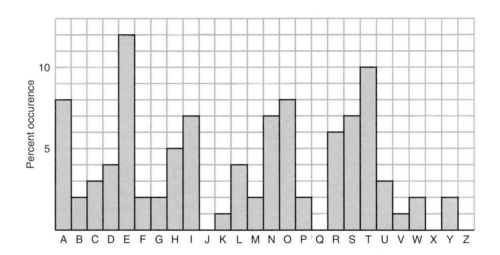

★ Make a frequency distribution of letters in the coded message. Predict the amount of shift by comparing this distribution with the one above, and by looking for patterns of high- and low-frequency letters. Try your prediction by deciphering a few words. When you have found the correct amount of shift, decipher the message.[6]

[6]For further techniques in cryptography, see A. Sinkov, *Elementary Cryptanalysis* (Washington, DC: Mathematical Association of America, 1966).

IDEAS FOR THE ELEMENTARY CLASSROOM

SUGGESTED CLASSROOM ACTIVITY: STUDENT-CENTERED DATA COLLECTION

Collecting, organizing, displaying, describing and interpreting of data can be done at all grade levels. At early grade levels, children can form living graphs as they stand in rows according to number of pets, month of birth, blouse or shirt color, and so forth. The "living graph" can be replaced by a similar display on a chart, with names in place of the children. Many mathematical terms arise in a discussion of the results, such as *more, less, fewer, greatest, how many, average,* and *frequency.*

As students get older and develop greater curiosity about themselves, their peers, and their environment, the list of topics for statistical study becomes much longer. Issues such as favorite television program, number of hours spent watching TV each day, and favorite advertisement can be explored for an entire school rather than one classroom.[7] This can help students understand the need for random sampling techniques.

PUZZLER

Label all faces of two cubes so that when the cubes are rolled, the sum of the top two numbers will always be 0, 1, 2, or 3, and all of these sums are equally likely to occur.

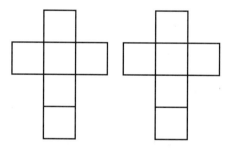

Readings for More Classroom Ideas

Bankard, Dianne, and Francis Fennell. "Ideas: Measurements, Surveys and Graphing." *Arithmetic Teacher* 39 (September 1991): 26–33.

Barson, Alan, and L. Barson. "Ideas: Collecting Data." *Arithmetic Teacher* 35 (March 1988): 19–24.

Bryan, Elizabeth H. "Exploring Data with Box Plots." *Mathematics Teacher* 81 (November 1988): 658–663.

Burrill, Gail, et al. *Data Analysis and Statistics Across the Curriculum,* in the *Curriculum and Evaluation Standards for School Mathematics Addenda Series.* Reston, VA: National Council of Teachers of Mathematics, 1992.

Finlay, Ellen, and Ian Lowe. *Chance and Data: Exploring Real Data.* Mathematics Curriculum and Teaching Program. Carlton, Australia: Curriculum Corporation, 1993.

Hitch, Chris, and Georganna Armstrong. "Daily Activities for Data Analysis." *Arithmetic Teacher* 41 (January 1994): 242–245.

---

[7]An interesting example of a statistical study done by middle school students is described by David Pagni in "A Television Programming Challenge: A Cooperative Group Activity That Uses Mathematics," *Arithmetic Teacher* 36 (January 1989), 7–9.

Lindquist, Mary M., et al. *Making Sense of Data,* in the *Curriculum and Evaluation Standards for School Mathematics Addenda Series: Grades K–6.* Reston, VA: National Council of Teachers of Mathematics, 1992.

Lovitt, Charles, and Ian Lowe. *Chance and Data: Investigations,* vol. II. Mathematics Curriculum and Teaching Program. Carlton, Australia: Curriculum Corporation, 1993.

Pagni, David L. "A Television Programming Challenge: A Cooperative Group Activity That Uses Mathematics." *Arithmetic Teacher* 36 (January 1989): 7–9.

Paull, Sandra. "Not Just An Average Unit." *Arithmetic Teacher* 38 (December 1990): 54–58.

Shaw, Jean M. "Let's Do It: Dealing with Data." *Arithmetic Teacher* 31 (May 1984): 9–15.

Shaw, Jean M. "Let's Do It: Making Graphs." *Arithmetic Teacher* 31 (January 1984): 7–11.

Young, Sharon. "Ideas: Bicycle Projects." *Arithmetic Teacher* 38 (September 1990): 23–33.

Young, Sharon. "Ideas: Dinosaur Projects." *Arithmetic Teacher* 38 (December 1990): 23–33.

CHAPTER 9

PROBABILITY

Students should actively explore situations by experimenting and simulating probability models. . . . Probability is rich in interesting problems that can fascinate students and provide settings for developing or applying such concepts as ratios, fractions, percents, and decimals.[1]

ACTIVITY SET 9.1

PROBABILITY EXPERIMENTS

Purpose To determine probabilities experimentally and then analyze the experiments to determine the theoretical probabilities, when possible

Materials A penny, 10 identical tacks, game grids on Material Cards 9 and 10, and the table of random digits on Material Card 8

Activity The word *stochastic*, strange sounding but currently very popular in scientific circles, means random, chancy, chaotic. It is pronounced "stoh-kastic." The stochastization of the world (forgive this tongue-twister) means the adoption of a point of view wherein randomness or chance or probability is perceived as real, objective and fundamental aspect of the world. . . .

Of the digits that crowd our daily papers many have a stochastic basis. We read about the percentage of families in New York City that are childless, the average number of cars owned by four-person families in Orlando, Florida, the probability that a certain transplant operation will succeed. We read about the odds that Nick the Greek is offering on a certain horse race, a market survey that estimated the monthly gross of a fast-food store in a certain location, and the fact that in a certain insurance pool favorable experience has lowered the rate by $.82 per thousand per month. It is

---

[1]*Curriculum and Evaluation Standards for School Mathematics* (Reston, VA: National Council of Teachers of Mathematics, 1989), 109.

implied that a certain attitude is to be engendered by these disclosures, that a course of action should be set in motion. If it is reported that the English scores of Nebraskan tenth-graders are such and such while that of Iowan tenth-graders are this and that, then presumably someone believes that something ought to be done about it.

The stochastization of the world so permeates our thinking and our behavior that it can be said to be one of the characteristic features of modern life. . . .[2]

The importance of stochastization (probability) in the education experience of youth has become widely recognized. The *Curriculum and Evaluation Standards for School Mathematics*[3] recommends that probability activities be included in all grades, kindergarten through 12th, and that a spirit of investigation, exploration, and discussion permeate this study. Lack of probabilistic thinking in the school curriculum appears to result in a lack of "probability sense" in students, and even misconceptions about probability.

In this activity set, we will consider both *experimental probabilities,* which are determined by observing the outcomes of experiments, and *theoretical probabilities,* which are determined by mathematical calculations. The theoretical probability of rolling a 4 on a die is $\frac{1}{6}$ because there are 6 faces on a die, each of which is equally likely to turn up, and only one of these faces has a 4. The experimental probability of obtaining a 4 is found by rolling a die many times and recording the results. Dividing the number of times a 4 comes up by the total number of rolls gives us the experimental probability.

1. Suppose someone wanted to bet that a tack would land with its point up when dropped on a hard surface. Would you accept the bet? Before you wager any money, try the following experiment. Take 10 identical tacks and

---

[2]P. J. Davis and R. Hersh, *Descartes Dream* (New York: Harcourt Brace Jovanovich, 1986), 18–19.
[3]This document was written by the National Council of Teachers of Mathematics to provide guidelines for reform in school mathematics in the next decade.

drop them on a hard surface. Count the number of tacks that land point up. Do this experiment 10 times and record your results in the table.

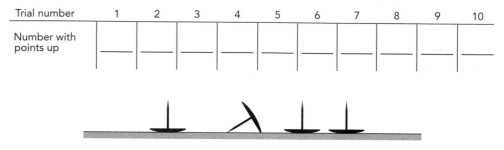

Trial number	1	2	3	4	5	6	7	8	9	10
Number with points up	——	——	——	——	——	——	——	——	——	——

a. Out of the 100 tacks you dropped, how many landed point up? On the basis of this experiment, explain why you would or would not accept the bet.

b. What is the experimental probability that this type of tack will land point up?

$$\frac{\text{Number with point up}}{\text{Total number dropped}} =$$

c. About how many tacks would you expect to land point up if you dropped 300?

d. What is the experimental probability that this type of tack will land point down? How is this probability related to the probability in part b?

2. Games of chance like the following are common at carnivals and fairs. A penny is spun on a square grid, and if it lands inside a square you win a prize. Compare the diameter of a penny to the width of the Two-Penny Grid (Material Card 9). Do you think there is a better chance that the penny will land inside a square or on a line? Make and record a conjecture before you begin the experiment.

Conjecture:

Conjecture:

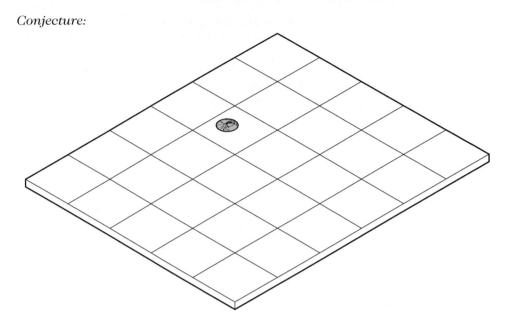

a. Spin a penny 24 times on the Two-Penny Grid and tally the results below.

	TALLY	TOTAL
Penny inside square		
Penny on line		

b. Based on your experiment, compute and record the experimental probability that a penny will land inside a square.

c. The length of a side of a square is twice the diameter of a penny. Which of the points labeled *A, B,* and *C* will be winning points if they represent the center of a penny?

★ **d.** Shade the region of the square in which the center of every *winning* penny must fall. What fractional part of the square is the shaded region?

★ **e.** Compare the area of the shaded region to the area of the whole square to determine the theoretical probability that a penny will land inside a square. Is this a fair game, in the sense that there is a 50 percent chance of winning?

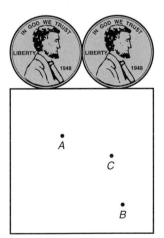

3. The sides of the squares on the Three-Penny Grid (Material Card 10) are three times the diameter of a penny. When a penny is spun on this grid, do you think the chances of its landing inside the lines are better than the chances of its landing on a line? Make and record a conjecture before you try the game.

Conjecture:

a. Spin a penny 24 times, tally your results, and compute the experimental probability of not landing on a line.

	TALLY	TOTAL
Penny inside square	_____	_____
Penny on line	_____	_____

★ **b.** Shade the region of the square in which the centers of winning pennies must fall. What is the theoretical probability that a penny will be a winning penny?

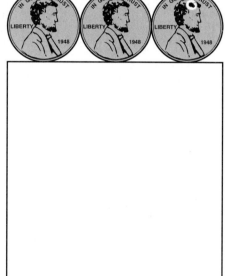

c. Explain how you would determine the theoretical probability that a spinning penny will not touch the lines on a Four-Penny Grid. Is this a fair game?

4. Cut out 3 cards of the same size. Label both sides of one with the letter A, both sides of the second with the letter B, one side of the third with A, and the other side of the third with B. Select a card at random and place it on the table. The card on the table will have either an A or a B facing up. What is the probability that the letter facing down will be different from the letter facing up? Take a guess. Then repeat this experiment 24 times and record the number of times that the letter facing down is different from the letter facing up. Compute and record the experimental probability.

Conjecture:

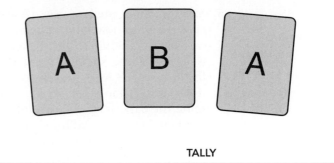

	TALLY	TOTAL
Same letter facing down	_____	_____
Different letter facing down	_____	_____

Experimental probability: $\dfrac{\text{Number of times different letter down}}{\text{Total number of random draws}} =$

Once a card has been selected and it is clear which letter is facing up, people often feel that there is a 50-50 chance that the letter facing down will be different. This is a false assumption. Notice that the 3 cards have 6 faces altogether. To distinguish between the two sides of the A-A card, let's refer to one side as A_1 and the other as A_2. Similarly, the two sides of the B-B card will be referred to as B_1 and B_2. We will continue to refer to the sides of the A-B card as A and B. When the first card is selected, 1 of 6 sides is facing up: A_1, A_2, B_1, B_2, A, B. For each of these 6 sides, record the letter of the side that would be facing down. Then answer the following questions.

Outcome	1	2	3	4	5	6
Top face	A_1	A_2	B_1	B_2	A	B
Bottom face	_____	_____	_____	_____	_____	_____

★ **a.** In how many of these outcomes is the top face of the card different from the bottom face? (Remember, the faces are labeled with only As and Bs.)

b. What is the probability of selecting a card on which the letter on the top face is different from the letter on the bottom face?

★ **c.** Suppose that a card has been selected and an A is face up. List the 3 outcomes from the table for this event.

d. What is the probability that the letter on the bottom face of the card in part c is a B?

★ **e.** Does knowing what letter is facing up help you determine the probability that the letter facing down is different? Explain.

5. Simulation: A student has 10 sweaters. If the student grabs a sweater at random each morning, what is the probability that the student will wear the same sweater more than once in a five-day week? Assign each sweater a digit from 0 through 9 and set up a simulation to determine the experimental probability. (*Hint:* Use 5 random digits selected from the table of random digits on Material Card 8 to represent 5 sweaters chosen at random in one week.)

- -

 ## JUST FOR FUN

RACETRACK GAME (2 or 3 players)
Each player chooses a track on the racetrack gameboard and places a marker on its starting square. In turn, the players roll two dice. If the sum of the numbers on the dice matches the number of the track on which the player's marker is located, the player may move 1 square toward the finish line. The first player whose marker reaches the last square on the track is the winner. Play the game a few times. Are you more likely to win on some tracks than on others?

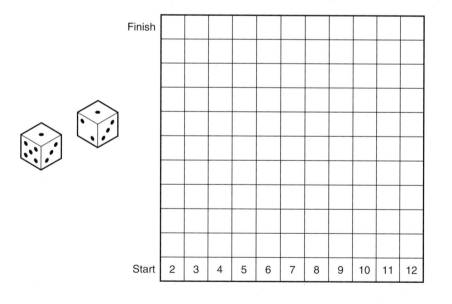

Variation 1: Play the game as above, but with an individual gameboard and 2 markers for each player. A player's markers may be placed on different tracks or on the same track. Is there a way to place your markers so as to increase your chances of winning?

Variation 2: Use the sum of the numbers on three dice rather than two. Do some tracks have better winning records than others?

Finish																
Start 3	4	5	6	7	8	9	10	11	12	13	14	15	16	17	18

Variation 3: Use the product of the numbers on the dice instead of the sum. Will you need more tracks on the game mat? Will certain tracks give you a better chance of winning?

· ·

PUZZLER

Have a friend grasp four identical shoelaces (or pieces of string) in the middle so that four ends extend on each side of the hand. If you tie them in pairs on each side of your friend's fist, are your chances of having one big loop when the laces are released greater or less than 50 percent?

ACTIVITY SET 9.2

MULTISTAGE PROBABILITY EXPERIMENTS

Purpose To perform multistage probability experiments and then compare the resulting experimental probabilities with the corresponding theoretical probabilities

Materials Green and red tiles from the Manipulative Kit, four coins, a pair of dice, and the simulation spinners on Material Card 30

Activity It once happened in Monte Carlo that red came up on 32 consecutive spins of a roulette wheel. The probability that such a run will occur is about one out of 4 billion.

The probability of two or more events occurring is called *compound probability* or *multistage probability*. When one event does not influence or affect the outcome of another event, the two are called *independent events*. For example, because the second spin of a roulette wheel is not affected by the first spin, the two are considered independent events. When one event does influence the outcome of a second, the events are said to be *dependent events*.

Consider, for example, the probability of drawing 2 red tiles from a box containing 3 red tiles and 4 green tiles.

On the first draw, the probability of obtaining a red tile is $\frac{3}{7}$. If the first tile is replaced before the second draw, the probability of drawing another red tile is $\frac{3}{7}$, because the numbers of each color of tiles in the box are the same as they were on the first draw. These two drawings are *independent* events because the result of the first draw does not affect the outcome of the second draw. The probability of drawing 2 red tiles in this case is $\frac{3}{7} \times \frac{3}{7} = \frac{9}{49}$, as illustrated by the following probability tree.

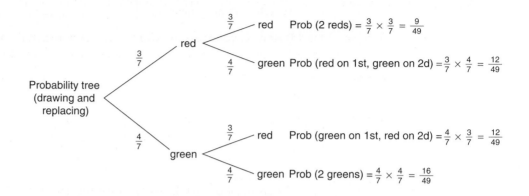

A completely different situation exists if the tile obtained on the first draw is not returned to the box before the second tile is drawn. In this case, the probability of drawing a red tile on the second draw depends on what happens on the first draw. That is, these events are *dependent*. For example, if a red tile is taken on the first draw, the probability of selecting a red tile on the second draw is $\frac{2}{6}$. In this case, the probability of drawing 2 red tiles is $\frac{3}{7} \times \frac{2}{6} = \frac{6}{42}$. The following probability tree illustrates this case.

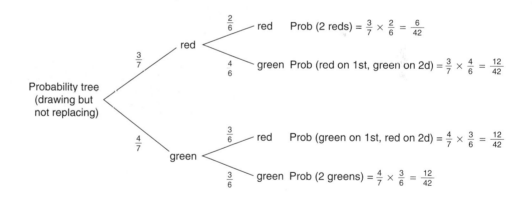

In the following activities, there are several experiments involving compound probabilities with both independent and dependent events. In each case, the experimental probability will be compared with the theoretical probability.

1. The following experiment has a result likely to be contrary to your intuition. Suppose that 3 red and 3 green tiles are placed in a container and that 2 are selected at random (both at once). What is the probability of getting 2 tiles of different colors? Make a conjecture about the probability, and then perform the experiment 40 times and tally your results.
   Conjecture:

	TALLY	TOTAL
Two tiles of different colors		
Two tiles of the same color		

a. Based on your results, what is the *experimental* probability of drawing the following?

2 tiles of different colors _____

2 tiles of the same color _____

★ **b.** One way to determine the *theoretical* probability is to systematically list all 15 possible pairs that could be drawn from the container. Complete the list of outcomes started below. (Notice that the tiles of each color have been numbered to preserve their identity.) Use the list to determine the theoretical probabilities by forming the following ratio. Compare these probabilities to the experimental probabilities from part a.

Probability of 2 tiles of a different color _____

Probability of 2 tiles of the same color _____

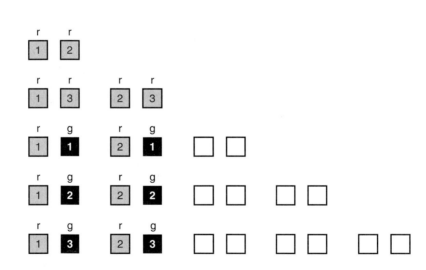

c. Drawing 2 tiles is the same as drawing 1 tile and then, without replacing it, drawing a second tile. The probability of drawing a red tile is $\frac{1}{2}$. The probability of then drawing a second red tile is $\frac{2}{5}$. The probability of drawing a red followed by a red is $\frac{1}{2} \times \frac{2}{5} = \frac{1}{5}$, as shown on the following probability tree. Determine the theoretical probabilities of the remaining three outcomes.

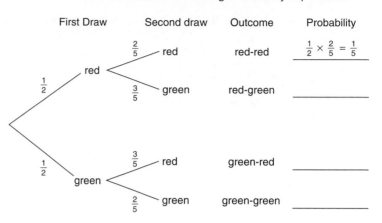

First Draw   Second draw   Outcome   Probability

$\frac{2}{5}$ red   red-red $\frac{1}{2} \times \frac{2}{5} = \frac{1}{5}$

red $\frac{3}{5}$ green   red-green   _____

$\frac{1}{2}$

$\frac{1}{2}$ $\frac{3}{5}$ red   green-red   _____

green $\frac{2}{5}$ green   green-green   _____

★ **d.** The theoretical probability of drawing 2 tiles of different colors can be obtained from the preceding tree diagram. Explain how this can be done and determine the probability. Compare this result to the theoretical probability determined in part b.

2. What is the probability that, on a toss of 4 coins, 2 will come up heads and 2 will come up tails? First make a conjecture about the probability and then perform the experiment by tossing 4 coins and recording the numbers of heads and tails in the table below. Do this experiment 32 times.

Conjecture:

	1	2	3	4	5	6	7	8	9	10	11	12	13	14	15	16	17	18	19	20	21	22	23	24	25	26	27	28	29	30	31	32
H																																
T																																

a. According to your table, what is the experimental probability of obtaining exactly 2 heads on a toss of 4 coins?

b. Tossing 4 coins at once is like tossing a single coin 4 times. Continue this tree diagram to show all possible outcomes when a coin is tossed 4 times in succession. There will be 16 possible outcomes. How many of these will have 2 heads and 2 tails?

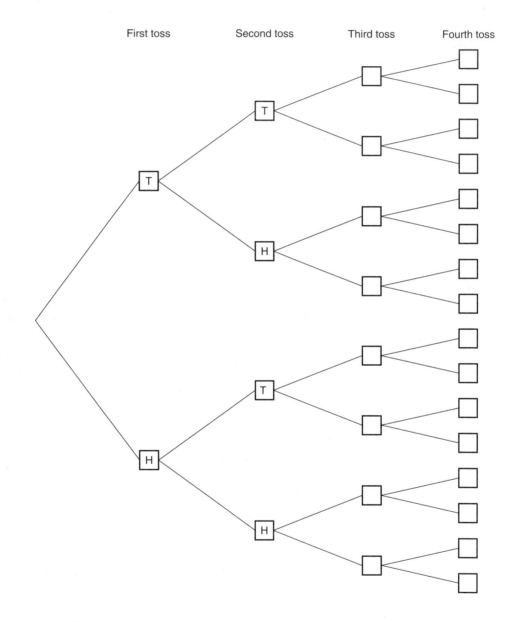

First toss   Second toss   Third toss   Fourth toss

★ **c.** What is the theoretical probability of getting 2 heads and 2 tails on a toss of 4 coins?

3. The chances of succeeding in compound events are often deceiving. You might expect that if a box had 7 red tiles and 3 green tiles, your chances of drawing 2 red tiles at the same time would be fairly good. Try this experiment 30 times and record your results. In this experiment you can either select two tiles at a time or select one tile and then, without replacing it, select another.

	TALLY	TOTAL
2 red tiles		
1 or more green tiles		

   a. What is the experimental probability of drawing 2 red tiles?

   b. Sketch a probability tree to determine the theoretical probability of drawing 2 red tiles.

4. Were you surprised in activity 3 that the chances of drawing 2 red tiles are so poor? Even if you replace the first tile before drawing the second, the chances of getting 2 red tiles are worse than you might expect. Carry out the experiment again, this time drawing the tiles separately and replacing the first tile each time. Repeat this procedure 30 times and record the results.

	TALLY	TOTAL
2 red tiles		
1 or more green tiles		

   a. What is the experimental probability of drawing 2 red tiles in succession when the first tile is returned?

   ★ **b.** Compute the theoretical probability of getting 2 red tiles when the first tile is returned. Explain your method.

5. Do you think that at least one double 6 is likely to occur in 24 rolls of two dice? This is one of the seventeenth-century gambling questions that led to the development of probability. Toss two dice 24 times and record the results of each toss. (Record a Y for a double 6 and an N otherwise.)

Record of 24 tosses

Did you roll a double 6? Even though this event may have occurred 1 or more times in your experiment, there is slightly less than a 50 percent chance of rolling one double 6 in 24 trials. The probability that an event will happen and the probability that it will not happen are called *complementary probabilities.* In calculating the following theoretical probabilities, you can make use of the fact that the sum of complementary probabilities is 1.

★ **a.** What is the probability of rolling a double 6 in 1 roll of the dice?

b. What is the probability of not rolling a double 6 in 1 roll of the dice?

★ **c.** What is the probability of not rolling a double 6 in 2 rolls of the dice?

d. Indicate how you would find the probability of not rolling a double 6 in 24 rolls of the dice. (Do not multiply your answer out.)

★ **e.** The product $\frac{35}{36} \times \frac{35}{36} \times \cdots \times \frac{35}{36}$, in which $\frac{35}{36}$ occurs 24 times, is approximately .51. What is the probability of rolling at least one double 6 in 24 rolls of the dice?

6. **Simulation:** A TV game show offers its contestants the opportunity to win a prize by choosing 1 of 3 doors. Behind 1 door is a valuable prize, but behind the other 2 doors is junk. After the contestant has chosen a door, the host opens 1 of the remaining doors, which has junk behind it, and asks if the contestant would like to *stick* with the initial choice or *switch* to the remaining unopened door. If you were the contestant, would you stick, switch, or, possibly, choose the options at random? You may be surprised to discover that your chances of winning vary depending on your strategy.

Door 1   Door 2   Door 3

a. *Experimental Probability of Sticking:* Suppose you always stick with your first choice. To simulate the sticking strategy, perform the following experiment using the spinner from Material Card 30. Anchor a paper clip to the center of the circle with your pencil point, and then spin the paper clip to simulate choosing a door at random. Perform the experiment 50 times and tally your results in the table. Determine the experimental probability of winning the prize if you always stick with your first choice.

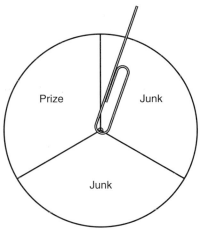

	TALLY	TOTAL
Prize		
No prize		

Experimental probability _____

b. *Experimental Probability of Switching:* No matter what door the contestant chooses, the host will always open a door with junk behind it and ask if the contestant wants to switch. Perform the following experiment to simulate a switching strategy. Choose the first door randomly, using the spinner as in part a. With the switch strategy, you win if the pointer stops on "junk," but you lose if the pointer stops on "prize." Explain why this happens. Then perform the experiment 50 times and compute the experimental probability of winning on a switch strategy.

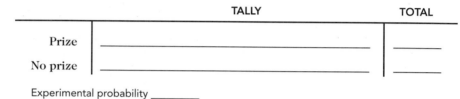

	TALLY	TOTAL
Prize		
No prize		

Experimental probability _____

c. *Experimental Probability of Randomly Sticking or Switching:* Maybe the best strategy would be to choose a door and then decide on a stick or switch strategy by chance. Perform the following experiment to simulate this strategy. Choose your first door randomly, using the spinner as above. Then use the second spinner (from Material Card 30) to decide whether you should stick or switch. What happens if your first spin selects "junk" and your second spin selects "switch"—do you win the prize or not? Then perform the experiment 50 times and compute the experimental probability of winning with this strategy.

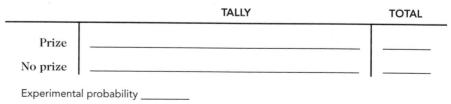

	TALLY	TOTAL
Prize		
No prize		

Experimental probability _____

★ **d.** The tree diagrams below represent the first stage of the game for the switch strategy and the stick strategy. Explain why we need show only one stage of the tree diagram to determine whether we have won or lost. For each strategy, determine the theoretical probability of winning the prize.

e. This two-stage tree diagram represents picking a door at random and then deciding to stick or switch at random. Notice that if you randomly choose a junk door and then randomly spin "switch," you switch choices when offered the opportunity and win the prize. Finish labeling the outcomes of the second stage and determine the theoretical probability of winning the prize with this strategy.

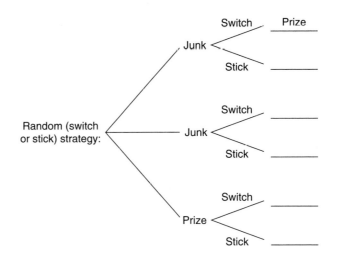

f. Suppose you were chosen to be a contestant for this game show. Write a short summary explaining what strategy you would choose and why you would choose it.

JUST FOR FUN

TRICK DICE

The four dice shown next have the following remarkable property: no matter which die your opponent selects, you can always select one of the remaining three dice so that the probability of winning is in your favor. (Winning means having a greater number of dots facing up.) Make a set of these dice, either by altering regular dice or by using the dice on Material Card 31.

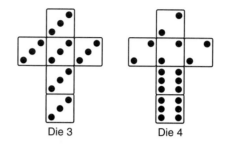

Die 1   Die 2   Die 3   Die 4

Try the following experiment with die 2 and die 4. Roll both dice 21 times and record the resulting numbers in the appropriate boxes of the following table. Then circle the numbers for which die 4 wins over 2. Before beginning the experiment, try to predict which die has the better chance of winning.

Die 2																					
Die 4																					

1. For the winning die in the experiment above, compute the experimental probability of winning.

★ 2. Complete this table to show all 36 pairs of numbers that can result from the two dice. Circle the pairs in which die 4 has the greater number. What is the theoretical probability that die 4 will win over die 2? Compare this result to the experimental probability in problem 1.

★ 3. If a 2 is rolled on die 4 and a 1 is rolled on die 2, then die 4 wins. What is the probability of these events happening? (Hint: Multiply the 2 probabilities.)

★ 4. If a 6 is rolled on die 4, it wins over every number on die 2. What is the chance of rolling a 6 on die 4?

★ 5. The theoretical probability that die 4 will win over die 2 is the sum of the probabilities in problems 3 and 4. What is this probability? Compare this result to your answer in problem 2.

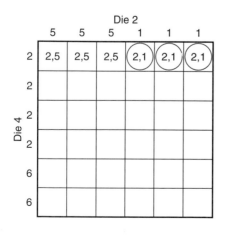

Similar approaches can be used to show that die 2 wins over die 1, die 1 wins over die 3, and die 3 wins over die 4. Surprisingly, the first die of each pair has a $\frac{2}{3}$ probability of winning over the second die. Try this experiment with some of your friends. Let them choose a die first, then you select one with a greater chance of winning.

IDEAS FOR THE ELEMENTARY CLASSROOM

SUGGESTED CLASSROOM ACTIVITY: RACETRACK PROBABILITY

The racetrack game (Just for Fun in Section 9.1) can be turned into a noncompetitive activity for young children involving addition, probability, and graphing. Post a chart like the one below at the front of the class. Each student, in turn, rolls a pair of dice (possibly large foam dice), adds the two top numbers, and marks the chart by putting an X in the square above the sum. The activity ends when one column becomes full of X's. The next time this activity is done, have the students each pick the number of the column they think will fill up first. Record their names beneath their chosen columns. Older students can engage in a similar activity with three dice. First have the students design the recording chart, deciding which sums can be obtained with three dice.

2	3	4	5	6	7	8	9	10	11	12

PUZZLER

If a string is cut at random into two pieces, what is the probability that one piece is less than or equal to half the length of the other?

Readings for More Classroom Ideas

Bright, George W. "Teaching Mathematics with Technology: Probability Simulations." *Arithmetic Teacher* 36 (May 1989): 16–18.

Bruni, James V., and H. J. Silverman. "Developing Concepts in Probability and Statistics—and Much More." *Arithmetic Teacher* 33 (February 1986): 34–37.

Dolan, Dan. "Implementing the Standards: Making Connections in Mathematics." *Arithmetic Teacher* 38 (February 1991): 57–60.

Horak, Virginia M., and W. J. Horak. "Let's Do It: Take a Chance." *Arithmetic Teacher* 30 (May 1983): 8–15.

Jones, Graham A., and Carol A. Thornton. *Data, Chance and Probability: Grades 1–3 Activity Book.* (Also grades 2–4 and 6–8 activity books) Lincolnshire, IL: Learning Resources, Inc., 1992.

Lovell, Robert. *Probability Activities.* Berkeley, CA: Key Curriculum Press, 1993.

Lovitt, Charles, and Ian Lowe. *Chance and Data: Investigations,* vol. I. Mathematics Curriculum and Teaching Program. Carlton, Australia: Curriculum Corporation, 1993.

Mason, Julia A., and Graham Jones. "The Lunch-Wheel Spin." *Arithmetic Teacher* 41 (March 1994): 404–408.

Phillips, Elizabeth, Glenda Lappan, Mary J. Winter, and William Fitzgerald. *Probability*. Middle Grades Mathematics Project. Menlo Park, CA: Addison-Wesley Publishing Company, 1986.

Shaughnessy, Michael, and M. J. Arcidiacono. "Visual Encounters with Chance," in *Math and the Mind's Eye* (Unit VIII). Salem, OR: The Math Learning Center, Box 3226, 1993.

Vissa, Jeanne M. "Probability and Combinations for Third Graders." *Arithmetic Teacher* 36 (December 1988): 33–37.

Woodward, Ernest. "A Second-Grade Probability and Graphing Lesson." *Arithmetic Teacher* 30 (March 1983): 23–24.

Zawojewski, Judith S. *Dealing with Data and Chance,* in the *Curriculum and Evaluation Standards for School Mathematics Addenda Series: Grades 5–8*. Reston, VA: National Council of Teachers of Mathematics, 1991.

CHAPTER 10

GEOMETRIC FIGURES

As they [children] explore patterns and relationships with models, blocks, geoboards, and graph paper, they learn about the properties of shapes and sharpen their intuitions and awareness of spatial concepts. . . . Folding paper cutouts or using mirrors to investigate lines of symmetry are other ways for children to observe figures in a variety of positions, become aware of their important properties, and compare and contrast them.[1]

ACTIVITY SET 10.1

FIGURES ON RECTANGULAR AND CIRCULAR GEOBOARDS

Purpose To use rectangular geoboards to illustrate geometric figures and circular geoboards to study inscribed and central angles

Materials A rectangular geoboard, a circular geoboard, and rubber bands (optional). Templates for making rectangular and circular geoboards are on Material Cards 27 and 33, respectively. Recording paper for activity 1 is on Material Card 11, and the three-circle Venn diagram is on Material Card 5. A protractor is on Material Card 32.

Activity The geoboard is a popular physical model for illustrating geometric concepts and solving geometric investigations. The most familiar type of geoboard has a square shape, with 25 nails arranged in a 5 by 5 array. Rubber bands can be placed on the nails to form models for segments, angles, and polygons. For example, here is a 12-sided polygon.

[1]*Curriculum and Evaluation Standards for School Mathematics* (Reston, VA: National Council of Teachers of Mathematics, 1989), 48–49.

The circular geoboard is very helpful for developing angle concepts. The one shown below has a nail at the center and an outer circle of 24 nails. Many of the angles and polygons that can be formed on this geoboard cannot be made on the rectangular geoboard. The circular geoboard will be used to form central and inscribed angles and to establish an important relationship between them.

Since most geoboard activities can be carried out on dot paper by drawing figures, the use of geoboards is optional in the following activities. However, geoboards provide insights because of the ease with which figures can be shaped and reshaped during an investigation. They also encourage experimentation and creativity. If geoboards are not available, you may wish to make them from boards and finishing nails using the templates on the Material Cards.

Rectangular Geoboards

1. This figure shows a geoboard triangle with its base along the bottom row of pins. Determine all possible geoboard triangles that have the same base. Record your results by drawing each triangle on geoboard recording paper (Material Card 11).

   a. Determine the area of each triangle using methods developed in Activity Set 6.4. Record the area inside the triangle.

★ **b.** Cut out each geoboard, that has a triangle drawn on it. (Cut around the entire geoboard, not just the triangles.) Group the triangles that have the same area. Describe the characteristics that triangles of equal area have in common.

★ **c.** The two triangles shown here are *congruent* because one can be cut out and placed on the other so that they coincide. Match all congruent triangles. Now, form the collection of all noncongruent triangles. How many noncongruent triangles are there? (If two or more triangles are congruent, select only one to represent that group.)

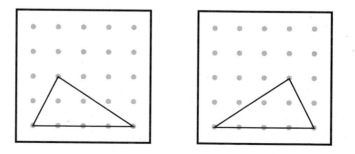

d. Label the three-circle Venn diagram, Material Card 5, as shown here. Sort the collection of non-congruent triangles by placing them in the appropriate regions of the Venn diagram. Record the number of triangles in each region on the diagram shown here. (A scalene triangle has all sides of different length; an isosceles triangle has at least two sides of equal length; and a right triangle has one right angle.)

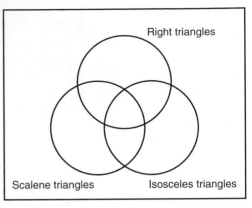

e. For the regions of the Venn diagram in part d which have no entries, can you draw triangles which could be placed in those regions? Explain how you arrived at your answer.

2. The first geoboard below shows three segments of different lengths. A geoboard segment has its endpoints on geoboard pins. Use your geoboard to determine how many geoboard segments of *different* lengths can be constructed. Record your solutions.

3. The geoboards following have a rubber band around the outer pins to form as large a square as possible. Additional rubber bands are used to divide the squares into two *congruent* halves. (Congruent figures have the same size and shape.)

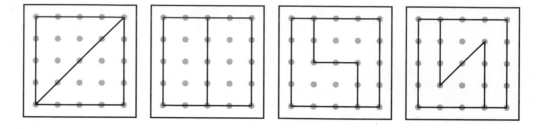

Find at least seven other ways to divide the square into congruent halves, and draw them below.

★ 4. There are 16 noncongruent quadrilaterals that can be formed on a 3 by 3 geoboard. Sketch them here.

Classify each of the above quadrilaterals by recording its letter following each description that applies to it. (A parallelogram has two pairs of opposite parallel sides, and a trapezoid has exactly one pair of parallel sides.)

Square   _____

Rectangle, but not square   _____

Parallelogram, but not rectangle   _____

Trapezoid   _____

Convex   _____

Nonconvex   _____

5. The first geoboard below shows a 21-sided polygon. Find polygons with more than 21 sides and draw them here.

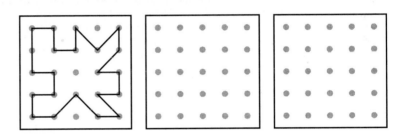

Circular Geoboards

6. **Central Angles:** An angle whose vertex is located at the center of the circle and whose sides intersect the circle is called a *central angle*. The portion of the circle that is cut off by the sides of the angle is called the *intercepted arc*. The central angle on this geoboard has a measure of 15 degrees (15°) because its intercepted arc is $\frac{1}{24}$ of a whole circle (360 ÷ 24 = 15).

★ **a.** Under each geoboard, write the number of degrees in the indicated central angle.

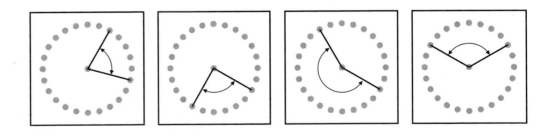

_____   _____   _____   _____

★ **b.** On your geoboard form central angles that have the following angle measures. Then draw them here.

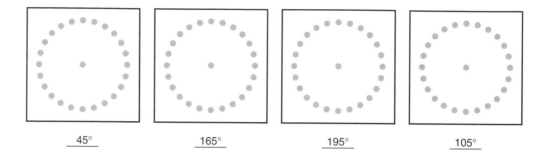

45°   165°   195°   105°

7. **Inscribed Angles:** An angle is *inscribed* in an arc of a circle when its vertex is on the arc and its sides contain endpoints of the arc.

★ **a.** Construct the following inscribed angles on your circular geoboard and measure them with your protractor. (There is a protractor on Material Card 32. If you do not have a circular geoboard, draw the angles lightly, in pencil, on the geoboard template on Material Card 33.)

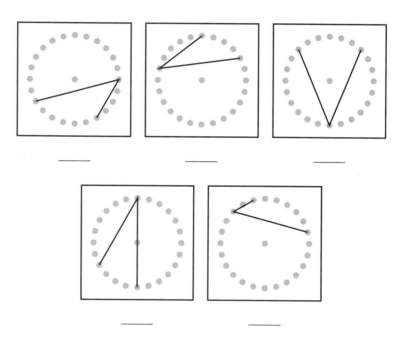

★ **b.** Look at the inscribed angles in part a that have the same angle measure. Make a conjecture about the *equality* of inscribed angles and the size of their corresponding intercepted arcs. Test your conjecture by drawing and measuring more inscribed angles. Record your conclusions.

Conjecture:

★ **c.** Angle *PQR* is inscribed in a semicircle (half a circle). Using your circular geoboard and protractor, construct and measure angle *PQR* and several other inscribed angles whose sides intersect the ends of a diameter. Record the angles and their measures below. Make a conjecture about such angles and record it below.

Conjecture:

Angle *AOC* _____

Angle *ABC* _____

8. Construct central angle *AOC* and inscribed angle *ABC* on your circular geoboard (or draw them on your circular geoboard template). Determine the measure of central angle *AOC*. Measure angle *ABC* with your protractor. Record both measures beneath the figure.

★ **a.** Form each of the following inscribed angles on your geoboard, measure the angle with your protractor, and record the inscribed angle measure below the figure. Then, on each geoboard, determine the measure of the central angle that intercepts the same arc as the inscribed angle and record it.

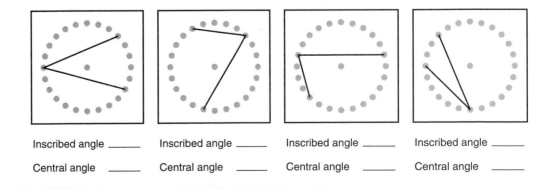

Inscribed angle _____   Inscribed angle _____   Inscribed angle _____   Inscribed angle _____

Central angle _____   Central angle _____   Central angle _____   Central angle _____

★ **b.** There is a relationship between the measure of an inscribed angle and that of its corresponding central angle. Write a conjecture about that relationship.

Conjecture:

. . . .

JUST FOR FUN

TANGRAM PUZZLES

Tangrams are one of the oldest and most popular of ancient Chinese puzzles. The 7 tangram pieces are shown in a square. There are 5 triangles, 1 square, and 1 parallelogram. Fold a standard piece of paper to get a square and cut out the square. Then fold the paper to obtain the 7 tangram pieces and cut them out for the following activities.

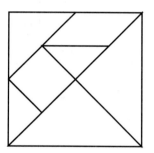

★ **1.** The 7 pieces are used in Chinese puzzles called *tangram puzzles*. The object of tangram puzzles is to use all of the tangram pieces to form figures. The tangram pieces should be placed so that they do not overlap. Try to form the following figures. There are many tangram figures.[2] You may wish to create and record a few of your own.

2. The tangram pieces below also can be used to create geometric shapes. For example:
   a. Use the 2 small triangles to make a square; a larger triangle; a parallelogram.
   b. Use the 2 small triangles and the medium-size triangle to make a rectangle; a parallelogram that is not a rectangle; a larger triangle.

3. The chart on the following page shows how a triangle can be created with 3 tangram pieces, a square with 5 tangram pieces, and a nonsquare rectangle with 4 pieces. Record your results from activity 2 and see if you can complete the chart. (There are no solutions for the entries that are crossed out.)

[2]R. Reed's *Tangrams* (New York: Dover, 1965) contains 330 tangram figures and their solutions.

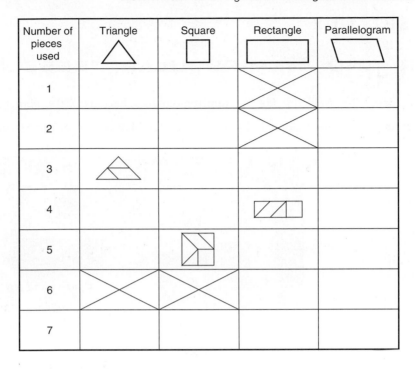

Number of pieces used	Triangle △	Square ☐	Rectangle ▭	Parallelogram ▱
1			✕	
2			✕	
3				
4				
5				
6				
7				

PUZZLER

Make one cut in this figure to create two congruent halves. (The cut does not have to be straight.)

ACTIVITY SET 10.2

REGULAR AND SEMIREGULAR TESSELLATIONS

Purpose To study regular and semiregular tessellations of the plane

Materials Pattern blocks and polygons for tessellations from the Manipulative Kit

A portion of the eye of a fruit fly.

Activity The hexagonal shapes in the accompanying photograph show a small portion of the eye of a fruit fly. The partitioning of surfaces by hexagons or nearly hexagonal figures is common in nature.[3] A figure, such as a regular hexagon, that can be used repeatedly to cover a surface without gaps or overlaps is said to *tile* or *tessellate* the surface. The resulting pattern is called a *tessellation.* An infinite variety of shapes can be used as the basic figure for a tessellation. The famous Dutch artist Maurits C. Escher (1898–1972) is noted for his tessellations with drawings of birds, fish, and other living creatures. Techniques for creating Escher-type tessellations are developed in Activity Set 12.2.

Pattern Block Tessellations

1. Figure 1 shows the beginnings of a tessellation with the yellow hexagon pattern block and figures 2 and 3 show the beginnings of two different tessellations with the red trapezoid.

[3]For some examples of hexagonal patterns and a discussion of why they occur in nature, see H. Weyl, *Symmetry* (Princeton: Princeton University Press, 1952), 83–89.

(1)   (2)   (3)

a. Find at least one other way to tessellate with the red trapezoid. Record your pattern.

b. All of the remaining pattern block pieces have more than one tessellation pattern like the trapezoid. For each of those, sketch enough of at least two patterns so that a reader will be able to extend them.

★ **2.** When 3 acute angles of white rhombuses are put together at a point, the sum of their measures is the same as one of the angles of an orange square. Since each angle of the square measures 90°, a small angle of the white rhombus measures 30°.

By comparing the angles of the various pieces (using no angle-measuring instruments), determine the measures of the other seven angles of the pieces in the pattern block collection. Record the measures on the pattern block diagrams and describe or show briefly how you reached your conclusions.

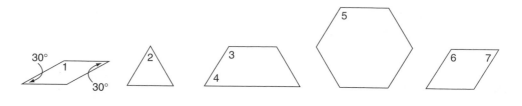

3. Both the figures below have been formed by taping two pattern blocks together to form new shapes. The first figure is a hexagon (6 sides and 6 interior angles) and the second is a pentagon (5 sides and 5 interior angles). On the diagrams record the measure of each interior angle in the new shapes.

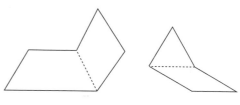

a. Form the shapes with your pattern blocks and test each of them to see if they will tessellate. If so, sketch enough of the beginnings of a pattern so the reader has sufficient information to extend it. If not, explain why it will not work.

b. "Tape" two other pieces together to create a new shape which will not tessellate. Record your figure and explain why it will not tessellate.

Tessellations with Regular Polygons

4. Here are the first six regular polygons. For each polygon, trace additional copies around the enlarged vertex point, as if to begin a tessellation.

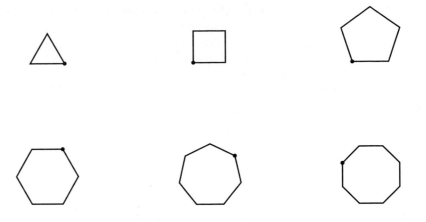

a. Which of these polygons will not tessellate?

b. What condition must the angles of a regular polygon satisfy in order for the polygon to tessellate?

★ c. Explain why regular polygons with more than 6 sides will not tessellate.

5. The equilateral triangle, square, and regular hexagon are the only regular polygons that tessellate. Although designs based on these patterns are common, more interesting tessellations can be formed by using two or three different regular polygons. A square and two octagons are around each vertex point of the tessellation shown here. Notice that the vertex angle of a square is 90° and of an octagon is 135°, and 90 + 135 + 135 = 360.

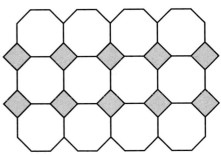

A tessellation that has two or more types of regular polygons arranged in the same order around every vertex point is called a *semiregular tessellation*. The five regular polygons that are used in semiregular tessellations are shown below. The number of degrees in a vertex angle of each polygon is recorded above the polygon. There are polygons for tessellating in the Manipulative Kit. Use them for the following activities.

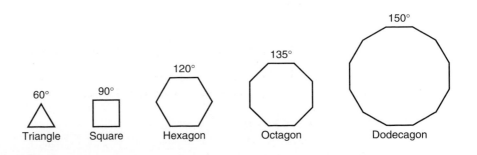

★ **a.** There are six semiregular tessellations that can be formed using combinations of two different regular polygons about each vertex. Find and sketch at least one of these tessellations. (*Hint:* Look for combinations of angles whose measures add up to 360°.)

★ **b.** There are two semiregular tessellations that use combinations of three different regular polygons about each vertex. Find and sketch one of these tessellations. (*Hint:* Look for combinations of angles whose measures add up to 360°.)

★ **c.** It is possible to tile a plane with combinations of polygons that do not form a semiregular tessellation. These tilings may have a regular pattern, but not every vertex point is surrounded by the same arrangement of polygons. Create such a tiling and sketch it here. (*Hint:* One such tiling uses dodecagons, triangles, and squares.)

JUST FOR FUN

THE GAME OF HEX (2 players)

Hex, a game of deductive reasoning, is played on a game board of hexagons similar to the 11 by 11 grid shown here (see Material Card 12). Player 1 and player 2 take turns placing their markers or symbols on any unoccupied hexagon. Player 1 attempts to form an unbroken chain or string of symbols from the left side of the grid to the right, and player 2 tries to form a chain of symbols from the top of the grid to the bottom. The first player to complete a chain is the winner. In this sample game, player 2 (using O's) won against player 1 (using X's).

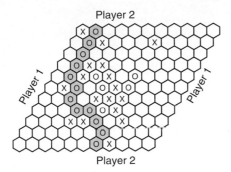

★**Winning Strategy:** There will always be a winner in the game of Hex, since the only way a player can prevent the other from winning is to form an unbroken chain of markers from one side of the grid to the other. On a 3 by 3 game board, the person who plays first can easily win in 3 moves. What should be the first move? Find a first move on the 4 by 4 and 5 by 5 game boards that will ensure a win regardless of the opponent's moves.

3 by 3   4 by 4   5 by 5

It is tempting to conclude that a winning strategy on an 11 by 11 game board begins with a first move on the center hexagon. However, there are so many possibilities for plays on a grid of this size that no winning strategy has yet been found. There is a type of proof in mathematics, called an *existence proof*, which shows that something exists even though no one is able to find it. It has been proved that a winning strategy does exist for the first player in a game of Hex on an 11 by 11 grid, but just what that strategy is, no one knows.[4]

PUZZLER

This 4 by 4 square has been divided into two congruent pieces. In how many different ways can this square be divided into two congruent pieces by drawing on the grid lines?

---

[4]For an elementary version of this proof, see M. Gardner, "Mathematical Games," *Scientific American* 197 (1) (1957), 145.

ACTIVITY SET 10.3

MODELS FOR REGULAR AND SEMIREGULAR POLYHEDRA

Purpose To construct and use models in order to observe and examine the properties of regular and semiregular polyhedra

Materials Patterns for constructing regular polyhedra are on Material Cards 34 and 35

Stars, *by M. C. Escher*
(© 1996 M. C. Escher/Cordon
Art—Baarn-Holland. All
rights reserved.)

[5]For the proof that there are exactly five regular polyhedra, see P. G. O'Daffer and S. R. Clemens, *Geometry: An Investigative Approach* (Reading, MA: Addison-Wesley, 1976), 115–119.

Activity The term *polyhedron* comes from Greek and means "many faces." A *regular polyhedron* is a convex polyhedron whose faces are regular polygons and whose vertices are each surrounded by the same number of these polygons. The regular polyhedra are also called *Platonic solids* because the Greek philosopher Plato (427–347 B.C.) immortalized them in his writings. Euclid (340 B.C.) proved that there were exactly five regular polyhedra.[5] Can you identify the Platonic solids in M. C. Escher's wood engraving *Stars?*

Platonic Solids

★ 1. There are several common methods for constructing the five Platonic solids. The polyhedra pictured here are see-through models similar to those in Escher's wood engraving. They can be made from drinking straws that are threaded or stuck together.

Another method is to cut out regular polygons and glue or tape them together. Material Cards 34 and 35 contain regular polygon patterns for making the Platonic solids. Cut out the patterns, use a ballpoint pen or sharp point to score the dashed lines, and assemble them by folding on the dashed lines and taping the edges. For each Platonic solid, record the number of faces (polygonal regions) and the name of the polygon used.

	NUMBER OF FACES	POLYGON
Tetrahedron	_____	_____
Cube	_____	_____
Octahedron	_____	_____
Dodecahedron	_____	_____
Icosahedron	_____	_____

2. The faces of the icosahedron and cube in the next photo were made from colorful greeting cards. (The triangular and square patterns for the faces are also shown. The corners of these patterns were cut with a paperpunch and scissors, and the edges bent up along the dashed lines. The adjoining faces of these polyhedra are held together by rubber bands on their edges.)

★ **a.** If you were to make your Platonic solids as described above, how many rubber bands would you need to make each one? (One band is used for each edge.)

Tetrahedron   _____

Cube   _____

Octahedron   _____

Dodecahedron   _____

Icosahedron   _____

b. You may enjoy planning colors for your Platonic solids so that no two faces with a common edge have the same color. For this condition to be satisfied, what is the least number of colors needed for the octahedron?

3. Euler's Formula

★ **a.** In the following table, record the numbers of vertices, faces, and edges for each of the Platonic solids.

	VERTICES (V)	FACES (F)	EDGES (E)
Tetrahedron	_____	_____	_____
Cube	_____	_____	_____
Octahedron	_____	_____	_____
Dodecahedron	_____	_____	_____
Icosahedron	_____	_____	_____

b. There is a relationship among the numbers of vertices, faces, and edges. Make a conjecture about this relationship. Try to express it in terms of the letters *V*, *F*, and *E*.

★ c. For each polyhedron shown here, count the vertices, faces, and edges. Test your conjecture from part a on these polyhedra, which are not Platonic solids. Record your results.

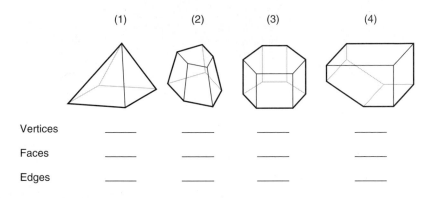

	(1)	(2)	(3)	(4)
Vertices	____	____	____	____
Faces	____	____	____	____
Edges	____	____	____	____

4. **Patterns for Cubes:** The patterns below were formed by joining 6 squares along their edges. Circle the patterns that can be folded into a cube. There are 11 such patterns. (You may wish to copy patterns, cut them out, and experiment by folding.)

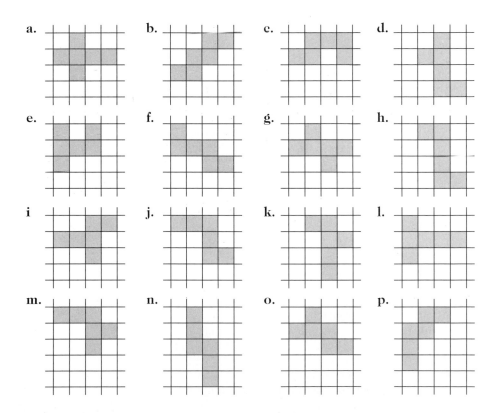

★ 5. **Archimedean Solids:** A *semiregular polyhedron* is a polyhedron that has as faces two or more regular polygons and the same arrangement of polygons about each vertex. The 13 semiregular polyhedra are shown below. They are also called *Archimedean solids*. Archimedes (287–212 B.C.) wrote a book on these solids, but the book has been lost.

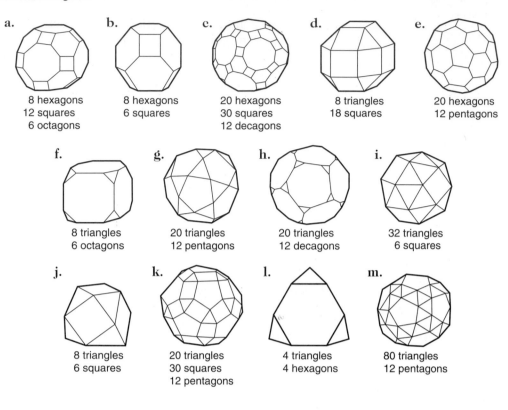

a.
8 hexagons
12 squares
6 octagons

b.
8 hexagons
6 squares

c.
20 hexagons
30 squares
12 decagons

d.
8 triangles
18 squares

e.
20 hexagons
12 pentagons

f.
8 triangles
6 octagons

g.
20 triangles
12 pentagons

h.
20 triangles
12 decagons

i.
32 triangles
6 squares

j.
8 triangles
6 squares

k.
20 triangles
30 squares
12 pentagons

l.
4 triangles
4 hexagons

m.
80 triangles
12 pentagons

The seven Archimedean solids shown in b, e, f, g, h, j, and l can be obtained by truncating Platonic solids. For example, if each corner of a tetrahedron is cut off, we obtain a truncated tetrahedron having 4 hexagons and 4 equilateral triangles as faces as in l.

★ Identify which Platonic solid is truncated to obtain each of the semiregular solids in b, e, f, g, h, and j. (It may be helpful to look at the Platonic solids you constructed in activity 1.)

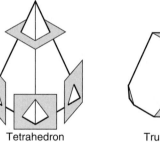

Tetrahedron

Truncated tetrahedron

- -

JUST FOR FUN

INSTANT INSANITY

Instant Insanity is a popular puzzle that was produced by Parker Brothers. The puzzle consists of four cubes with their faces colored either red, white, blue, or green. The object of the puzzle is to stack the cubes so that each side of the stack (or column) has each of the four colors.

Material Card 36 contains patterns for a set of four cubes. Cut out and assemble the cubes and try to solve the puzzle.

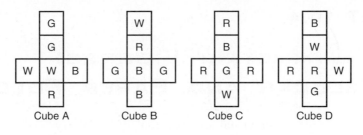

Cube A   Cube B   Cube C   Cube D

Robert E. Levin described the following method for solving this puzzle.[4] He numbered the faces of the cubes, using 1 for red, 2 for white, 3 for blue, and 4 for green, as shown below. To solve the puzzle you must get the numbers 1, 2, 3, and 4 along each side of the stack.

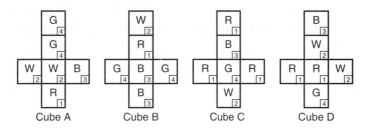

Cube A   Cube B   Cube C   Cube D

The sum of these numbers is 10, and the sum of the numbers on opposite sides of the stack must be 20.

Levin made the following table showing opposite pairs of numbers on each cube and their sums. For example, 4 and 2 are on opposite faces of cube A and their sum is 6. The bottom row of the table contains the sums of opposite faces for each cube. For one combina-

tion of numbers whose sum is 20, the sums have been circled. Notice that above these circled numbers, the numbers 1, 2, 3, and 4 each occur only twice. This tells you how to stack the cubes so that two opposite sides of the stack will have a total sum of 20. (Both of these sides will have all four colors.) The two remaining sides of the stack must also have a sum of 20. Find four more numbers from the bottom row (one for each cube) such that their sum is 20 and each of the numbers 1, 2, 3, and 4 occurs exactly twice among the faces. The remaining two faces of each cube will be its top and bottom faces when it is placed in the stack.

	CUBE A			CUBE B			CUBE C			CUBE D		
Pairs of opposite faces	4	4	3	4	1	2	1	1	3	1	1	4
	2	1	2	4	3	3	1	4	2	3	2	2
Sums of pairs	⑥	5	5	8	4	⑤	2	⑤	5	④	3	6

• •

PUZZLER

One square is subdivided into 7 smaller squares. Subdivide the other square into 6 smaller squares.

[4]R. Levin, "Solving Instant Insanity," *Journal of Recreational Mathematics* 2 (July 1969), 189–192.

ACTIVITY SET 10.4

CREATING SYMMETRIC FIGURES: PATTERN BLOCKS AND PAPER FOLDING

Purpose To introduce visual investigations of symmetry

Materials Pattern blocks from the Manipulative Kit, Material Card 13, scissors, and pieces of paper

Activity The *wind rose,* shown here, is a mariner's device for charting the direction of the wind. The earliest known wind rose appeared on the ancient sailing charts of the Mediterranean pilots, who charted eight principal winds. These are marked on our eight-pointed wind rose. Later, half-winds led to a wind rose with 16 points, and quarter-winds brought the total number of points to 32.[5]

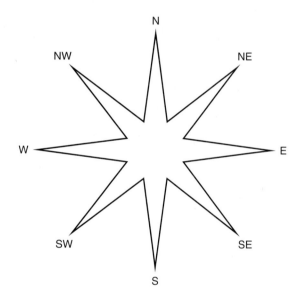

The eight-pointed wind rose is highly symmetric. It has eight lines of symmetry and eight rotational symmetries. For example, a line through any two opposite vertices of the wind rose is a *line of symmetry* because when the wind rose is folded on this line, the two sides will coincide. The wind rose has *rotational symmetries* of 45°, 90°, 135°, 180°, 225°, 270°, 315°, and 360° because, when rotated about its center through any one of these angles, the figure will coincide with the original position of the wind rose.

Activities 4 to 6 have several basic patterns for cutting out symmetric figures. The variety of figures that can be obtained from slight changes in the angles of the cuts is surprising. The eight-pointed wind rose can be cut from one of the patterns—try to predict which one as you do the folding and cutting.

---

[5]M. C. Krause, "Wind Rose, the Beautiful Circle," *Arithmetic Teacher* 20 (May 1973), 375.

Pattern Block Symmetries

1. Use the square and the white rhombus from your pattern block pieces to form figure 1 below. Notice that when another rhombus is attached as in figures 2 and 3, the new figures each have one line of symmetry. When the rhombus is attached as in figure 4, there are no lines of symmetry but there is rotational symmetry of 180°. Finally, when the rhombus is attached as in figure 5, there are no lines of symmetry or rotational symmetries.

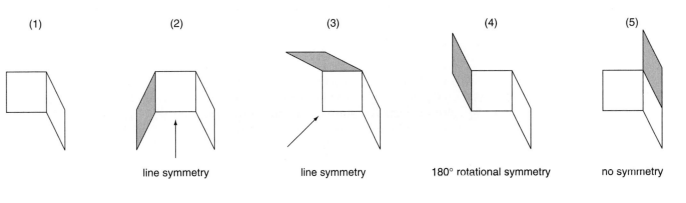

(1)　　　(2)　　　(3)　　　(4)　　　(5)

line symmetry　　　line symmetry　　　180° rotational symmetry　　　no symmetry

★ **a.** Form the following figure with your pattern block pieces. Determine the different ways you can attach another trapezoid to create figures with line symmetry. Use diagrams to record your results.

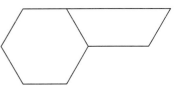

b. Do the same as in part a but find ways to create rotational symmetry (other than 360°).

★ **c.** By attaching 6 trapezoids to the hexagon, create figures that have the following four properties. Make a sketch to record your results.

　　(1) One line of symmetry and no rotational symmetries

　　(2) Six rotational symmetries but no lines of symmetry

(3) Three rotational symmetries and three lines of symmetry

(4) No symmetries

2. a. Use your pattern blocks and Material Card 13 to build this design. Complete the design by adding additional pattern blocks so that the design is symmetric about both perpendicular lines. Sketch the completed design here. Does the completed design have any rotational symmetries? If so, how many?

b. Build the design shown here and use additional pattern blocks to complete a design which has rotational symmetries of 90°, 180°, and 270° about the intersection of the perpendicular lines. Sketch the completed design on the figure. Does the completed design have any line symmetries?

c. Arrange the pattern blocks as shown in this figure. Add additional pattern blocks so that the completed design has rotational symmetry of 90°, 180°, and 270°. Sketch the completed design here.

Paper-Folding Symmetries

3. Fold a rectangular piece of paper in half twice, making the second fold perpendicular to the first. Let C be the corner of all folded edges. Hold the folded paper at corner C and make one cut across as shown by segment AB on the diagram. Before opening the folded corner, predict what the shape will be and how many lines of symmetry it will have.

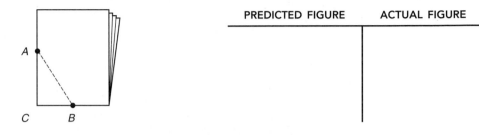

	PREDICTED FIGURE	ACTUAL FIGURE

a. Is it possible to draw a segment AB and make one cut across the folds so that the piece will unfold to a square? If so, describe how you made your cut. If not, explain why it cannot be done.

b. Experiment with other single cuts that start at point A but which exit from any of the other three sides of the twice-folded paper. Continue to predict before you unfold. Make a list of the different types of figures you obtain.

	PREDICTED FIGURE	ACTUAL FIGURE
(1)		
(2)		
(3)		

4. Fold a rectangular piece of paper in half twice, making the second fold perpendicular to the first. Let C be the corner of all the folded edges. Prepare to make two cuts from the edges to an inside point, as shown here. Before cutting the paper, predict what kind of polygon you will get, how many lines of symmetry the figure will have, and whether the figure will be convex or nonconvex. Cut and check your predictions.

	PREDICTED RESULT	ACTUAL RESULT
Type of polygon	————	————
Number of lines of symmetry	————	————
Convex or not	————	————

★ **a.** Find a way to make two cuts into an inside point so that you get a regular octagon; a regular hexagon. Sketch the location of your cuts on these folded-paper diagrams.

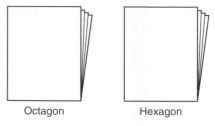

Octagon   Hexagon

b. Make a sketch of the figure you think will result when you cut a piece of double-folded paper as shown below. Then cut the paper and sketch the result.

PREDICTED RESULT   ACTUAL RESULT

c. Vary the angle of the cuts in part b. Sketch lines to show what cuts will result in a rhombus inside a square; a square inside a rhombus. Sketch the resulting figures.

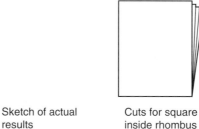

Cuts for rhombus   Sketch of actual   Cuts for square   Sketch of actual
inside square   results   inside rhombus   results

5. The following pattern leads to a variety of symmetrical shapes. Begin with a standard sheet of paper as in figure a, and fold the upper right corner down to produce figure b. Then fold the upper vertex *R* down to point *S* to obtain figure c. To get figure d, fold the two halves inward so that points *S* and *T* are on line *ℓ*.

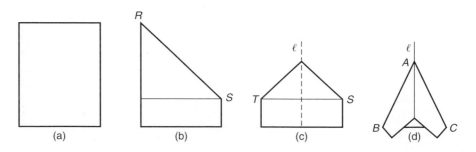

(a)   (b)   (c)   (d)

Make a horizontal cut, as indicated on this diagram, and draw a sketch of the resulting figure.

RESULTING FIGURE

For parts a–d, draw a sketch of the figure you predict will result from the indicated cut. Then fold the paper, make the cut, and draw the actual result. Determine the number of lines of symmetry for each.

a. Slanted cut

PREDICTED FIGURE   ACTUAL RESULT

b. Slanted cut (reversed)

PREDICTED FIGURE   ACTUAL RESULT

c. Combination of two slanted cuts

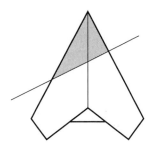

PREDICTED FIGURE   ACTUAL RESULT

★ **d.** Two cuts to an inside point on the center line

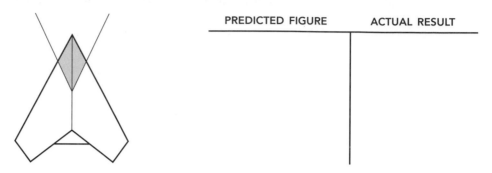

PREDICTED FIGURE	ACTUAL RESULT

★ **e.** Find two cuts into a point on the center line that will produce a regular 16-sided polygon, and sketch them on this diagram.

6. The five-pointed star has been used for badges and national symbols for centuries. It appears today on the flags of 41 countries and was once used on the back of a United States $4 piece.

The four steps pictured in figures a through d illustrate a paper-folding approach to making a five-pointed star. To obtain figure a, fold a standard sheet of paper perpendicular to its longer side. Next, fold point C over to midpoint M of side $\overline{AD}$, as shown in figure b. To get figure c, fold up the corner containing point D and crease along $\overline{MZ}$. For the final step, fold the right side of figure c over to the left side so that edge $\overline{NZ}$ lies along edge $\overline{MZ}$.

(a)   (b)   (c)   (d)

a. Fold a piece of paper according to the instructions, make a cut from X to Y, and sketch the resulting figure.

b. Find a way to make a single cut so that the resulting figure is a regular pentagon; a regular decagon. Sketch the cut lines on the figures below.

Cut line to produce
a regular pentagon

Cut line to produce
a regular decagon

JUST FOR FUN

SNOWFLAKES

Snow is the only substance that crystallizes in many different figures. Yet in spite of the variations in the figures, all snow crystals have a common characteristic—their hexagonal shape.

A New England farmer, W. A. Bentley, began looking at snowflakes when he was given a microscope at the age of 15. A few years later he was given a camera, which he adapted to his microscope to take photographs of snowflakes. Shortly before his death in 1931, Bentley published a book containing 2500 pictures of snow crystals. His work has been used by artists, photographers, illustrators, jewelers, meteorologists, and crystallographers.[6]

To create your own snowflake, fold a standard-size sheet of paper according to the following directions. (Tracing paper or lightweight paper is easiest to fold and cut.)

1. Fold the paper in half twice, making the second fold perpendicular to the first. In figure a the corner C is also the center of the original piece of paper.

2. Fold to find the center line parallel to the longer edges, as indicated in figure b.
3. Bring corner X up to the center line and crease the paper along $\overline{CY}$, as shown in figure c.
4. Fold corner B *back* until side $\overline{CB}$ lies along side $\overline{CY}$, and crease along $\overline{CX}$, as in figure d.
5. Cut off the portion of paper above $\overline{XY}$, as shown in figure e.

Now cut out designs along sides $\overline{CY}$, $\overline{CX}$, and $\overline{XY}$. Unfold the finished product carefully to examine your snowflake design. What is its shape? What lines of symmetry and what rotational symmetries does it have? Experiment with other designs.

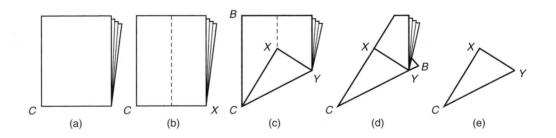

(a)   (b)   (c)   (d)   (e)

[6]F. Hapgood, "When Ice Crystals Fall from the Sky Art Meets Science," *Smithsonian* (January 1976), 67–72.

ACTIVITY SET 10.5

COMPUTER GAMES IN LOGO

Purpose   To use a LOGO game to practice angle and distance estimation

Materials   A computer and Apple or Terrapin LOGO software

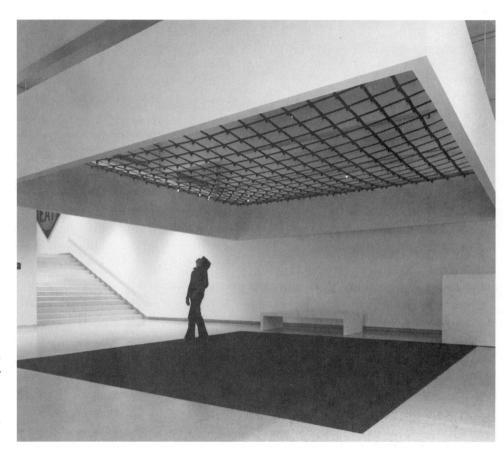

Network III, a computer-generated environment, Walker Art Center, Minneapolis. (Photo by Eric Sutherland, Courtesy of Walker Art Center, Minneapolis.)

Activity   The network of lights in this photograph is activated by a computer as people walk on the carpet. The carpet is subdivided into small squares, each containing a pressure-actuated switch that detects the presence of a person on that square. The computer is programmed to determine where people are within the space, which direction they are moving, how fast they are traveling, and so forth. The computer uses this information to generate patterns in the network of lights. The sense of a highly elaborate abstract game is conveyed, tempting the person into testing the environment to see how the computer responds to one's movements.

LOGO Target Game

A target, which is a circle of radius 9, and the turtle, which is represented by a triangle, are randomly placed on the screen. The object is to get the turtle completely inside the circle in as few tries as possible.[7]

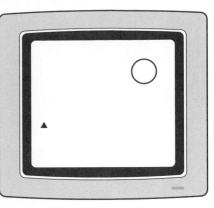

The procedure TARGETGAME sets up the screen for this game. TARGETGAME is defined by using two other procedures: CIRCLE9 draws a circle of radius 9, and PLACERAN-DOMLY places the turtle and the circle in random locations on the screen.

1. Type the commands for CIRCLE9, PLACERANDOMLY, and TARGETGAME as they are shown here.[8]

TO CIRCLE9
  REPEAT 360 [FD .0174* 9 RT 1]
END

TO TARGETGAME
  CLEARGRAPHICS
  PLACERANDOMLY CIRCLE9
  PENUP HOME
  PLACERANDOMLY
END

TO PLACERANDOMLY
  PENUP
  RT 90 FD RANDOM 110 BK RANDOM 110
  LT 90 FD RANDOM 60 BK RANDOM 60
  PENDOWN
END

2. Play the game, typing TARGETGAME to set the game up. A move consists of giving the turtle a direction and a distance. For example, RT 60 FD 150 is 1 move. The object of the game is to get the turtle *completely* inside the circle in as few moves as possible. When you have succeeded, your opponent types TARGETGAME and attempts to hit the target in fewer moves.

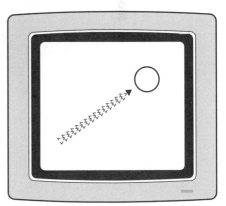

★ 3. The definition of PLACERANDOMLY uses the command RANDOM, which randomly selects whole numbers from 1 up to a given number. For example, RANDOM 360 selects a whole number from 1 up to and including 359, and

---

[7]For additional information about LOGO procedures see section 10.5 in this book's companion text, *Mathematics for Elementary Teachers: A Conceptual Approach*, or consult a LOGO manual.
[8]For Macintosh computers press Enter to execute commands rather than Return. Pressing Return will put the cursor at the beginning of the next line.

RANDOM 100 selects a number from 1 up to and including 99. Explain why the numbers 110 and 60 were used in definition of PLACERANDOMLY.

4. Revise the game so that the target is a square with sides of length 18.

IDEAS FOR THE ELEMENTARY CLASSROOM

SUGGESTED CLASSROOM ACTIVITY: PAPER-FOLDING SYMMETRIES

Children can become actively involved in investigating symmetry through folding and cutting paper.

1. Single or double fold a sheet of paper, and have students cut a design and display the symmetries of the result.

2. Do as in activity 1, but ask the students to draw a sketch of what they think their design will look like before they unfold the paper.

3. Have the students double fold (folds perpendicular) a sheet of paper (a); draw a design on one side (b); draw a sketch to predict the outcome before cutting; and then cut, unfold, and compare the result to their prediction.

(a)   (b)

4. Show the students some symmetric patterns you have made and ask them to make similar patterns by folding and cutting.

Readings for More Classroom Ideas

Arcidiacono, Michael, D. Fielker, and E. Maier. "Seeing Symmetry," in *Math and the Mind's Eye* (Unit X). Salem, OR: The Math Learning Center, Box 3226, 1996.

Barson, Alan, and L. Barson. "Ideas: Geometry Activities." *Arithmetic Teacher* 35 (April 1988): 27–36.

Battista, Michael, and Douglas Clements. "Research into Practice: Constructing Geometric Concepts in Logo." *Arithmetic Teacher* 38 (November 1990): 15–17.

Bennett, A., E. Maier, and L. Ted Nelson. "Looking at Geometry," in *Math and the Mind's Eye* (Unit V). Salem, OR: The Math Learning Center, Box 3226, 1988.

Bidwell, James K. "Using Reflections to Find Symmetric and Asymmetric Patterns." *Arithmetic Teacher* 34 (March 1987): 10–15.

Bradley, Claudette. "Teaching Mathematics with Technology: The Four Directions Indian Beadwork Design with Logo." *Arithmetic Teacher* 39 (May 1992): 46–49.

Bright, George W. "Teaching Mathematics with Technology: Logo and Geometry." *Arithmetic Teacher* 36 (January 1989): 32–34.

Carroll, William M. "Cross Sections of Clay Solids." *Arithmetic Teacher* 35 (March 1988): 6–11.

Claus, Alison. "Exploring Geometry." *Arithmetic Teacher* 40 (September 1992): 14–17.

Clauss, Judith Enz. "Pentagonal Tessellations." *Arithmetic Teacher* 38 (January 1991): 52–56.

Clements, Douglas, and Julie S. Meredith. "One Point of View: My Turn: A Talk with the Logo Turtle." *Arithmetic Teacher* 41 (December 1993): 189–191.

Cook, Marcy. "Ideas [Rectangle Activities]." *Arithmetic Teacher* 36 (March 1989): 27–32.

Del Grande, John, and Lorna Morrow. *Geometry and Spatial Sense,* in the *Curriculum and Evaluation Standards for School Mathematics Addenda Series: Grades K–6.* Reston, VA: National Council of Teachers of Mathematics, 1993.

Dutch, Steven I. "Folding n-pointed Stars and Snowflakes." *Mathematics Teacher* 87 (November 1994): 630–637.

Evered, Lisa J. "Folded Fashions: Symmetry in Clothing Design." *Arithmetic Teacher* 40 (December 1992): 204–206.

Flores, Alfinio. "Bilingual Lessons in Early-Grades Geometry." *Teaching Children Mathematics* 1 (March 1995): 420–424.

Geddes, Dorothy, et al. *Geometry in the Middle Grades,* in the *Curriculum and Evaluation Standards for School Mathematics Addenda Series: Grades 5–8.* Reston, VA: National Council of Teachers of Mathematics. 1992.

Happs, John, and Helen Mansfield. "Research into Practice: Estimation and Mental-Imagery Model in Geometry." *Arithmetic Teacher* 40 (September 1992): 44–46.

Kriegler, Shelley. "The Tangram—It's More Than an Ancient Puzzle." *Arithmetic Teacher* 38 (May 1991): 38–43.

Leeson, Neville J. "Improving Students' Sense of Three-Dimensional Shapes." *Teaching Children Mathematics* 1 (September 1994): 8–11.

Maupin, Sue. "Middle-Grades Geometry." *Mathematics Teaching in the Middle School* 1 (May 1996): 790–796.

McClintock, Ruth. "Animating Geometry Discussions with Flexigons." *Mathematics Teacher* 87 (November 1994): 602–606.

Miller, William A. "Puzzles That Section Regular Solids." *Mathematics Teacher* 81 (September 1988): 463–468.

Morrow, Lorna J. "Implementing the Standards: Geometry Through the Standards." *Arithmetic Teacher* 38 (April 1991): 21–25.

Onslow, Barry, "Pentominoes Revisted." *Arithmetic Teacher* 37 (May 1990): 5–9.

Reys, Robert E. "Discovery with Cubes." *Mathematics Teacher* 81 (May 1988): 377–381.

Rubenstein, Rheta N., Glenda Lappan, Elizabeth Phillips, and William Fitzgerald. "Angle Sense: A Valuable Connector," *Arithmetic Teacher* 40 (February 1993): 352–358.

Serra, Michael. *Patty Paper Geometry.* Berkeley, CA: Key Curriculum Press, 1994.

Seymour, D., and J. Britton. "Creating Escher-Like Tessellations." *Introduction to Tessellations.* Palo Alto, CA: Dale Seymour Publications, 1989, 1–59.

Souza, Ronald. "Golfing with a Protractor." *Arithmetic Teacher* 35 (April 1988): 52–56.

Wheatley, Grayson H. "Research into Practice: Spatial Sense and the Construction of Abstract Units in Tiling." *Arithmetic Teacher* 39 (April 1992): 43–45.

Wilson, Patricia, and Verna Adams. "A Dynamic Way to Teach Angle and Angle Measure." *Arithmetic Teacher* 39 (January 1992): 6–13.

Zaslavsky, Claudia. "Symmetry in American Folk Art." *Arithmetic Teacher* 38 (September 1990): 6–12.

CHAPTER 11

MEASUREMENT

Children can see the usefulness of measurement if classroom experiences focus on measuring real objects, making objects of given sizes, and estimating measurements. Textbook experiences cannot substitute for activities that use measurement to answer questions about real problems.[1]

ACTIVITY SET 11.1

MEASURING WITH METRIC UNITS

Purpose   To use estimation and measurement activities to introduce the basic metric units

Materials   A metric ruler is on Material Card 32, and a metric measuring tape is on Material Card 14

© 1974 United Feature Syndicate, Inc.

Activity   The metric system of measurement is used by most nations of the world. The basic metric units for length, weight, and volume are the *meter* (a little longer than a yard), the *gram* (about the weight of a paper clip), and the *liter* (a little

---

[1]*Curriculum and Evaluation Standards for School Mathematics* (Reston, VA: National Council of Teachers of Mathematics, 1989), 53.

more than a quart). Larger and smaller measures are obtained by using the following prefixes. The four prefixes marked with an asterisk are most commonly used. There are additional prefixes which extend this system to even larger and smaller measures for scientific purposes.

kilo*	1000 times
hecto	100 times
deka	10 times
deci*	$\frac{1}{10}$
centi*	$\frac{1}{100}$
milli*	$\frac{1}{1000}$

The prefixes differ by powers of 10. For example,

10 millimeters (mm) = 1 centimeter (cm)
10 centimeters = 1 decimeter (dm)
10 decimeters = 1 meter (m)
1000 meters = 1 kilometer (km)

There is a simple relationship among the metric units for length, weight, and volume:

The following activities involve the metric units for length and volume. If you are not familiar with the metric system and are unaccustomed to thinking of length in terms of centimeters and meters, the estimation and measuring game in activity 1 will give you expertise quickly. Another measuring game is in Just for Fun, at the end of this activity set.

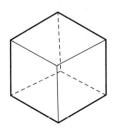

One cubic centimeter (1 cm³) equals 1 milliliter (ml) and, if water, has a mass of 1 gram (g).

1. **Centimeter and Meter Guessing Games (2 players):** One player marks two points on a sheet of paper. The opponent guesses the distance in centimeters between these two points. The distance is then measured with a ruler. If the guess is within 1 centimeter of being correct, the guessing player scores 1 point. If not, there is no score. The players alternate picking points and guessing distances until someone has scored 11 points.

Challenging: If a player thinks an opponent's guess is not within 1 centimeter, that player may challenge the guess by giving his or her own estimate of the distance. If the challenger's estimate is within 1 centimeter and the opponent's is not, then the challenger receives 1 point and the opponent receives no score. However, if the opponent is within 1 centimeter, he or she receives 2 points for the insult, regardless of the challenger's estimate, and the challenger receives no score.

Variation 1: Players estimate the lengths of objects around them. Since they will be estimating in centimeters, these objects should be reasonably small, such as pencils, books, and dollar bills.

Variation 2: This game is called the Meter Guessing Game. On a player's turn, he or she selects an object in the room, and the opponent guesses its length in meters. If the guess is within $\frac{1}{2}$ meter, the guessing player scores 1 point. If not, there is no score. The players alternate picking objects and guessing lengths. As before, a player's guess may be challenged.

2. Your handspan is a convenient ruler for measuring lengths. Stretch out your fingers and use your metric ruler or metric measuring tape to measure the maximum distance from your little finger to your thumb in centimeters.

a. Use your handspan to approximate the width and length of this page in centimeters. Record your results below and then check your approximations by measuring.

	WIDTH	LENGTH
Approximation	_____	_____
Measurement	_____	_____

b. Select some objects around you and estimate their lengths in centimeters. Check your estimates by measuring. Repeat this activity 10 times, and see how many distances you can predict to within 1 centimeter. Record the objects, your estimates of lengths, and your measurements. In the last column record the difference between your estimation and measurement as a positive number, and then compute the average difference.

OBJECT	ESTIMATION	MEASUREMENT (nearest cm)	DIFFERENCE
_____	_____	_____	_____
_____	_____	_____	_____
_____	_____	_____	_____
_____	_____	_____	_____
_____	_____	_____	_____
_____	_____	_____	_____
_____	_____	_____	_____
_____	_____	_____	_____
_____	_____	_____	_____
_____	_____	_____	_____

Average of differences _____

3. A millimeter is the smallest unit on your metric ruler. Obtain the measurements of the objects in parts a through c to the nearest millimeter.

★ a. The length of a dollar bill

★ b. The diameter of a penny

c. The width of one of your fingernails. Do you have one with a width of 1 centimeter?

d. What fraction of a millimeter is the thickness of one page of this book? (*Hint*: Measure several pages at once.)

4. This table contains some body measurements that are useful for buying and making clothes. Estimate or use your handspan to approximate these measurements. Then use your metric measuring tape and your metric ruler to obtain these measurements to the nearest centimeter.

	ESTIMATE	MEASUREMENT
Waist	_____	_____
Height	_____	_____
Arm length	_____	_____
Foot length	_____	_____
Width of palm	_____	_____
Circumference of head	_____	_____

5. Use your metric measuring tape (Material Card 14) for the following.

a. Measure the distance from the middle of your chest to your fingertips with your arm outstretched. Is this distance greater than or less than 1 meter? This body distance was once used by merchants to measure cloth. It is the origin of the English measure called the yard.

b. Measure the distance from the floor up to your waist. How does this distance compare with a meter?

c. Select some objects around you whose lengths are greater than 1 meter, and try to estimate their length to within $\frac{1}{2}$ meter (50 cm). For example, estimate the height, width, and length of a room and then measure these distances with your metric measuring tape. Repeat this activity for 10 different objects, and see how many distances you can predict to within $\frac{1}{2}$ meter in the following table. Record the objects, your estimates of lengths, and the measurements. In the last column of the table, record the difference between your estimation and measurement, as a positive number, and then compute the average of the differences.

OBJECT	ESTIMATION	MEASUREMENT (nearest $\frac{1}{2}$ cm)	DIFFERENCE
_____	_____	_____	_____
_____	_____	_____	_____
_____	_____	_____	_____
_____	_____	_____	_____
_____	_____	_____	_____
_____	_____	_____	_____
_____	_____	_____	_____
_____	_____	_____	_____
_____	_____	_____	_____
_____	_____	_____	_____

Average of differences _____

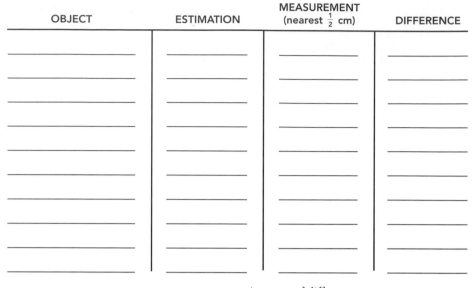

6. Your *pace* is the distance you cover in one normal step. To gather information about your pace, measure off a distance of 10 meters. Record the time in seconds and the number of paces it takes you to walk this distance.

Number of paces needed to walk 10 meters: _____

Time, in seconds, needed to walk 10 meters: _____

Using this information, explain how to determine each of the following.

a. The length of a single pace, in centimeters

b. The number of paces it will take you to walk 1 kilometer

c. The time in minutes that it will take you to walk 1 kilometer

Single pace

7. A liter is very close to the English measure the quart. A liter is equal to 1000 cubic centimeters, the volume of a 10 cm by 10 cm by 10 cm cube.

★ **a.** Use the dimensions on this drawing of a quart container to approximate the number of cubic centimeters in a quart. Which is greater, a liter or a quart?

One quart container

19.3 cm

7 cm   7 cm

★ **b.** What height should be marked on a two-quart container to measure 1 liter?

Two quart container

20.5 cm

9.6 cm   9.6 cm

JUST FOR FUN

CENTIMETER RACING GAME (2 or more players)

This game is played on a racing mat (Material Card 15). The object of the game is to go from the center of the circle to a point inside the triangle, square, pentagon, and hexagon, in that order. Each player in turn rolls two dice. The two numbers may be added, subtracted, multiplied, or divided. The resulting computation is the number of centimeters the player moves. A metric ruler (Material Card 32) should be used to draw the line segment whose length is the player's number.

On each subsequent turn, players draw another line segment, beginning at the end of their last line segment. Before players can pass through a polygon or proceed from one polygon to the next, they must land inside the polygon with the end of a line segment. The first player to draw a line segment that ends inside the hexagon is the winner.

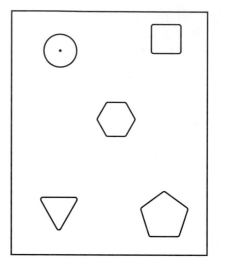

ACTIVITY SET 11.2

AREAS ON GEOBOARDS

Purpose To use rectangular geoboards to develop area concepts

Materials A rectangular geoboard and rubber bands. A template for making a rectangular geoboard is on Material Card 27.

Activity The rows and columns of nails on a rectangular geoboard, like the one shown here, outline 16 small squares. In this activity set, these small squares will serve as the unit squares for the areas of the geoboard figures. Finding the area of a geoboard polygon means determining the number of unit squares and partial squares needed to cover the polygon.

It takes 6 unit squares and 7 halves of unit squares to cover the figure on this geoboard, so its area is $9\frac{1}{2}$ unit squares.

In the following activities, you will examine different methods for determining areas of polygons and discover how the formulas for the areas of rectangles, parallelograms, and triangles are related.

---

1. Form each polygon on your geoboard, determine its area by counting squares and halves of squares, and record the area beneath the figure.

★ **a.**   **b.**   ★ **c.**

  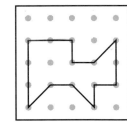

_____   _____   _____

d.   ★ **e.**   **f.**

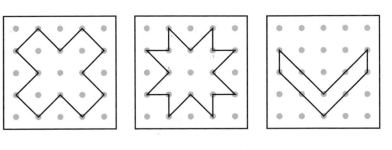

_____   _____   _____

2. In the figure for part a, the upper shaded triangle has an area of 1 square unit because it is half of a 2 by 1 rectangle. Similarly, the lower shaded triangle has an area of $1\frac{1}{2}$ square units because it is half of a 3 by 1 rectangle. Determine the areas of these figures by subdividing them into squares, halves of squares, and triangles that are halves of rectangles.

★ a.   b.   ★ c.

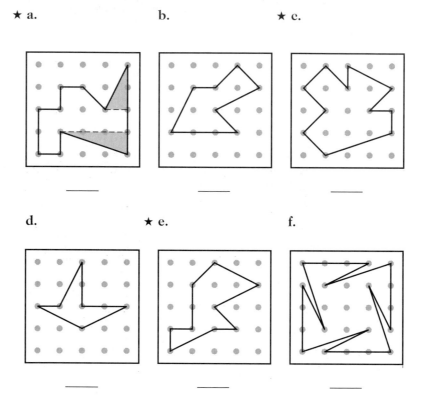

d.   ★ e.   f.

3. Sometimes it is easier to find the area outside a figure than the area inside. The hexagon in part a has been enclosed inside a square. What is the area of the shaded region? Subtract this area from the area of the 3 by 3 square to find the area of the hexagon. Use this technique to find the areas of the following figures.

★ a.   b.   ★ c.

d.   ★ e.   f.

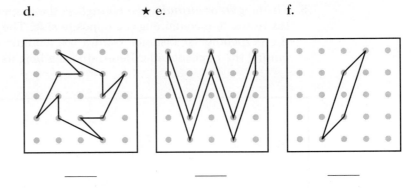

_____   _____   _____

4. Determine the areas of the following figures using any technique or combination of techniques. Notice that the hexagon in part a has a vertical line of symmetry, so you can determine the area of half the region and double the result.

★ a.   b.   ★ c.

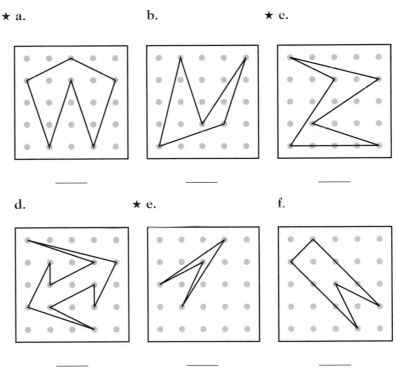

_____   _____   _____

d.   ★ e.   f.

_____   _____   _____

5. The *height,* or *altitude, of a triangle* is the perpendicular distance from a vertex to the line containing the opposite side. The *height of a parallelogram* is the perpendicular distance from a line containing one side to the line containing the opposite side. Determine the heights indicated below.

From vertex *A*   From vertex *E*   From side *ZW*   From side *RS*
_____   _____   _____   _____

6. Use your geoboard techniques to determine the area of each of these parallelograms.

_____   _____   _____   _____

Each of the preceding parallelograms has one pair of sides of length 2 and a common height. Make a conjecture about how to determine the area of a parallelogram if you know the length of a side and the height from that side. Sketch additional parallelograms below to test your conjecture. If your conjecture appears to be valid, record it.

Conjecture:

7. Use geoboard techniques to determine the areas of these triangles.

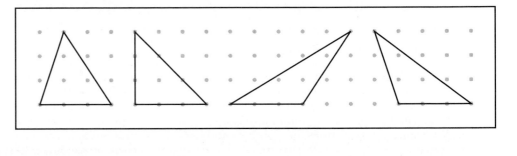

——————   ——————   ——————   ——————

Make and test conjectures about triangles with bases of equal length and common heights. Record your conjecture below.

Conjecture:

8. The triangle in part a is enclosed in a parallelogram that shares two sides with it. Enclose each triangle in a parallelogram that shares two sides with it. Then, using geoboard techniques, record the areas of the triangle and its parallelogram.

★ **a.**   **b.**   ★ **c.**   **d.**

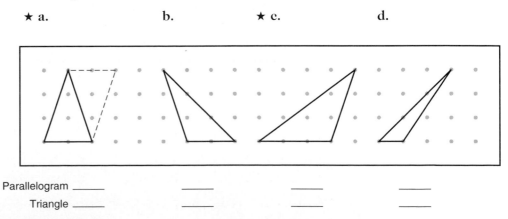

Parallelogram _____   _____   _____   _____

Triangle _____   _____   _____   _____

★ 9. The formula for the area of a triangle is one-half of the base length times the height to that base [$A = (\frac{1}{2})bh$]. Based on the observations you have made in activities 5, 6, 7, and 8, write a statement that explains this formula.

JUST FOR FUN

PENTOMINOES

Pentominoes are polygons that can be formed by joining five squares along their edges. Surprisingly, there are 12 such polygons. Pentominoes can be used in puzzles, games, tessellations, and other problem-solving activities.

A complete set of pentomino pieces is on Material Card 37. Material Card 16 has a grid that can be used for activities 2, 3, and 4. Note: Pieces can be turned over.

1. Selecting the appropriate pieces from your pentomino set, form the 4 by 5 rectangular puzzle shown here. Outline this rectangle with pencil, and see how many other combinations of pieces will exactly fill the outline.

2. The best-known challenge is to use all 12 pieces to form a 6 by 10 rectangle. Supposedly there are over 2000 different solutions. Find one solution and record it on this grid.

3. It is possible to form several puzzles by constructing an 8 by 8 grid of squares and then removing four unit squares. In one of these, the unit squares are missing from the corners, as shown here. Use all 12 pieces to cover a grid with this shape. Record your solution here.

★ 4. **Pentomino Game (2 players):** This game is played on an 8 by 8 grid. The players take turns placing a pentomino on uncovered squares of the grid. Play continues until someone is unable to play or all the pieces have been used. The player who makes the last move wins the game. The first seven plays of a game are shown on this board. Player A has made four moves, and player B has made three moves. Find a way player B can make the eighth move (with one of the remaining pentominoes) so that no more moves can be made. Play a few games and look for strategies.

★ 5. It is possible to place 5 different pentomino pieces on an 8 by 8 grid so that no other piece from the same set can be placed on the grid. Can you find 5 such pieces?

PUZZLER

Make one straight cut so that the two resulting pieces can be put together to form a square.

ACTIVITY SET 11.3

MODELS FOR VOLUME AND SURFACE AREA

Purpose To construct three-dimensional figures and measure their volume

Materials Patterns for a prism, pyramid, and cylinder are on Material Card 38, and a compass and protractor are on Material Card 32.

Activity One of the greatest mathematicians of all time was Archimedes (287–212 B.C.), a native of Syracuse on the island of Sicily. You may have heard the story of how Archimedes was able to solve a problem King Hieron had with his crown. The king had weighed out the exact amount of pure gold he wanted used for a crown, but upon receiving the crown he became suspicious that it was a mixture of gold and silver. The crown weighed as much as the original amount of gold, so there seemed to be no way of exposing the fraud. Archimedes was informed of the problem, and a solution occurred to him while he was taking a bath. He noticed that the amount of water that overflowed the tub depended on the extent to which his body was immersed. In his excitement to try his solution with gold and silver, Archimedes leaped from the tub and ran naked to his home, shouting, "Eureka! Eureka!"

As Archimedes discovered, the volume of a submerged object is equal to the volume of the displaced water. Finding the volumes of objects by submerging them in water is especially convenient with metric units, because the number of milliliters of water that is displaced is equal to the volume of the object in cubic centimeters. This relationship will be used in the following activities. You may also need the formulas for volumes of prisms and cylinders (area of base × height), pyramids and cones ($\frac{1}{3}$ × area of base × height), and spheres [$(\frac{4}{3})\pi r^3$].

★ **1.** To understand Archimedes' solution, consider two cubes both weighing the same amount, one of pure gold and one of pure silver. Since gold is about twice as heavy as silver, the cube of gold will be smaller than the cube of silver. Therefore, when each is submerged in water, there will be more water displaced for the cube of silver. To apply his theory, Archimedes used the crown and an amount of pure gold weighing the same as the crown. He submerged them separately in water and measured the amount of overflow. There was more water displaced for the crown than for the pure gold. What does this show about the volume of the crown as compared to the volume of the gold? Was King Hieron cheated?

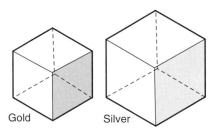

Gold   Silver

★ **2.** Patterns for prisms, pyramids, and cylinders are easy to make. Three such patterns are contained on Material Card 38. Cut them out and tape their edges. Compute the volumes and surface areas of these figures. You may wish to fill them with sand or salt to check your answers. (The area of the base of a cylinder is πr^2. Use 3.14 for π.)

	HEXAGONAL PRISM	HEXAGONAL PYRAMID	CYLINDER
Area of base	_____	_____	_____
Height (altitude)	_____	_____	_____
Volume	_____	_____	_____
Surface area	_____	_____	_____

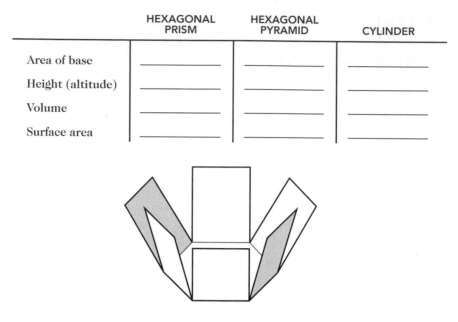

★ **3.** A sheet of paper can be made into a cylinder in the two ways shown in the following figures. Make a cylinder (without bases) from a standard sheet of paper so that its circumference is 21.5 centimeters and its height is 28 centimeters. Then use another sheet of paper to form a cylinder with a circumference of 28 centimeters and a height of 21.5 centimeters. Predict which cylinder has the greater volume. As you compute the volume of each cylinder, record your steps and answers below.

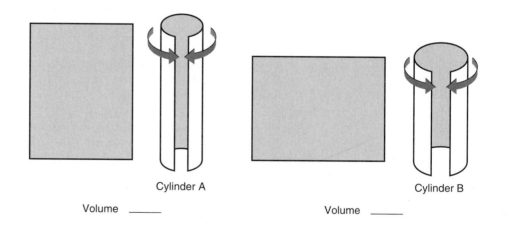

Cylinder A

Volume _____

Cylinder B

Volume _____

4. Cut a standard sheet of paper in half lengthwise and tape the two halves end to end, as shown next. Make a cylinder without bases and compute its volume. Compare the volume of this cylinder with that of cylinder B in activity

3. What happens to the volume of a cylinder as the height is halved and the circumference (thus, radius and diameter) is doubled?

5. Make a set of six different cones by cutting out three disks, each of radius 10 centimeters. (There are a compass and protractor on Material Card 32.) Each disk can be used for making two cones, as shown here. Cut from these disks sectors with central angles of 45°, 90°, 135°, 225°, 270°, and 315°, and *number the sectors from 1 to 6 according to the size of the central angle.* After cutting each disk into two parts, bend it and tape the edges to form the cones.

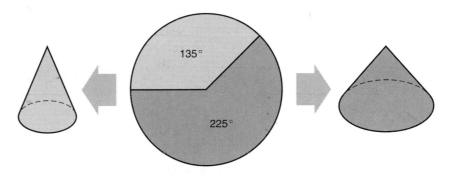

a. Without computing, line the cones up from left to right in what you estimate to be increasing volume. Record your estimated order by recording the numbers of the cones.

_____   _____   _____   _____   _____   _____

Least volume   Greatest volume

★ b. Compute the base areas and volumes (to the nearest two decimal places) of the cones, and enter them in the following table. Use the results to check the estimated order of the cones in part a. (The area of the base of a cone is πr^2. Use 3.14 for π.)

	1	2	3	4	5	6
Central angle of disk	45°	90°	135°	225°	270°	315°
Base area (cm²)	____	____	____	____	____	____
Height (cm)	9.92	9.68	9.27	7.81	6.61	4.84
Radius (cm)	1.25	2.50	3.75	6.25	7.50	8.75
Volume (cm³)	____	____	____	____	____	____

★ **c.** What will happen to the volume of the cone as sectors with central angles of less than 45° are used? as sectors with central angles of greater than 315° are used?

6. Choose one of your cones from activity 5, and place a mark on the surface halfway from the vertex to the base.

   a. If the cone were filled to this mark, estimate what fractional part of the total volume would be filled. Circle the fraction that best represents your estimate.

$$\frac{1}{8} \quad \frac{1}{7} \quad \frac{1}{6} \quad \frac{1}{5} \quad \frac{1}{4} \quad \frac{1}{3} \quad \frac{1}{2}$$

   b. To experimentally test your estimate, fill the cone up to the mark with water (or sand or rice) and then pour its contents into an identical cone, repeating the process until the second cone is full. How many "fillings" are required?

★ **c.** Compute the volume of your "half cone" and compare it to the volume of the whole cone. What do you discover?

7. A basketball displaces 7235 milliliters of water.

★ **a.** What is its volume in cubic centimeters?

b. What is the diameter of this ball? [Sphere volume = $(\frac{4}{3})\pi r^3$, where r is the radius. Use 3.14 for π.] Explain how you arrived at your conclusions.

c. Submerge a baseball in water and measure the displaced water in milliliters. According to this experiment, what is the volume of a baseball in cubic centimeters? A baseball has a diameter of approximately 7.3 centimeters. Compute its volume in cubic centimeters, and compare this answer with the results of your experiment. Record your results.

d. Submerge an unopened cylindrical can in water and measure the overflow. Then measure the diameter and height of the can and compute its volume. Compare the computed volume with the results of your experiment. Record your results.

8. Spherical objects such as Christmas tree ornaments and basketballs are packed in cube-shaped compartments and boxes.

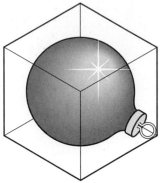

a. If a sphere just fits into a box, estimate what fraction of the box is "wasted space." Circle the fraction that best represents your estimate.

$$\frac{1}{6} \quad \frac{1}{5} \quad \frac{1}{4} \quad \frac{1}{3} \quad \frac{1}{2}$$

Compute the amount of wasted space when a sphere of diameter 25 centimeters is placed in a box. What fraction of the total volume of this box is wasted space?

b. Spheres are also packed in cylinders. A cylinder provides a better fit than a box, but there is still extra space. If 3 balls are packed in a cylindrical can whose diameter equals that of a ball and whose height is 3 times the diameter, estimate what fraction of the space is unused.

$$\frac{1}{6} \quad \frac{1}{5} \quad \frac{1}{4} \quad \frac{1}{3} \quad \frac{1}{2}$$

Compute the amount of unused space.

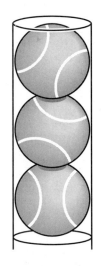

★ **c.** Tennis ball cans hold 3 balls. Determine the amount of wasted space in these cans if the balls have a diameter of 6.3 centimeters and the can has a diameter of 7 centimeters and a height of 20 centimeters. Check the reasonableness of your answer by experimenting with a can of balls and water.

JUST FOR FUN

SOMA CUBES

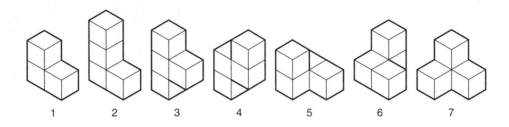

1   2   3   4   5   6   7

Soma cubes are a seven-piece puzzle invented by the Danish author Piet Hein. Piece 1 has 3 cubes, and the other pieces each have 4 cubes. Soma cubes can be purchased, or they can be constructed by gluing together cubes, such as sugar cubes, wooden cubes, or dice.

Surprisingly, these 7 pieces can be assembled to form a 3 by 3 by 3 cube. You may wish to try this challenging puzzle.

A common activity with soma cubes is constructing certain well-

known figures. Each of the shapes in figure 1 below requires all 7 pieces. Try to build them.

There are several elementary techniques for determining when a figure cannot be constructed with soma cubes. The simplest of these is counting the number of cubes. For example, a figure with 18 cubes cannot be formed because there is no combination of 4s and one 3 that adds up to 18. Use this approach to find which of the shapes in Figure 2 cannot be formed with soma cubes.[2]

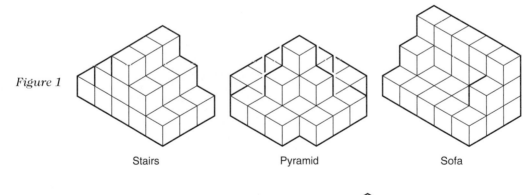

Figure 1

Stairs   Pyramid   Sofa

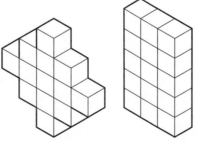

Figure 2

---

[2]Additional techniques can be found in G. Carson, "Soma Cubes," *The Mathematics Teacher* 66 (November 1973), 583–592.

PUZZLER

This solid is made from 1000 cubes. The solid is spray-painted on all sides, including the bottom. What percent of the cubes have no paint on them?

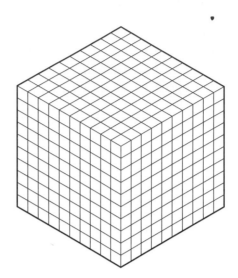

IDEAS FOR THE ELEMENTARY CLASSROOM

SUGGESTED CLASSROOM ACTIVITY: FOLDING BOXES

Building and filling boxes helps students understand the concepts of volume and surface area. By cutting squares from the corners of a grid sheet and folding and taping sides, students can construct boxes without tops. Seven boxes that can be formed by cutting whole numbers of squares from the corners of a 16 by 16 sheet of grid paper are shown here.

After the boxes have been constructed, have students do the following:

1. Arrange them in order from least capacity to greatest capacity by simply looking and comparing (estimating).

2. Order them by filling each with foam nuggets and comparing relative volumes.

3. Stack cubic centimeters or other cubical objects inside to compare volume.

4. (Older students) Compute the volume of each box once they understand the concept of volume.

5. Obtain the surface area of each box by counting squares or computing from the dimensions. Students may be surprised to discover that the surface area of the boxes from left to right in the photo decreases, whereas the volume increases and then decreases.

6. Use grid paper with other dimensions to construct boxes with different dimensions.

7. Cut patterns that will fold into boxes with tops.

Readings for More Classroom Ideas

Badger, Elizabeth. "More Than Testing." *Arithmetic Teacher* 39 (May 1992): 7–11.

Barson, Alan, and L. Barson. "Ideas: Measurement Activities." *Arithmetic Teacher* 35 (May 1988): 20–29.

Cook, March. "Ideas: Rectangle Activities." *Arithmetic Teacher* 36 (March 1989): 27–32.

Fay, Nancy, and C. Tsairides. "Metric Mall." *Arithmetic Teacher* 37 (September 1989): 6–11.

Fitzgerald, William, and Janet Shroyer. *Mouse and Elephant: Measuring Growth.* Middle Grades Mathematics Project. Menlo Park, CA: Addison-Wesley Publishing Company, 1986.

Geddes, Dorothy, et al. *Measurement in the Middle Grades,* in the *Curriculum and Evaluation Standards for School Mathematics Addenda Series: Grades 5–8.* Reston, VA: National Council of Teachers of Mathematics, 1994.

Holcomb, Joan. "Using Geoboards in the Primary Grades." *Arithmetic Teacher* 27 (April 1980): 22–25.

Horak, Virginia M., and W. J. Horak. "Let's Do It: Making Measurement Meaningful." *Arithmetic Teacher* 30 (November 1982): 18–23.

Jensen, Rosalie, and D. R. O'Neil. "Let's Do It: Meaningful Linear Measurement." *Arithmetic Teacher* 29 (September 1981): 6–12.

Lamphere, Patricia. "Geoboard Patterns and Figures." *Teaching Children Mathematics* 1 (January 1995): 282–286.

Lindquist, Mary M. "Implementing the Standards: The Measurement Standards." *Arithmetic Teacher* 37 (October 1989): 22–26.

Shaw, Jean M. "Let's Do It: Exploring Perimeter and Area Using Centimeter Squared Paper." *Arithmetic Teacher* 31 (December 1983): 4–11.

Shaw, Jean M. "Let's Do It: Student-Made Measuring Tools." *Arithmetic Teacher* 31 (November 1983): 12–15.

Shaw, Jean M. "Meaning Metrics: Measure, Mix, Manipulate, and Mold." *Arithmetic Teacher* 28 (March 1981): 49–50.

Stix, Andi. "Pic-Jour Math: Pictorial Journal Writing in Mathematics." *Arithmetic Teacher* 41 (January 1994): 264–269.

Whitin, David J., and Cassandra Gary. "Promoting Mathematical Explorations Through Children's Literature." *Arithmetic Teacher* 41 (March 1994): 394–399.

Zaslavsky, Claudia. "People Who Live in Round Houses." *Arithmetic Teacher* 37 (September 1989): 18–21.

CHAPTER 12

MOTIONS IN GEOMETRY

Students discover relationships and develop spatial sense by constructing, drawing, measuring, visualizing, comparing, transforming, and classifying geometric figures. Discussing ideas, conjecturing, and testing hypotheses precede the development of more formal summary statements.[1]

ACTIVITY SET 12.1

LOCATING SETS OF POINTS IN THE PLANE

Purpose   To locate and sketch sets of points in a plane that satisfy given conditions

Materials   A ruler, compass, and protractor from Material Card 32, an index card, and scissors

Activity   Look at the two identical coins below. If the left coin is carefully rolled halfway around the other, what will be the position of the point *A?* Make a conjecture and test it by experimenting with two identical coins.

In this activity set, we will be locating the positions of points in the plane. Many geometric figures are described or defined as sets of points with certain

[1]*Curriculum and Evaluation Standards for School Mathematics* (Reston, VA: National Council of Teachers of Mathematics, 1989), 112.

conditions placed on them. Suppose, for example, that we are asked to locate and sketch *the set of points in the plane that are 2 cm from a given point P.* We can begin to identify points by using a ruler to locate points 2 cm from point *P,* as shown in figure a. As more and more points are added to the collection of points, we can see that a smooth curve drawn through the points, as in figure b, visually describes the set of all points 2 cm from *P* as a circle with center *P* and radius 2 cm.

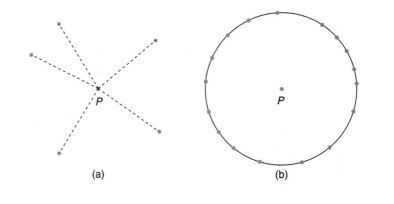

      (a)   (b)

1. For parts a and b, place on each figure 10 to 20 points that satisfy the stated condition. Then draw a smooth curve through all points satisfying the condition and describe the outcome in your own words.

   a. The set of all points in the plane that are the same distance from point *K* as from point *L*

   K •

   L •

   ★ b. The set of all points in the plane that are the same distance from line *m* as from line *n*

2. A chord is a line segment joining two points on a circle. Parts a through c involve chords of circles. Locate as many points as you need to feel confident about sketching the curve that satisfies the conditions. Describe each result in words, as specifically as possible.

★ **a.** The set of all points that are midpoints of chords of length 4 cm on this circle

b. The midpoints of all chords of this circle that have point *R* as one endpoint

★ **c.** The midpoints of all chords of this circle that pass through point *S*

3. Draw and cut out a circle with radius 1.5 cm.

  a. Suppose the circle rolls around the inside of the square in part b, always tangent to at least 1 edge. Sketch the path traced by the center of the circle and then describe it in words.

  b. Sketch and describe the path of the circle's center if the circle rolls around the outside of the square.

★ **4.** Point B is the center of a circle with radius 1 cm, and point A is the center of a circle with radius 2 cm. Both X and Y, which are the intersections of these two circles, are twice as far from point A as from point B. Find more points that are twice as far from A as from B. (*Hint*: You may find it helpful to locate these points by drawing circles about A and B, with the radius about A twice the radius about B.) Sketch and describe the set of all points in the plane that satisfy the conditions.

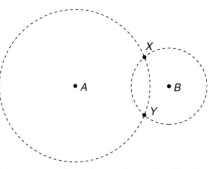

5. Cut out a narrow strip of paper having a length of 10 cm and punch a small hole at its midpoint. Place this strip on two perpendicular lines so that each end touches one of the lines. Place a pencil at the midpoint, *M*, and with the help of a classmate, move the strip so that its endpoints always touch the two perpendicular lines. What curve is traced by *M*?

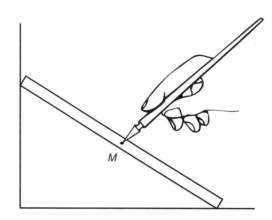

6. The line segment $\overline{PQ}$ is 7 cm long. Point *X* is the corner of an index card (any piece of paper with a square corner will work), placed on top of segment $\overline{PQ}$ so that its adjacent sides pass through points *P* and *Q*. It is possible to shift the index card to new positions so that *P* and *Q* are still on adjacent edges but the corner of the card is at a different point, such as point *Y*. Locate and mark several different corner points.

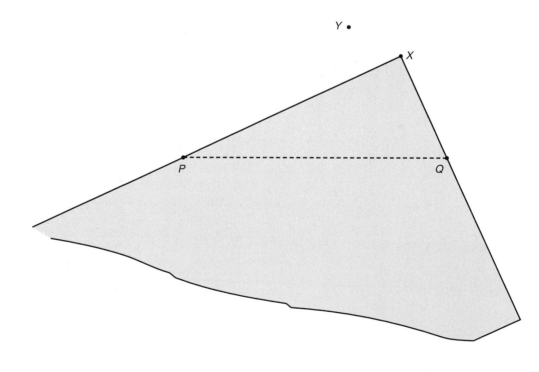

★ **a.** Describe what the curve made up of all the corner points will look like.

b. Bisect one corner of the index card, and cut along the angle bisector to obtain a 45° angle. The point W is the vertex point of the 45° angle. This card is placed on top of segment $\overline{RS}$ so that its sides pass through points R and S. Shift the card to locate other vertex points with R and S on the adjacent sides of the 45° angle. Describe the set of all such vertex points.

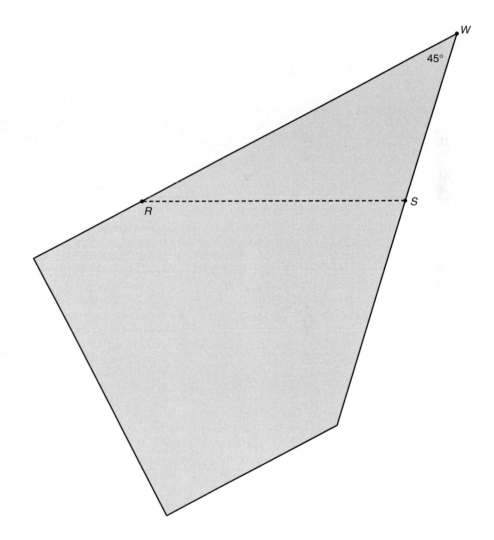

c. Suppose the vertex angle of the card described above were greater than 90°. Draw a sketch of what you think the set of vertex points would look like. Test your conjecture by cutting an index card angle greater than 90° and locating points.

JUST FOR FUN

LINE DESIGNS

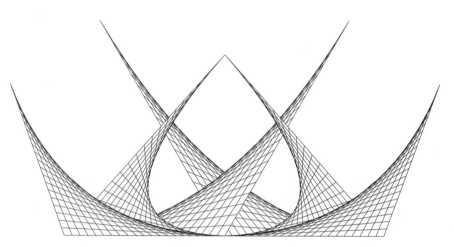

Line designs are geometric designs formed by connecting sequences of points with line segments. One common method is to connect equally spaced points on the sides of an angle, as shown in figure a. These points are connected in the following order: *A* to *a*, *B* to *b*, *C* to *c*, and so on. The resulting design gives the illusion of a curve. This curve is a parabola. Experiment with different types of angles. For the obtuse angle in figure c, the curve will be closer to the angle than for the acute angle in figure b. Combining several angles, as in the figure above, produces beautiful designs.

Another way to create line designs is to draw chords in a circle according to certain rules. The design in Figure d is being formed in a circle whose circumference has been divided into 36 equal parts. The first chord connects point 1 to point 2; the second chord connects point 2 to point 4; the third chord connects point 3 to point 6; and so on. This figure shows the first 18 chords, with point 18 connected to point 36. Continue drawing chords by connecting point 19 to point 2, point 20 to point 4, etc., until you reach point 36. The resulting figure gives the illusion of a heart shape. A curve with this shape is called a cardioid.

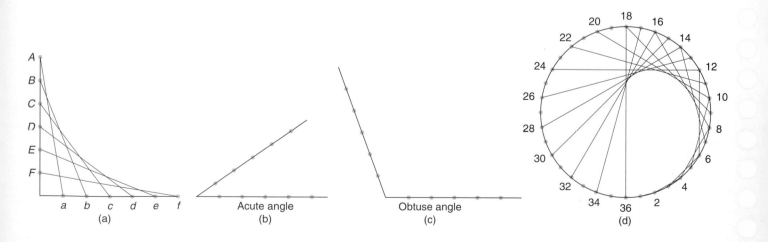

The front ends of the chords for this cardioid traveled twice as fast around the circle as the back ends of the chords. This time we will let the front ends of the chords travel 3 times as fast. That is, connect point 1 to point 3, 2 to 6, 3 to 9, and so forth. Continue drawing these chords until the back ends of the chords have made one revolution and the front ends have made three revolutions. The cardioid above has 1 cusp (inward point). How many cusps will this curve have?

Experiment with some more patterns. For example, let the front ends of the chords move 4 times faster $(1 \rightarrow 4, 2 \rightarrow 8, 3 \rightarrow 12, \ldots)$ or 5 times faster $(1 \rightarrow 5, 2 \rightarrow 10, \ldots)$. Can you predict the number of cusps in each case? (The 36 spaces around a circle will work for 2, 3, 4, or 6 cusps. For 5 cusps, use 40 spaces or some other multiple of 5 that conveniently divides into 360.) Many of these designs can be stitched with colored thread or yarn on cloth or posterboard or formed with nails and string or rubber bands. Below are some examples. The first one was formed by rubber bands and nails, the second by yarn and nails, and the third by white thread stitched into black silk.

- -

PUZZLER

You ride your bike straight across a strip of fresh wet paint 10 inches wide. What pattern of marks will your bike tires leave?

ACTIVITY SET 12.2

DRAWING ESCHER-TYPE TESSELLATIONS

Purpose　To create nonstandard tessellations and Escher-type drawings that illustrate motions in geometry

Materials　A ruler, compass from Material Card 32, and tracing paper

Alhambra drawings by M. C. Escher (© 1996 M. C. Escher/ Cordon Art—Baarn-Holland. All rights reserved.)

Activity　The Dutch artist M. C. Escher was fascinated by the tile patterns he observed on the walls, floors, and ceilings of the Alhambra—a thirteenth-century Moorish palace in Granada, Spain. He considered the pure geometric tessellations his "richest source of inspiration." Escher thought it a "pity" that the talented Islamic artists were restricted, by religious beliefs, to geometric forms. His own works are filled with images of living things.

Two Intersecting Planes, by M. C. Escher (© 1996 M. C. Escher/Cordon Art—Baarn-Holland. All rights reserved.)

Escher-type drawings can be constructed by altering polygons that tessellate (triangles, quadrilaterals, and regular hexagons) by using congruence mappings (translations, rotations, reflections, and glide reflections). In this activity set, you will devise drawings and have the opportunity to create your own artistic work.

1. **Translation Tessellations:** The rectangle in figure a tessellates. In figure b, one side of the rectangle is modified by a jagged line design. The design is then *translated* to the opposite side of the rectangle as a modification in figure c.

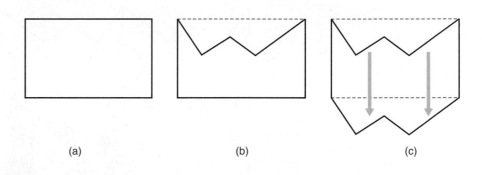

(a)   (b)   (c)

★ **a.** Explain why the new shape in figure c will also tessellate the plane.

In figure d, one of the remaining parallel sides of the rectangle is altered by a different design. This design is then translated to the opposite side in figure e, producing the final shape in figure f.

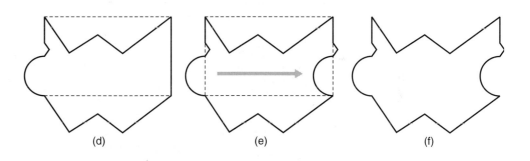

(d)   (e)   (f)

The tessellation formed by the modified rectangle is shown below. This tessellation becomes an Escher-type drawing when details and/or color are added to the basic design.

b. Create your own translation tessellation by modifying and translating the sides of this parallelogram.

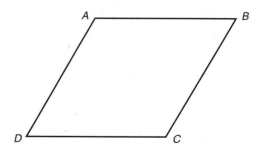

(1) Modify side $\overline{AB}$.

(2) Translate the design to $\overline{DC}$. Place a piece of tracing paper over the parallelogram. Mark points A and B and trace your modification for side $\overline{AB}$. Then slide the tracing paper so that point A coincides with D and point B coincides with C. Take a pointed object (ballpoint pen, compass point) and make enough imprints through the tracing paper so that when you remove the paper you can draw the translated design on $\overline{DC}$.

(3) Repeat steps 1 and 2 to translate a modification of side $\overline{AD}$ to side $\overline{BC}$.

c. Use the pattern you have just created to form a tessellation. An easy way to do this is to place a clean piece of tracing paper over the pattern you created and carefully trace the pattern. Then move the tracing paper up, down, right, or left, and trace additional patterns adjacent to your first copy on the tracing paper. Make an Escher-type drawing by sketching in details.

2. **Rotation Tessellations.** The following figures illustrate the modification and rotation of the sides of an equilateral triangle. First, side $\overline{AB}$ is modified as in figure a. Then the design is rotated about vertex A to adjacent side $\overline{AC}$, as shown in figure b, so that vertex B is mapped onto vertex C.

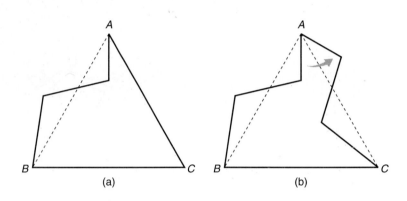

Side $\overline{BC}$ can be modified by rotating a design about its midpoint. In figure c, a design is created between the midpoint M and vertex C. The pattern is completed by rotating this design 180° about midpoint M so that vertex C is mapped onto vertex B, as shown in figure d.

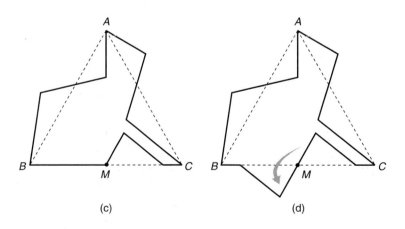

This pattern was used to create the following tessellation. Notice that this tessellation can be mapped onto itself by rotations about certain vertex points. List all the rotations about point *P* that will map this tessellation onto itself.

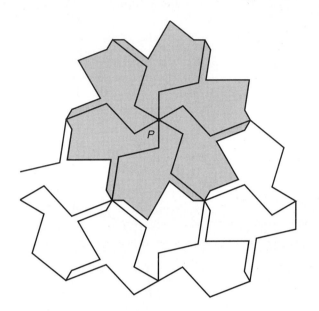

a. Create a rotation tessellation from square *ABCD* by first modifying side $\overline{AB}$ and rotating the design about vertex *B* to adjacent side $\overline{BC}$ and then modifying side $\overline{AD}$ and rotating the design about vertex *D* to adjacent side $\overline{DC}$. Use your pattern to form a tessellation.

b. Use the following scalene triangle to design a rotation tessellation figure. Because no two sides have equal length, you cannot rotate one side to another about a vertex, as in figure b at the beginning of activity 2. However, half a side can be rotated about the midpoint of that side, as was done in figures c and d of activity 2. The midpoint of each side has been marked. For each side, create a design between a vertex and the midpoint, and then rotate the design 180° about the midpoint. Show that this pattern tessellates.

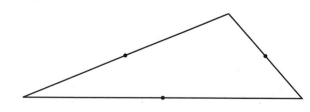

c. Convert one or both of your tessellations to an Escher-type drawing.

3. **Glide-Reflection Tessellations:** A *glide reflection* can be used to create a tessellating figure from parallelogram *ABCD*. Side $\overline{AD}$ is modified in figure a, and the design is translated to side $\overline{BC}$ in figure b. Next, side $\overline{DC}$ is modified as shown in figure c.

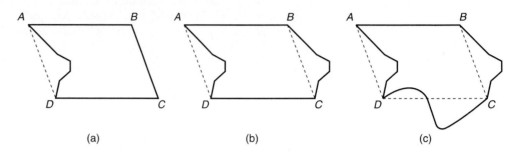

(a)   (b)   (c)

The design on $\overline{DC}$ is then translated to side $\overline{AB}$, as shown in figure d (this is the *glide part*). Finally, the design along side $\overline{AB}$ is *reflected* about a line ℓ perpendicular to the midpoint of $\overline{AB}$, as illustrated in figure e. The two motions shown in figures d and e comprise a *glide reflection*.

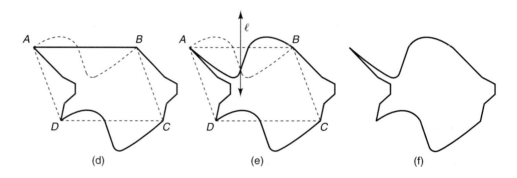

(d)   (e)   (f)

a. The pattern created in figures a–f produces the following tessellation. What mapping will map the top row of this tessellation onto the second row? The top row onto the third row?

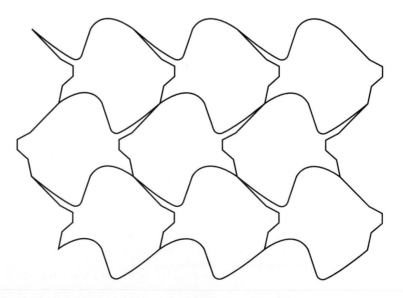

b. Modify the square *ABCD*, using two glide reflections to produce a figure that tessellates. Create a design along side $\overline{AD}$, translate the design to side $\overline{BC}$, and then reflect it about a line perpendicular to the midpoint of $\overline{BC}$. Similarly, modify side $\overline{AB}$ and translate that design to side $\overline{DC}$ through a glide reflection. (*Suggestion:* Use tracing paper to perform the glide and reflection.)

JUST FOR FUN

PAPER PUZZLE 1: PAPER-STRIP CUBE

Draw a strip of 8 squares that each measure 3 cm on a side. Cut out the strip of squares, and fold it to make a cube that measures 3 cm on each edge.

PAPER PUZZLE 2: FOLDING NUMBERS IN ORDER

The following rectangle with the eight numbered squares can be folded so that the numbers are in order from 1 through 8 by carrying out the three folds shown in figures a, b, and c. (*Note:* The numbers will be in order, but not all will be facing up.)

Design a similar puzzle. One method is to *work backwards* by creatively folding a rectangle with blank squares, numbering the squares in order, and then unfolding it to write the numbers right side up on the rectangle.

PAPER PUZZLE 3: STEPPING THROUGH A PIECE OF PAPER

It is possible to cut a piece of $8\frac{1}{2}$-by-11-inch paper in such a way that you create a hole large enough to step through. A paper and scissors are all you need. No taping, gluing, or refastening the paper is needed or permitted. Try it. (*Hint:* Fold a sheet of paper and mark three points, *A, B,* and *C,* on the fold line. Make three cuts, as indicated by the dotted lines. Then cut along the fold from *A* to *C.* To create a larger hole, extend this procedure by making more cuts.)

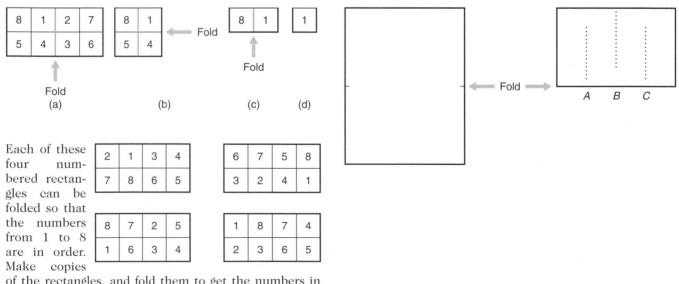

Each of these four numbered rectangles can be folded so that the numbers from 1 to 8 are in order. Make copies of the rectangles, and fold them to get the numbers in order. Devise a way to record your solutions so that another person can understand your procedures.

ACTIVITY SET 12.3

DEVICES FOR INDIRECT MEASUREMENT

Purpose   To devise methods and simple instruments for measuring distances based on knowledge of similar triangles

Materials   Tape, drinking straw, paper-towel tube, hypsometer-clinometer from Material Card 39 and ruler and protractor from Material Card 32 (depending on which instruments you make)

Activity   It was in the second century B.C. that the Greek astronomer Hipparchus applied a simple theorem from geometry to measure distances indirectly. He computed the radius of the earth, the distance to the moon, and many other astronomical distances. The theorem that Hipparchus applied states that if two triangles are *similar* (have the same shape), their sides are proportional. This important theorem is used in surveying, map-making, and navigation.

All that is needed to establish that two triangles are similar is that two angles of one are congruent to two angles of the other. The two triangles shown below are similar because ∡ A is congruent to ∡ D and ∡ C is congruent to ∡ F. (When two angles of one triangle are congruent to two angles of another, the remaining angles also must be congruent. Why?)

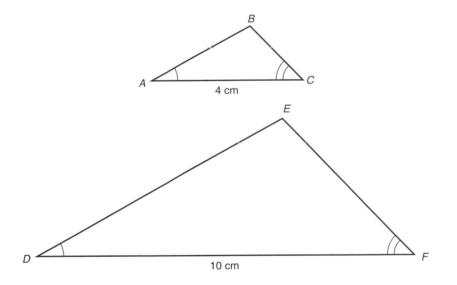

What Hipparchus knew about two such similar triangles is that their side lengths are proportional. For example, side $\overline{DF}$ corresponds to side $\overline{AC}$ and is 2.5 times as long. You can check by measuring that this same relationship holds for the other corresponding sides. That is,

$$DF = 2.5 \times AC \qquad FE = 2.5 \times CB \qquad ED = 2.5 \times BA$$

Notice also that the ratios of the lengths of sides in one triangle are equal to the corresponding ratios in a similar triangle. For example,

$$\frac{AB}{AC} = \frac{DE}{DF} \qquad \text{since} \qquad \frac{AB}{AC} = \frac{3}{4} \qquad \text{and} \qquad \frac{DE}{DF} = \frac{2.5 \times 3}{2.5 \times 4}$$

Similarly, the following ratios are also equal.

$$\frac{AB}{BC} = \frac{DE}{EF} \quad \text{and} \quad \frac{BC}{AC} = \frac{EF}{DF}$$

All of the estimating methods and instruments in this activity set use the fact that the length of corresponding sides of similar triangles are proportional.

---

1. **Sighting Method:** Artists hold out their thumbs to estimate the sizes of objects they are painting. Let's examine the theory behind this method. Stretch your arm out in front of you, holding a ruler in a vertical position. Select some distant object such as a person and estimate his or her height. Hold the ruler so that the top is in line with your eye and the top of the person's head. Position your thumb on the ruler so that it is in line with the person's feet.

★ **a.** The lines of sight from your eye (point *E*) to the top of your ruler and your thumb form triangle *EAB*. The lines of sight from *E* to the head and feet of the observed person form triangle *EA'B'*. *Why are these triangles similar?*

b. Obtain the length of $\overline{EA}$ by measuring the distance from your eye to a ruler, as shown in the figure.

c. The two similar triangles are represented separately in the diagram below.

Since triangle *EAB* is similar to triangle *EA′B′*, their sides are proportional. Assume that *AB* is 4 cm and the height of the person is 160 cm. Use your measurement for $\overline{EA}$ from part b to determine the distance *EA′* between the two people.

2. **Scout Sighting Method:** Here is an old scout trick for getting a rough estimate of the distance to an object. This variation of the sighting method does not require a ruler. The scout stretches out his or her arm and, with the left eye closed, sights with the right eye along the tip of one finger to a distant object. Next the scout closes the right eye and sights with the left eye along this finger to another object. The scout then estimates the distance between the two objects and multiplies by 10 to get the distance from these objects.[2]

a. If the scout estimates the distance between the tree *(T)* and the rock *(R)* to be 90 m (about the length of a football field), how far is the scout from the tree?

b. In the following diagram, E_1 and E_2 represent the eyes, *F* the finger, *T* the tree, and *R* the rock. The two isosceles triangles that are formed are similar. What is the ratio, E_1F/E_1E_2, for the measurements on this diagram?

7.5 cm — E_1 75 cm T
E_2 F   90 meters
R

---

[2]For several more elementary sighting methods, see C. N. Shuster and F. L. Bedford, *Field Work in Mathematics* (East Palistine, OH: Yoder Instruments, 1935), 56–57.

★ **c.** Explain why 10×90 gives the distance from F to T in meters.

d. The scout sighting method is based on the assumption that E_1F (the distance from eye to fingertip) is 10 times E_1E_2 (the distance between the eyes). Stretch your arm out in front of you and measure the distance from your eye to your raised index finger. Then measure the distance between your eyes. Should you be using the number 10 for the scout sighting method? If not, what number should you be using?

★ **e.** When you measure your distance from an object you are fairly close to, such as something in a room, you should add the distance from eye to finger to the result obtained from the scout sighting method. In approximating greater distances, you can ignore the distance from eye to finger, E_1F. Explain why.

3. Stadiascope: The stadiascope works on the same principle as the sighting method with the ruler (see activity 1). This instrument has a peep sight at one end and cross threads at the other. The stadiascope shown here was made from a paper-towel tube having a length of 27 cm. At one end of the tube, six threads have been taped in horizontal rows. These threads are 1 cm apart. A piece of paper has been taped over the other end, and a peep sight has been punched on the same level as the lowest thread.

Peep sight

27 cm

Threads, 1 cm apart

Stadiascope

The following diagram shows a stadiascope being used to measure the distance to a truck. The truck fills 4 spaces at the end of the stadiascope. Let's assume that the truck has a height of 3 m.

a. Point *E* is the peep sight, and points *A* and *B* mark the upper edge and lower edge of the 4 spaces of the stadiascope in which the truck is seen. Triangle *EBA* and triangle *EDC* are right triangles. Explain why they are similar.

★ b. Since triangle *EBA* is similar to triangle *EDC,* the ratios of their corresponding sides are equal. Use the ratios given here to compute the length of $\overline{ED}$ in meters. (*Note:* *EB* and *AB* can be left in centimeters and *CD* in meters.)

$$\frac{ED}{EB} = \frac{CD}{AB}$$

★ c. Suppose you sight a person who fills 2 spaces of the stadiascope and you estimate this person's height to be 180 cm. How many meters is this person from you?

d. Make a stadiascope and use it to measure some heights or distances indirectly. Check your results with direct measurements.

4. **Clinometer:** The clinometer, used to measure heights of objects, is an easy device to construct (see Material Card 39). It is a simplified version of the quadrant, an important instrument in the Middle Ages, and the sextant, an instrument used for locating the positions of ships. Each of these devices has arcs that are graduated in degrees for measuring angles of elevation. The arc of the clinometer is marked from 0 to 90°. When an object is sighted through the straw, the number of degrees in angle *BVW* can be read from the arc. Angle *BAC* is the angle of elevation of the clinometer. What will happen to angle *BVW* as angle *BAC* increases?

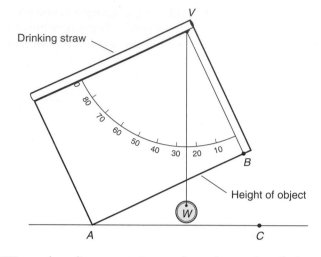

Drinking straw

Height of object

Angle *BVW* on the clinometer is equal to the angle of elevation of the clinometer, angle *BAC*. In the next figure, the clinometer was used to find the angle of elevation from eye level to the top of the tree. This angle is 18°. The distance from the person's feet to the base of the tree is 60 m.

a. Right triangle *ETR* in the drawing is similar to the real triangle that the observer sees outdoors. Explain why.

★ **b.** Use a ruler to set up a scale on $\overline{ET}$. For example, $\overline{ET}$ can be marked off in millimeters. If $\overline{ET}$ represents a distance of 60 m, what distance does each millimeter unit of your scale represent? Use your scale to find the length of $\overline{TR}$.

c. The observer's eye is 150 cm above the ground. What is the height of the tree?

d. Make a clinometer by pasting Material Card 39 onto a solid backing. Use this device to measure the heights of some objects. (*Note:* Draw a similar triangle and set up a scale.)

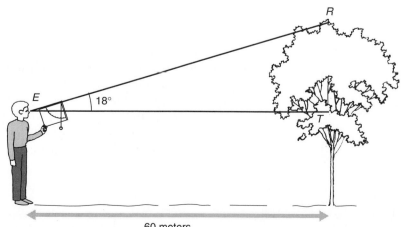

60 meters

5. **Hypsometer:** The hypsometer is used for the same purpose as the clinometer, but it eliminates the need to measure angles (see Material Card 39). The grid is used to set up a scale on the sides of the hypsometer. For example, suppose that you sight to the top of a building and that the string of the hypsometer falls in the position shown here. If you are standing 55 m from the base of the building, this distance is represented on the right side of the hypsometer by letting each space be 10 m. By beginning at distance 55 on the right side of the hypsometer and following the arrow in to the plumb line (weighted string) and then down to the lower edge of the grid, you can see that the height of the building is 25 m plus the distance from the ground to the viewer's eye.

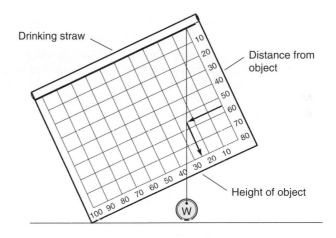

★ **a.** Given the position of the string shown on this hypsometer, determine the height of an object that is at a distance of 70 m.

b. If you know the height of an object, you can use the hypsometer to find the distance to its base. Given the position of the string on this hypsometer, determine the distance to the base of a tree that is 30 m tall.

c. Make a hypsometer from Material Card 39 and use it to measure the heights of some objects.

6. **Transit:** The transit (or theodolite) is the most important instrument for measuring horizontal and vertical angles in civil engineering. In its earliest form, this instrument was capable of measuring only horizontal angles, much like the simplified version shown here. To make a transit, tape a protractor (Material Card 32) to one end of a meter stick (or long thin board) and pin a drinking straw at the center point of the protractor.

The next diagram shows how the transit can be used to find the distance between two points. Line segment $\overline{AB}$ has been marked by posts on the left bank of the river. By holding the stick of the transit parallel to $\overline{AB}$, you can measure angle *FAB* and angle *FBA*. The distance between the posts can be found by using a tape measure or by pacing off. This distance is 500 m. On paper, a triangle can be drawn (like the one in the figure) to represent the real triangle formed by the fort and the posts. This small triangle is similar to the real triangle because angle *A* and angle *B* have been drawn to be congruent to the angles measured with the transit.

a. Use a ruler to set up a scale on $\overline{AB}$ in the diagram. The actual distance from *A* to the fort can be found by using your scale. What is this distance?

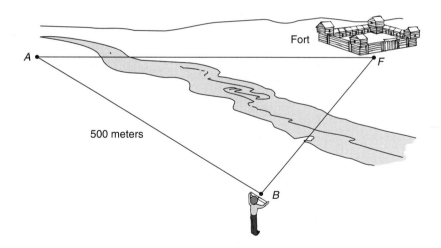

★ **b.** Explain how you would use the transit to make a map of the objects in this field. What is the least number of angles and distances you would have to measure?

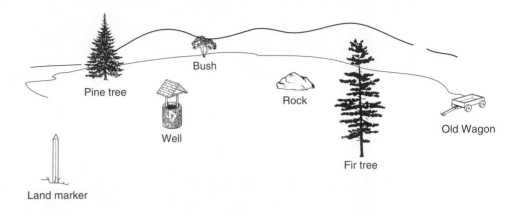

JUST FOR FUN

ENLARGING DRAWINGS

Figure a shows a drawing of a bunny. Suppose you wish to copy and double the size of the drawing. Here is one method that works when you do not have immediate access to a copy machine that automatically enlarges. Draw or place a transparent grid over the bunny as shown in figure b.

(a)

(b)

A grid similar to the grid in figure b, but whose edges are 2 times as long as those in figure b, is drawn below. The sketch of the bunny is then copied square by square from the small grid to the larger grid. On the grid below, five squares have been copied from figure b above. Complete the enlargement by copying the remaining squares. Choose a picture, cartoon, or drawing of your own and enlarge it using the grid method. You can make it as large as you wish by choosing an appropriate grid to copy upon.

ACTIVITY SET 12.4

TOPOLOGICAL INVESTIGATIONS AND ENTERTAINMENT

Purpose   To investigate properties of the one-edged and one-sided Moebius band and analyze party tricks that have topological explanations

Materials   Strips of paper, scissors, tape, and string

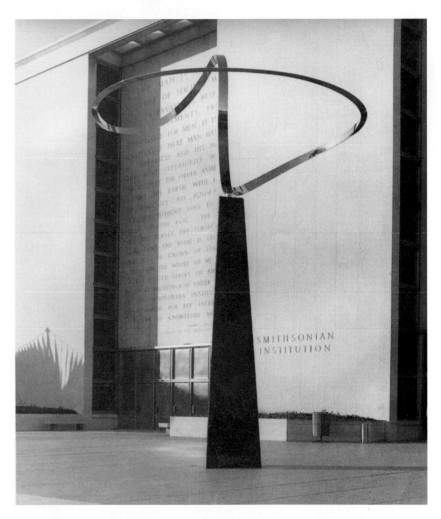

Eight-foot steel Moebius band by Rivera at the History and Technology, Smithsonian Institute, rotates once every six minutes. (Smithsonian Institute Photo no. 72-233.)

Activity   In the middle of the nineteenth century, the geometer A. F. Moebius (1790–1868) submitted to the Paris Academy a paper that expressed new ideas about one-sided surfaces. Even though his paper contained surprising results about a new kind of geometry, it lay buried for years in the files of the academy before it was made public.

Moebius had made his discoveries in what was later to become an important field of mathematics: topology. Topology is the study of properties of figures that remain after the figures have been deformed and have lost most of their geometric properties.

This activity set begins with investigations into the Moebius band—a one-sided geometric figure. The Moebius band is constructed by putting a half-twist in a strip of paper and fastening its ends, as shown below.

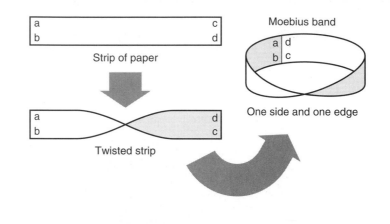

1. One of the many stories about the legendary Paul Bunyan involves the Moebius band. Paul was using a Moebius-band-shaped conveyor belt to bring uranium ore out of a mine in Colorado. The belt ran $\frac{1}{2}$ km into the mine and was a little over 1 m wide. After several months of operation, the mine gallery had become twice as long and Paul decided to cut the belt down the middle to increase its length. He told Ford Fordsen to take his chain saw and cut the belt lengthwise.

   "That will give us two belts," said Ford Fordsen. "We'll have to cut them in two crosswise and splice them together. That means I'll have to go to town and buy the materials for two splices." "No," said Paul. "This belt has a half-twist—which makes it what is known in geometry as a Moebius strip."[3]

   ★ a. Make a Moebius band from a strip of paper by putting a half-twist in it and taping together the two ends of the strip. Cut it lengthwise down the middle as pictured here. Who was right, Fordsen or Bunyan? Describe your results.

[3]W. H. Upson, "Paul Bunyan Versus the Conveyor Belt," *Ford Times,* Ford Motor Company.

★ **b.** The Moebius band has only one side. Is the band you get in part a, after cutting, one-sided or two-sided? (To check, draw a line lengthwise down the middle of the band until it returns to the starting point.)

   c. Later in the story Paul cut the conveyor belt lengthwise a second time to make it even longer. This time a character called Loud Mouth Johnson disagreed with Paul on the number of pieces that would be produced. Take your band from part b and cut it lengthwise down the middle. Do you get one or two bands? Describe your result, including the number of sides.

2. The B. F. Goodrich Company manufactures the Turnover Conveyor Belt System. This belt, with two half-twists, has an advantage over conventional belt systems in that only the clean side of the belt is in contact with the idlers on the underside.

a. Make a band from a strip of paper by putting in two half-twists and taping together the ends of the band. How many sides does it have? (Save this band for activity 3, part b.)

b. Form a band with three half-twists. How many sides does it have? (Save this band for activity 3, part c.)

c. Make a conjecture about the numbers of sides of bands with even and odd numbers of half-twists.

3. If you were surprised by the results in activity 1, you may wish to try predicting the outcomes for the following types of cuts. After each cut, describe the number of bands and the number of sides to each band.

★ **a.** Form a Moebius band. Draw a line, beginning one-third of the way in from one edge and continuing until you return to the starting point. This continuous line will produce two tracks, as shown in this drawing. Describe what will be produced by cutting along this line.

b. Take the band with two half-twists, which you made in part a of activity 2. Describe what happens when this band is cut lengthwise down the middle.

c. Take your band from part b of activity 2. Predict what you will get when it is cut lengthwise down the middle. Cut it and describe your results.

4. Double Moebius Band: Place two strips of paper together (as pictured here), give them a half-twist (as if they were one strip), and tape the edges together (ends taped in pairs—top two and bottom two). The result is a double Moebius band. Run your fingers or a pencil all the way around the double band between the two layers. Is this two separate bands or one band?

a. What will happen when the double band is opened? Describe the results and the number of sides.

b. Make a triple Moebius band out of three strips of paper. Try to predict what will happen when it is opened. Describe what you get. (*Note:* When the six ends are brought together, they are taped in pairs: top two, middle two, and bottom two.)

★ 5. **Party Trick:** Cut two pieces of string with lengths of about 50 cm. Tie the two ends of one of these strings around someone's wrists. Then tie another person's wrists with the second piece of string so that they are linked together as shown in this picture. The object is to get unlinked without untying or cutting the string. Try it. Explain how this can be done.

★ 6. **Card and Ring Puzzle:** Make the object pictured here using a piece of cardboard, a string, and a ring that is too large to pass through the hole in the panel. The problem is to move the ring from loop A to loop B without cutting or untying the string. Try this and explain how the puzzle can be solved. (The ends of the string are not involved in the solution.)

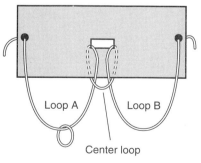

Loop A   Loop B

Center loop

7. **Vest Trick:** One of the important concepts in topology is the distinction between inside and outside. For example, the solution to the party trick in activity 5 shows that the strings and arms never were interlinked in the sense that links have to be cut or broken in order to be separated. The following demonstration shows a woman taking off her vest without removing her coat. This shows that, topologically speaking, the vest was never inside the coat.

★ 8. **Closed Curve Experiment or Party Game:** Several people (three or more) stand around in a circle. On command, everyone extends both arms across the circle, taking hold of the hands of two other people. Without breaking grips, is it possible for the people to rearrange themselves so that they form a circle (simple closed curve) with each person holding hands with the people on his or her right and left? Can this always be done? Can it ever be done? Try this experiment and form a conjecture.

PUZZLER

Cut this figure into four congruent pieces.[4]

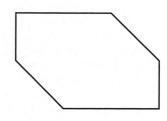

JUST FOR FUN

GALE GAME[5] (2 players)

This game, devised by David C. Gale of Brown University, is played on a grid of alternately colored rows of dots (in this case, white and black). One player connects only white dots, and the other player connects only black dots. The players take turns connecting any two adjacent dots. The objective is to construct a path from one edge of the square to the opposite edge, with one player trying to connect the top edge of the square to the bottom and the other player trying to connect the left edge to the right. Only one line between two dots is drawn on each turn, and no line is permitted to cross an opponent's line. Try playing this game. Is it possible for two players to block each other so that no one wins, or will there always be a winner?

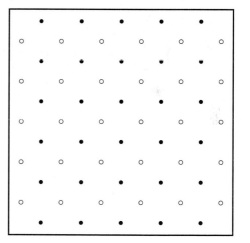

---

[4]From the "October Calendar" of *The Mathematics Teacher* 81 (October 1988), 556–557.
[5]The Gale game is described by M. Gardner, "Four Mathematical Diversions Involving Concepts of Topology," *Scientific American* 199 (April 1958), 124–129.

SPROUTS: A NETWORK GAME[6] (2 players)

This is a game in which two players draw a network. Before the game begins, several arbitrary vertex points are drawn on paper. Our example begins with points *r*, *s*, and *t*. The players take turns drawing an arc connecting two vertex points or from one vertex point back to itself (a loop), subject to the following conditions:

★ **1.** Each time an arc is drawn, another vertex point is placed on it.
2. An arc must not cross itself or any other arc.
3. There can be no more than three arcs at each vertex point. (You may find it helpful to circle those vertex points with three arcs.)

The winner is the last person who is able to draw an arc. In the game shown here, player A is the winner, since only one more turn can be taken after play 6. Draw the final arc in this game.

Play a few games of Sprouts. Start with a two-point game. Then move to a three-point game and a four-point game. After you feel comfortable with this game, try to analyze it by answering the following questions:

★ **1.** What is the greatest number of turns possible in a game started with two vertex points? What is the least number of turns?

2. Answer the questions in part 1 for three vertex points.

★ **3.** For a game started with *n* points, there are simple formulas for determining the greatest and least numbers of moves. Can you find them?

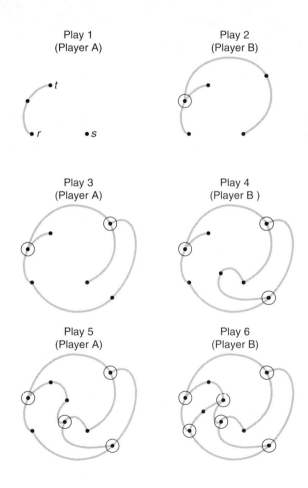

Play 1
(Player A)

Play 2
(Player B)

Play 3
(Player A)

Play 4
(Player B)

Play 5
(Player A)

Play 6
(Player B)

[6]M. Gardner, *Mathematical Carnival* (New York: Knopf, 1975), Chapter 1.

IDEAS FOR THE ELEMENTARY CLASSROOM
SUGGESTED CLASSROOM ACTIVITY: ANALYZING SHAPES

Once students are able to recognize geometric shapes in different contexts, they can analyze properties of particular geometric shapes. Provide pairs of scissors, rulers, and copies of large parallelograms.

1. Ask the students to investigate the parallelograms and make a list of everything they observe. Encourage them to measure, cut (along diagonals and through the center), fold, and roll up their parallelograms. Make a master list of all observations on the chalkboard or butcher paper.

2. Discuss whether all the properties listed are true for all parallelograms.

3. Do a similar investigation of squares, rectangles, rhombuses, trapezoids, triangles, and other shapes.

Readings for More Classroom Ideas

Bidwell, James K. "Using Reflections to Find Symmetric and Asymmetric Patterns." *Arithmetic Teacher* 34 (March 1987): 10–15.

Britton, Jill, and Walter Britton. *Teaching Tessellating Art.* Palo Alto, CA: Dale Seymour Publications, 1992.

Geddes, Dorothy, et al. *Geometry in the Middle Grades,* in the *Curriculum and Evaluation Standards for School Mathematics Addenda Series: Grades 5–8.* Reston, VA: National Council of Teachers of Mathematics, 1992.

Hirsch, Christian R. "Graphs, Games, and Generalizations." *Mathematics Teacher* 81 (December 1988): 741–745.

Horak, Virginia M., and W. J. Horak. "Let's Do It: Using Geometry Tiles as a Manipulative for Developing Basic Concepts." *Arithmetic Teacher* 30 (April 1983): 8–15.

Kaiser, Barbara. "Explorations with Tessellating Polygons." *Arithmetic Teacher* 36 (December 1988): 19–24.

Phillips, Elizabeth, Glenda Lappan, Mary J. Winter, and William Fitzgerald. *Similarity and Equivalent Fractions,* Middle Grades Mathematics Project. Menlo Park, CA: Addison-Wesley Publishing Company, 1986.

Sawada, Daiyo. "Symmetry and Tessellations from Rotational Transformations on Transparencies." *Arithmetic Teacher* 33 (December 1985): 12–13.

Schattschneider, Doris. *Visions of Symmetry: Notebooks, Periodic Drawings, and Related Work of M. C. Escher.* New York, NY: W. H. Freeman and Company, 1990.

Seymour, D. and J. Britton. "Creating Escher-like Tessellations," in *Introduction to Tessellations,* pp. 181–236. Palo Alto, CA: Dale Seymour Publications, 1989.

Sovchik, Robert, and L. J. Meconi. "Ideas: Measurement." *Arithmetic Teacher* 41 (January 1994): 253–262.

Woodward, E., V. Gibbs, and M. Shoulders. "A Fifth-Grade Similarity Unit." *Arithmetic Teacher* 39 (April 1992): 22–25.

Woodward, Ernest, and P. G. Buckner. "Reflections and Symmetry—A Second-Grade Miniunit." *Arithmetic Teacher* 35 (October 1987): 8–11.

Zaslavsky, Claudia. "Networks—New York Subways, a Piece of String, and African Traditions." *Arithmetic Teacher* 29 (October 1981): 42–47.

ANSWERS TO PUZZLERS

P. 6 Move toothpicks A and B as indicated.

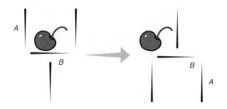

P. 12 Move toothpicks A, B, and C as shown here.

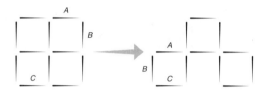

P. 13 Move toothpicks A and B as shown here.

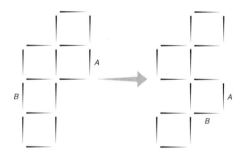

P. 27 Draw one coin from the container marked "Nickel and Penny." If it is a nickel, then that container must contain two nickels and the container marked "Two Nickels" must contain two pennies—otherwise the third container would be labeled correctly. If a penny is drawn from the "Nickel and Penny" container, then that container holds two pennies and the container marked "Two Pennies" contains two nickels.

P. 37

P. 52 On the back of the disk marked 1 is a 5; on the back of 2 is a 4; on the back of 3 is a 4.

P. 64 9 coins

P. 75 Here is one way:

	Start	H	T	H	T	H	T			
Move 1		H	T	H	–	–	T	T	H	
Move 2		–	–	H	H	T	T	T	H	
Move 3		–	–	–	–	T	T	T	H	H	H

P. 84 The same number of committees of 2 as committees of 8.

P. 100 120 first-year students

P. 110 All the listed lengths can be obtained.

P. 139 The 5 by 10 rectangle

P. 147

P. 154 $142

P. 160 30 inches. *Hint:* Set one table with its block on top of the other table to determine the heights of the two tables.

P. 161 You have 7 pennies and your friend has 5.

P. 170 They are equally likely.

P. 188 Here is one way. There are many others.

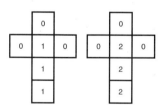

P. 197 Greater than 50%. The probability of obtaining one big loop is $\frac{2}{3}$, or 67%.

P. 209 $\frac{2}{3}$

P. 219

P. 225 Six different (noncongruent) ways

P. 231

P. 256

P. 264 51.2%

P. 273 Strips of paint 10 inches long, where the distance from the beginning of one strip to the beginning of the next is the circumference of the circle.

P. 297 2-dimensional solution

3-dimensional solution

ANSWERS TO SELECTED ACTIVITIES

ACTIVITY SET 1.1

1. a. Here are some of the many ways they differ:
    (1) The 7th pattern has one more triangle than the 6th.
    (2) The 6th has the same number of triangles pointing up as pointing down.
    (3) The 6th figure forms a parallelogram, the 7th a trapezoid.

2. c. 13 triangles and 12 rhombuses. Each even-numbered figure has the same number of triangles as rhombuses, and a rhombus on the right end. The 24th figure has 12 triangles and 12 rhombuses and a triangle attached to the right end produces the 25th figure.

3. b. A rhombus. The pattern repeats after 3 steps so every 3rd figure has a square on the right. The 15th figure has a square on the right, the 16th a hexagon on the right, and the 17th a rhombus.

  d. 19 of each shape.

4. b. Any figure number that is a multiple of 3 has $\frac{1}{3}$ that number of hexagons and $\frac{2}{3}$ that number of triangles. If the figure number is 1 more than a multiple of 3 determine the number of pieces for the previous figure (which is a multiple of 3) and then add another hexagon. If the figure number is 1 less than a multiple of 3, determine the number of pieces for the following figure (which is a multiple of 3) and then subtract 1 triangle.

6. Here are 3 ways. There are other possibilities.
Sequence I: Add one square to the top of each column in the previous figure.

Sequence II: Form 3 columns with 4 squares and make the 4th column 1 square more than the preceding 4th column.

Sequence III: Form a square array and remove 1 square from the upper right corner.

7. Sequence II: 10 squares, 19 triangles, and 9 rhombuses, with a triangle on the right end. The 36th figure looks like 9 copies of the 4th figure so it contains 9 squares, 18 triangles, and 9 rhombuses. To get the 38th figure we need 1 more square and 1 more triangle.

JUST FOR FUN 1.1

1. With 1 red peg and 1 black peg and 3 holes, it takes 3 moves. With 2 red pegs and 2 black pegs and 5 holes, it takes 8 moves.

ACTIVITY SET 1.2

1. c. Here is one way to describe it: The 50th figure will have a horizontal row of 50 tiles with a vertical column of 49 tiles on its left end. It will contain a total of 49 + 50 = 99 tiles.

3. b. The fourth term in the sequence is 20 and the tenth term is 44.

4. a. 110 tiles. It will be 10 tiles wide and 11 tiles high. 55 tiles of each color.

5. c. The 100th stairstep.

JUST FOR FUN 1.2

1. If the sequence begins with "loves me," the last response will be "loves me" for daisies with an odd number of petals.

ACTIVITY SET 1.3

1. Student A
  a. Student A may have been looking at colors row by row.
  b. So starting at the bottom row of the 7th figure and going up one row at a time this student would see 4 + 3 + 4 + 3 + 4 + 3 + 4 yellows and 3 + 4 + 3 + 4 + 3 + 4 + 3 greens. The 8th figure would have 4 + 4 + 4 + 4 + 4 + 4 + 4 + 4 greens and the same number of yellows.
  c. The 11th figure would have
6 + 5 + 6 + 5 + 6 + 5 + 6 + 5 + 6 + 5 + 6 yellows and
5 + 6 + 5 + 6 + 5 + 6 + 5 + 6 + 5 + 6 + 5 greens.

3. Sequence II

	FIG. 1	FIG. 2	FIG. 3	FIG. 4
red	1	3	5	7
blue	0	2	4	6
green	0	4(1)	4(1 + 3)	4(1 + 3 + 5)

The 30th figure will have
59 red   58 blue
$4(1 + 3 + 5 + 7 + \cdots + 55 + 57) = 3364$ green

JUST FOR FUN 1.3

1. Spirolaterals b and e cannot be completed. If the numbers are reversed, the two spirolaterals will be in different positions but they will be congruent. One will have to be flipped over to coincide with the other.

2. **a.** 1, 2, 3   **b.** 1, 2, 3, 4   **c.** 1, 2, 3, 4, 5, 6

E	S	W	N	E	S	W	N	E	S	W	N
1	2	3	1	1	2	3	4	1	2	3	4
2	3	1	2	1	2	3	4	5	6	1	2
3	1	2	3	1	2	3	4	3	4	5	6
6	6	6	6	3	6	9	12	9	12	9	12

ACTIVITY SET 2.1

2. **a.** By asking yes or no questions that refer to a single attribute, a player can identify any piece in at most 6 guesses. For example: Is it large? Is it red? Is it blue? Is it triangular? Is it square? Is it circular?

4. **b.** LRC, SRT, SBT, LRS, LRH, SRC, SRS, SRH, LRT, SYT, LYT, LBT

5. **a.** LRC, LYC, SRC, SYC

6. **b.** LARGE RED pieces, or LARGE AND RED pieces
   c. LYT, SYT, LBT, LBS, LBC, LBH, SBT, SBS, SBC, SBH, LRT, LRH, LRS, LRC, SRT, SRH, SRS, SRC

7. **b.** (2) (H∩NY)∩L: LBH, LRH
   (5) H∩(NY∪L): SBH, SRH, LBH, LRH, LYH

ACTIVITY SET 2.2

1. **b.** (1) 4
   b. (2) approximately 1.3; when the wheel makes 1 complete revolution, the distance along the cycloid is 1.3 times the horizontal distance.
   c. For every unit of horizontal distance a point on the cycloid travels 1.3 units. So, a point on the tire travels about 130 miles along its path on a 100-mile bike trip.
   e. When a point on the tire touches the ground it changes direction.

2. **b.** The curve repeats itself after 1 revolution.
   d. About 37.5 feet (12.5 + 25) above ground after 34 seconds and 50 feet above ground after $2\frac{1}{2}$ minutes.

ACTIVITY SET 2.3

3. Math—*Robinson*, English—*Smith*, French—*Brown*, Logic—*Jones*.

4. Pilot—*Jones*, Copilot—*Smith*, Engineer—*Robinson*.

ACTIVITY SET 3.1

1. **c.** 0 long-flats, 0 flats, 4 longs, 4 units
2. **c.** 1 long-flat, 0 flats, 0 longs, 1 unit
   f. 453 unit squares
3. **c.** 1001_{five}
   f. 3303_{five}

4. **b.** 142 unit squares
5. **a.** base three

6. **b.** 425_{seven} Total number of unit squares: 215

7. **b.**

123_nine

JUST FOR FUN 3.1

Mind-Reading Cards

2. 27 = 1 + 2 + 8 + 16, cards 1, 2, 8, and 16
4. A number k is on a card if and only if the number of the card is a term in the sum of the binary numbers that equals k. So the sum of the numbers of the cards on which a person's age appears is the person's age.
5. Since 44 = 32 + 8 + 4, the number 44 must be written on cards 4, 8, and 32.

Game of Nim

3. Crossing out 1 stick in the second row leaves an even number of binary groups.

4. It is not possible in 1 turn to change an even situation into another even situation. Therefore, if you leave your opponent with an even situation, there will be an odd situation on your turn.

ACTIVITY SET 3.2

2. **b.** Since the maximum amount you can win in a roll is 2 longs and 2 units, it will take you at least 11 turns to win the game. (If you win the maximum amount on each turn, then in 2 turns you will be 1 unit short of a flat. So in 10 turns you will be 5 units short of a long-flat, and it will take at least 1 more turn to win.)

d. Your winnings of 4 flats, 2 longs, and 1 unit are 2 longs and 4 units short of a long-flat. You cannot win on the next turn because the maximum amount you can win on 1 turn is 2 longs and 2 units.

3. a. 122_{five} c. 1021_{five}
4. a. 1010_{three} c. 433_{six}
6. b. Comparing the base pieces for 313_{five} and 242_{five} shows that the difference is 2 longs and 1 unit. So the player must have rolled 5 on one die and 6 on the other.
8. a. 424_{five} c. 3414_{five}
9. a. 1022_{three} c. 101_{two}

JUST FOR FUN 3.2

If you cross off 16, then no matter what your opponent does, you will be able to cross off numbers through 20 on your next turn and win the game. To ensure that you are able to cross off 16, you must be the player to cross off 12. Similarly, you can be sure of crossing off 12 if you cross off 8, and you can be sure of crossing off 8 if you cross off 4. The only way you can be sure of crossing off 4 is if your opponent begins the game.

ACTIVITY SET 3.3

2. Any two-digit number can be represented by, at most, 9 longs and 9 units. Multiplication of a one-digit number by a two-digit number can be done concretely by laying out the specified number (1 to 9) of copies of longs and flats for the two-digit number. The product of the numbers can then be determined by regrouping the base pieces. Since 10 units can be regrouped as 1 long, 10 longs as 1 flat, and so on, it is not necessary to count beyond 10.
3. b. 483

4. Products can be determined by counting the numbers of flats, longs, and units in rectangular arrays. Use the numbers being multiplied to outline a rectangle. Then fill in the rectangle with your base pieces. Regroup the pieces to determine the product. The following example shows this procedure for 21×33.

So 21×33 is represented by 6 flats, 9 longs, and 3 units, and $21 \times 33 = 693$.

5. a.

6. b.

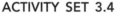

8 flats, 14 longs, and 6 units $22 \times 43 = 946$

ACTIVITY SET 3.4

1. b.

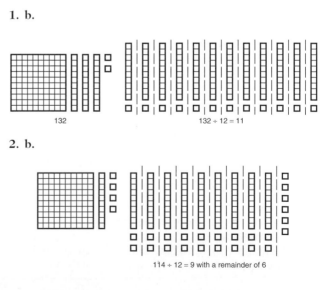

132        $132 \div 12 = 11$

2. b.

$114 \div 12 = 9$ with a remainder of 6

3. b.

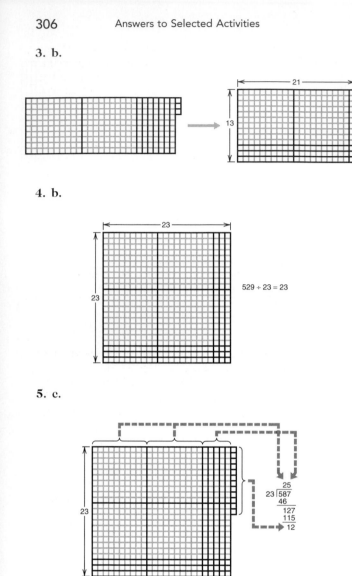

4. b.

$529 \div 23 = 23$

5. c.

$$\begin{array}{r} 25 \\ 23\overline{)587} \\ 46 \\ \hline 127 \\ 115 \\ \hline 12 \end{array}$$

ACTIVITY SET 4.1

2. **b.** The 125th even number has two rows of 125 tiles. The 125th even number is 250.
3. **b.** The 15th odd number has a horizontal row of 15 tiles on the bottom and a row of 14 tiles on the top. The 15th odd number is 29.
   d. 79 is the 40th position; 117 is in the 59th position.
4. **b.** Even   **e.** Even
5. **b.** The L-shapes representing the first 10 consecutive odd numbers form a 10 by 10 square, so the sum of the first 10 consecutive odd numbers is 100.
8. **b.** 1 is the only nonzero whole number with exactly 1 factor.
   e. Numbers with an odd number of factors have a square among their rectangles. That is, they are square numbers.
10. The numbers 6, 8, 10, 14, 15, 21, 22, 26, 27, and 33 are a few of the numbers that have exactly 4 factors.

These numbers are the product of two different primes or the cube of a prime.

ACTIVITY SET 4.2

1. **b.** 1, 2, 3, 6, 9, 18
2. **b.** GCF(18, 25) = 1
5. **a.** 8
7. **b.** GCF(280, 168) = GCF(112, 168) = GCF(112, 56) = GCF(56, 56) = 56
   d. GCF(306, 187) = GCF(119, 187) = GCF(119, 68) = GCF(51, 68) = GCF(51, 17) = GCF(34, 17) = GCF(17, 17) = 17
8. **b.** LCM(14, 21) = 42
   d. LCM(8, 10) = 40

9. a.

A	B	GCF(A, B)	LCM(A, B)
(3) 14	21	7	42
(5) 8	10	2	40

10. **a.** GCF(9, 15) = 3 and $9 \times 15 = 135$, $135 \div 3 = 45$. So LCM(9, 15) = 45.
    c. GCF(14, 35) = 7 and $14 \times 35 = 490$, $490 \div 7 = 70$. So LCM(14, 35) = 70.

JUST FOR FUN 4.2

1. Yes

Star (8, 3)   Star (9, 4)   Star (7, 2)   Star (7, 4)

2. Star (n, s) is congruent to (has the same size and shape as) star (n, r).

Star (12, 5)   Star (12, 7)   Star (10, 3)   Star (10, 7)

3. Star (5, 1) has one path; star (10, 4) has 2 paths; star (12, 4) has 4 paths; and star (6, 3) has 3 paths.

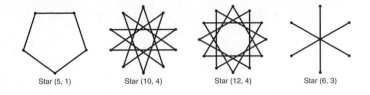

Star (5, 1)   Star (10, 4)   Star (12, 4)   Star (6, 3)

4. n and s must be relatively prime; that is, GCF(n, s) = 1. These stars have 1 continuous path: (1) star (15, 2) = star (15, 13); (2) star (15, 4) = star (15, 11); and (3) star (15, 7) = star (15, 8).

Star (15, 2)   Star (15, 4)   Star (15, 7)

5. Star (9, 2) has 1 path and requires 2 orbits. Star (7, 3) has 1 path and requires 3 orbits. Star (14, 4) has 2 paths and each path requires 2 orbits.

Star (9, 2)   Star (7, 3)   Star (14, 4)

6. b. The number of orbits for star (n, s) is LCM(n, s) divided by n.

7. b. 15

ACTIVITY SET 5.1

2. a. 37   8   29   21
   c. 20   6   14   8
   f. 24   13   11   ⁻2

3. c. 13; ⁻59; ⁻62

4. b. If there are more red tiles than black tiles, subtract the number of black tiles from the number of red tiles and make the answer negative. If the number of black tiles is greater than or equal to the number of red tiles, subtract the number of red tiles from the number of black tiles.

5. b.

⁺5 − ⁻2 = 7

6. Notice that in each of the preceding examples, taking out a given number of tiles of one color is equivalent to putting in the same number of tiles of the opposite color. For example, in 5b, 2 red tiles and 2 black tiles were put in the set and then 2 red tiles were withdrawn from the set. The same result could be accomplished by simply adding 2 black tiles to the set.

7. b.

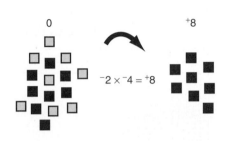

⁻2 × ⁻4 = ⁺8

9. c. In the sharing approach, ⁻3 represents the number of groups, which is not possible. In the measurement approach, groups of 3 red tiles cannot be formed from 12 black tiles.

10. c. $91 \div {}^-7 = {}^-13$ ${}^-4 \div {}^-4 = {}^+1$ ${}^-1001 \div 11 = {}^-91$
   $221 \div {}^-17 = {}^-13$ $0 \div {}^-9 = 0$

ACTIVITY SET 5.2

1. a.

FRACTION	NO. OF BARS WITH EQUAL FRACTIONS
$\frac{0}{4}$	5
$\frac{1}{2}$	4
$\frac{2}{3}$	3
$\frac{6}{6}$	5
$\frac{1}{4}$	2

2. a. $\frac{1}{12} < \frac{1}{6} < \frac{1}{4} < \frac{1}{3} < \frac{5}{12} < \frac{1}{2} < \frac{7}{12} < \frac{2}{3} < \frac{3}{4} < \frac{5}{6} < \frac{11}{12}$

3. b. Here are 10 inequalities; there are others.
$\frac{1}{2} < \frac{2}{3}, \frac{1}{2} < \frac{3}{4}, \frac{1}{2} < \frac{4}{6}, \frac{1}{2} < \frac{5}{6}, \frac{1}{3} < \frac{2}{4}, \frac{1}{3} < \frac{3}{4}, \frac{1}{4} < \frac{1}{2},$
$\frac{1}{4} < \frac{1}{3}, \frac{1}{4} < \frac{2}{6}, \frac{1}{4} < \frac{3}{6}$

4. b. $\frac{5}{11}$ is less than $\frac{1}{2}$ and $\frac{4}{6}$ is greater than $\frac{1}{2}$, so $\frac{5}{11}$ is less than $\frac{4}{6}$.

   d. Cutting a bar into 50 pieces produces smaller pieces than does cutting the same bar into 30 pieces, so $\frac{1}{50}$ is less than $\frac{1}{30}$.

5. a. Nearest whole number, 4
   Diagram:

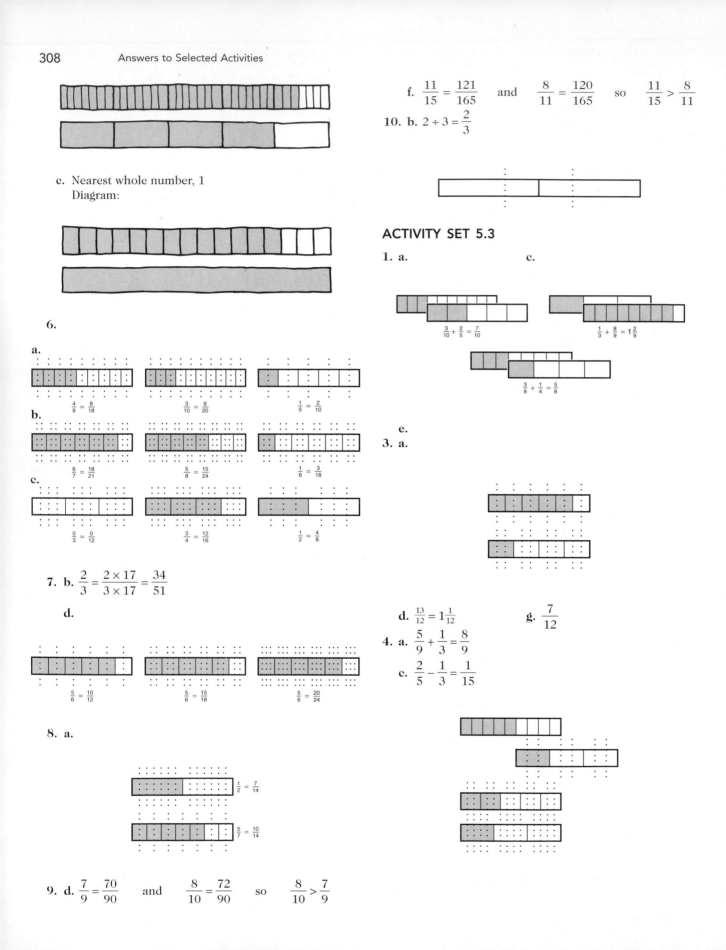

c. Nearest whole number, 1
   Diagram:

f. $\dfrac{11}{15} = \dfrac{121}{165}$ and $\dfrac{8}{11} = \dfrac{120}{165}$ so $\dfrac{11}{15} > \dfrac{8}{11}$

10. b. $2 \div 3 = \dfrac{2}{3}$

ACTIVITY SET 5.3

1. a.   c.

   $\dfrac{3}{10} + \dfrac{2}{5} = \dfrac{7}{10}$ $\dfrac{1}{3} + \dfrac{8}{9} = 1\dfrac{2}{9}$

   $\dfrac{3}{8} + \dfrac{1}{4} = \dfrac{5}{8}$

6.

a.

   $\dfrac{4}{9} = \dfrac{8}{18}$ $\dfrac{3}{10} = \dfrac{6}{20}$ $\dfrac{1}{5} = \dfrac{2}{10}$

b.

   $\dfrac{6}{7} = \dfrac{18}{21}$ $\dfrac{5}{8} = \dfrac{15}{24}$ $\dfrac{1}{6} = \dfrac{3}{18}$

c.

   $\dfrac{0}{3} = \dfrac{0}{12}$ $\dfrac{3}{4} = \dfrac{12}{16}$ $\dfrac{1}{2} = \dfrac{4}{8}$

e.
3. a.

d. $\dfrac{13}{12} = 1\dfrac{1}{12}$ g. $\dfrac{7}{12}$

4. a. $\dfrac{5}{9} + \dfrac{1}{3} = \dfrac{8}{9}$

   c. $\dfrac{2}{5} - \dfrac{1}{3} = \dfrac{1}{15}$

7. b. $\dfrac{2}{3} = \dfrac{2 \times 17}{3 \times 17} = \dfrac{34}{51}$

d.

   $\dfrac{5}{6} = \dfrac{10}{12}$ $\dfrac{5}{6} = \dfrac{15}{18}$ $\dfrac{5}{6} = \dfrac{20}{24}$

8. a.

   $\dfrac{1}{2} = \dfrac{7}{14}$

   $\dfrac{5}{7} = \dfrac{10}{14}$

9. d. $\dfrac{7}{9} = \dfrac{70}{90}$ and $\dfrac{8}{10} = \dfrac{72}{90}$ so $\dfrac{8}{10} > \dfrac{7}{9}$

5.

a.

$\frac{1}{2} \times \frac{1}{3} = \frac{1}{6}$ $\frac{1}{2} \times \frac{4}{5} = \frac{4}{10}$ $\frac{1}{2} \times \frac{6}{8} = \frac{6}{16}$

b.

$\frac{1}{3} \times \frac{1}{4} = \frac{1}{12}$ $\frac{2}{3} \times \frac{1}{6} = \frac{2}{18}$ $\frac{2}{3} \times \frac{9}{10} = \frac{18}{30}$

c.

$\frac{1}{4} \times \frac{1}{2} = \frac{1}{8}$ $\frac{3}{4} \times \frac{1}{5} = \frac{3}{20}$ $\frac{3}{4} \times \frac{8}{9} = \frac{24}{36}$

7. b. 5

   d. $1\frac{1}{2}$

   f. $3\frac{1}{2}$

8.

b.

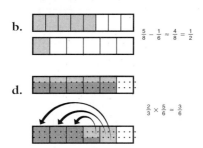

$\frac{5}{8} - \frac{1}{6} \approx \frac{4}{8} = \frac{1}{2}$

d.

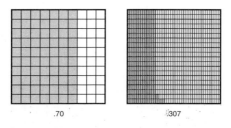

$\frac{2}{3} \times \frac{5}{6} \approx \frac{3}{6}$

9. a. $\frac{1}{6} + \frac{1}{4} = \frac{5}{12}$ $3 \times \frac{3}{12} = \frac{3}{4}$ $\frac{2}{4} + \frac{0}{3} = \frac{1}{2}$ $3 \times \frac{1}{4} = \frac{3}{4}$

   or

   $\frac{2}{4} - \frac{1}{2} = \frac{0}{3}$ $\frac{2}{3} \div \frac{2}{6} = 2$ $\frac{5}{12} - \frac{3}{12} = \frac{1}{6}$ $\frac{2}{3} \div \frac{2}{6} = 2$

ACTIVITY SET 6.1

1. d.   **f.**

      .70   .307

2. b. .33   **f.** .09   **h.** .090
3. a. 3 parts out of 10 is equal to 30 parts out of 100; .3 = .30
   c. 470 parts out of 1000 is equal to 47 parts out of 100; .470 = .47
   e. 1 part out of 100 is equal to 10 parts out of 1000; .01 = .010

4. b.

      .055

TENTHS	HUNDREDTHS	THOUSANDTHS
0	5	5

   d. Every collection of 10 like parts (thousandths, hundredths, or tenths) can be regrouped to form 1 larger part and is recorded in the adjacent column, to the left.
5. b. Each part would be $\frac{1}{100,000}$ of the unit square. The decimal is written as .00001 and named 1 hundred-thousandth.
6. b. .042 > .04
   e. .0420   .0047   .0400
8. c.

   .2   .17   .167

ACTIVITY SET 6.2

2. a. .4 + .29 = .69

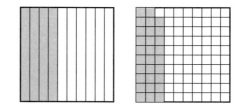

   c. .07 + .605 + .2 = .875

   .07   .605   .2

4. a. .5 − .07 = .43. If 3 hundredths and 4 tenths are added to the square for .07, you get the square for .5.

c. .435 − .3 = .135. Add 1 tenth, 3 hundredths, and 5 thousandths to .3.

5. b. 4 × .725 = 2.9 because 4 thousandth squares, each with 725 parts shaded, yield a total of 2900 shaded parts. Since there are 1000 parts in 1 whole square, the total shaded amount would be equal to 2 whole squares and 900 parts shaded out of 1000.

d. Multiplying by 10 makes each shaded tenth column of a decimal square equal to a unit square. Similarly, multiplying by 10 makes each hundredth square equal to a tenth column and each thousandth piece equal to a hundredth square.

6. c.

1 unit square, 7 tenths, and 12 hundredths
1.4 × 1.3 = 1.82

9. The decimal 2.87 can be represented by 2 whole squares and a square with 87 hundredths shaded (8 tenth columns and 7 hundredth squares). Dividing a unit square by 10 results in a region equivalent to 1 tenth column. Dividing a tenth column by 10 results in a region equal to 1 hundredth square, and dividing a hundredth square by 10 results in a region equal to 1 thousandth piece. When the squares representing 2.87 are divided by 10, the result is 2 tenth columns, 8 hundredth squares, and 7 thousandth pieces.

10. d. Five tenths can be measured off or subtracted from each unit twice. Since there are 250 units, .5 can be subtracted 500 times.

ACTIVITY SET 6.3

1. a. 30% **c.** 103% **d.** 130%

2. a. **c.** **f.**

3. a. The value is 45. One strip (10 squares) has value 30 and one-half strip has value 15.

c. The value is 288. Each small square has value 3 and 300 − 12 = 288.

4. a. Value 37.5: each strip (10%) has value 15 and one-half strip (5%) has value 7.5.

c. Value 10.5: every pair of small squares has value 3, and 3 + 3 + 3 + 1.5 = 10.5.

5. a. 270 is 60% of 450: each strip has value 45, so 6 strips (60%) have value 270.

c. 441 is 98% of 450: each small square has value 4.5, so 98 (98%) small squares have value 441.

6. a. Value of grid is 400: since 6% has value 24, 1% has value 4, and the value of the 10 by 10 grid is 400.

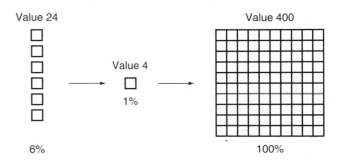

Value 24 — 6%

Value 4 — 1%

Value 400 — 100%

c. Value of the grid is 240: since 55% has value 132, 1% has value 2.4 (132 ÷ 55), and 100% has value 240.

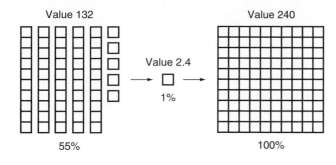

Value 132   Value 240
Value 2.4
1%
55%   100%

7. a. Some possible observations: there are 208 women employees; 35% of the employees are men; there are 112 men employees.

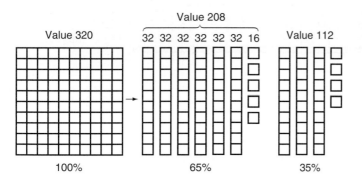

Value 320   Value 208
32 32 32 32 32 32 16   Value 112
100%   65%   35%

b. Some observations: 35% of the students were absent; 65% of the students were present.

Value 800   Value 280
80 80 80 40
100%

8. b. $\frac{2}{5} = 40\% = .4$

20 parts   20 parts   20 parts   20 parts   20 parts

d. $\frac{13}{20} = 65\% = .65$

5 parts
5 parts | 5 parts   . . .   5 parts
5 parts | 5 parts

9. b. $\frac{5}{6} \approx 85\% = .85$

17 parts

ACTIVITY SET 6.4

1. b. 7 square units   **e.** 4 square units   **h.** 2 square units
2. b. 4 square units   **e.** 2 square units   **g.** 10 square units
4. a. $\sqrt{13}$ **b.** 5   **g.** $\sqrt{17}$

6.

	SQUARE A	SQUARE B	SQUARE C
b. Fig. 2	9	4	13
d. Fig. 4	45	20	65

7. b.

	AREA OF SQUARE ON HYPOTENUSE	LENGTH OF HYPOTENUSE
b. Fig. 2	26	$\sqrt{26}$
d. Fig. 4	58	$\sqrt{58}$

ACTIVITY SET 7.1

1. a. The length of the rectangle is twice its width.
  b. Six algebra pieces represent the perimeter of the rectangle, so each algebra piece represents 9 units (54 ÷ 6). Therefore, the length is 18 units and the width 9 units.
  c.

3. a.

b. The perimeter of the triangle can be represented with 5 algebra pieces and 6 units. The perimeter is 66, so the 5 algebra pieces represent 60 units. Therefore, each single algebra piece represents 12 units. The sides of the triangle are 12 units, 24 units, and 30 units.

5.

The short piece is 34 m and the long piece is 41 m.

7.

Suppose Greg exchanges his dimes for nickels.

Greg has 80 cents.

10. The numbers are 23 and 41.

ACTIVITY SET 7.2

1. b. $x^2 + 2xy + y^2$

2. a.

$(3y)(3y) = 9y^2$

$x(x + y) = x^2 + xy$

3. a.

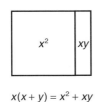

$y(2x + y) = 2yx + y^2$

4. b. A rectangle cannot be formed.

c. A rectangle can be formed.

5. a. $(x + 2)(x + 4) = x^2 + 6x + 8$

c. $(x + 1)(2x + 3) = 2x^2 + 5x + 3$

6. a.

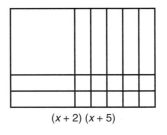

$(x + 2)(x + 5)$

d. Neither a square nor a rectangle can be formed.

ACTIVITY SET 8.1

4. b. $117,333.33 is the average for the 6 greatest incomes; $18,666.67 is the average for the 6 smallest.

d. $73,166.67 is the greatest average and $41,833.33 is the least. Both are closer to the mean of $56,444.44 than the greatest and least from part b.

ACTIVITY SET 8.2

1. a. 60 inches
  d. For two couples the woman was taller. One couple had the same height.

2. b.

ACTIVITY SET 8.3

1. c. *At least 3* means 3, 4, 5, or 6 girls. Count the number of outcomes in the chart that have 3, 4, 5, or 6 heads and divide that number by 64.

2. a. The pulse rate distribution comes close to satisfying this property because 68.3% of the population is within ±1 standard deviation of the mean, and 95% is within ±2 standard deviations of the mean.

3. a.

Letter	e	s	c	w	k
Percent	16.3%	7.2%	2.6%	1.7%	.6%

  c. This assignment of code symbols requires 43 time units, as compared to 47 time units for Morse code.

e	t	a	o	n	i	s
•	—	• •	• —	— •	• • •	— —

s	r	h	h
• • —	• — •	• • • •	— • •

4. a.

INTERVAL	WIN OR LOSE	NO. OF NUMBERS
5,132 to 9,999	Lose	4,868
10,000 to 49,999	Win	40,000
50,000 to 99,999	Lose	50,000
100,000 to 260,350	Win	160,351

  c. You win on 73 populations and your opponent wins on 39 populations.

JUST FOR FUN 8.3

Here is a frequency distribution for the letters that occur in the message.

The letter M occurs most frequently, so it is reasonable to guess that this is the enciphered letter for E. If M represents E, then I represents A and Q represents I. This agrees with one of the patterns for the distribution of letters in large samples. Also notice that the fifth and sixth letters beyond M did not occur in the message. This also agrees with the fact that the fifth and sixth letters beyond E are the low-frequency letters J and K. It appears that the message has been coded by replacing each letter by the letter that is 8 letters beyond. The message can be decoded by reversing that process. The result is:

"Galileo showed men of science that weighing and measuring are worthwhile. Newton convinced a large portion of them that weighing and measuring are the only investigations that are worthwhile."

Charles Singer

ACTIVITY SET 9.1

2. d. $\frac{1}{4}$ **e.** No. There is only a 25% chance of winning.

3. b. $\frac{4}{9}$

4. a. 2   **c.** $\begin{matrix} A_1 & A_2 & A \\ A_2 & A_1 & B \end{matrix}$ **e.** No

ACTIVITY SET 9.2

1. b. Probability of 2 of different colors: $\frac{3}{5}$

  Probability of 2 of the same color: $\frac{2}{5}$

  d. From the probability tree, we see that the probability of drawing first a red and then a green is $\frac{1}{2} \times \frac{3}{5} = \frac{3}{10}$, and the probability of drawing first a green and then a red is $\frac{1}{2} \times \frac{3}{5} = \frac{3}{10}$. So the probability of drawing 2 squares of different colors is $\frac{3}{10} + \frac{3}{10} = \frac{3}{5}$.

2. c. $\frac{6}{16}$ or $\frac{3}{8}$

4. b. $\frac{49}{100}$

5. a. $\frac{1}{36}$ **c.** $\frac{35}{36} \times \frac{35}{36}$ or $\left(\frac{35}{36}\right)^2$
  e. Approximately $1 - .51 = .49$

6. d. The probability of choosing a junk door on your first pick is $\frac{2}{3}$. But, using the switch strategy, you automatically win if your first choice is a junk door (the host must open the remaining junk door, so when you switch you win). So the probability of winning with the switch strategy is $\frac{2}{3}$.

  The probability of winning with the stick strategy is $\frac{1}{3}$.

JUST FOR FUN 9.2

2. $\frac{2}{3}$ 3. $\frac{1}{3}$ 4. $\frac{1}{3}$ 5. $\frac{2}{3}$

ACTIVITY SET 10.1

1. **b.** All triangles that have their third vertex on the same row parallel to the base have the same area.
   c. There are 12 noncongruent triangles that can be formed on the given base.

4.

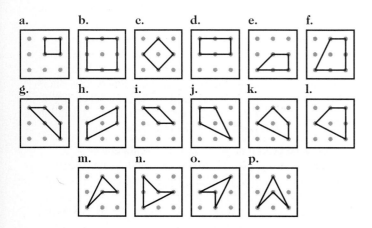

a.   b.   c.   d.   e.   f.
g.   h.   i.   j.   k.   l.
m.   n.   o.   p.

Figures a, b, and c are squares; figure d is a rectangle but not a square; figures h and i are parallelograms but not rectangles; figures e, f, and g are trapezoids; figures a, b, c, d, e, f, g, h, i, j, k, and l are convex; figures m, n, o, and p are nonconvex.

6. **a.** 75°; 90°; 210°; 120°
   b.

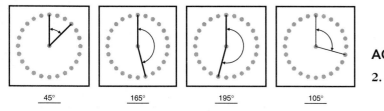

45°   165°   195°   105°

7. **a.** 45°; 30°; 45°; 30°; 45°
   b. Inscribed angles that intercept arcs of equal length in the same or congruent circles have the same measure.
   c. Inscribed angles whose sides intersect the ends of a diameter are right angles.

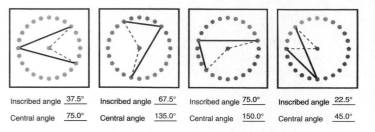

Inscribed angle 37.5°   Inscribed angle 67.5°   Inscribed angle 75.0°   Inscribed angle 22.5°
Central angle 75.0°   Central angle 135.0°   Central angle 150.0°   Central angle 45.0°

b. The measure of an inscribed angle is half the measure of the central angle that intercepts the same arc.

JUST FOR FUN 10.1

1. The 7 tangram pieces have been numbered (see the square below) in the solutions to the puzzles.

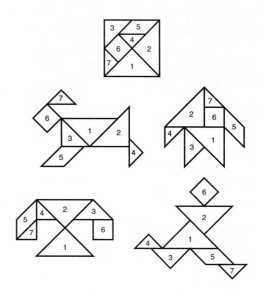

ACTIVITY SET 10.2

2.

ANGLE	MEASURE
1	150°
2	60°
3	120°
4	60°
5	120°
6	120°
7	60°

4. c. Each interior angle of a regular polygon with more than 6 sides is greater than 120° and less than 180°. The measures of such angles are not factors of 360.

5. a.

b.

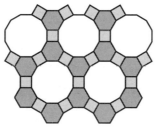

c. Here is one example. There are others.

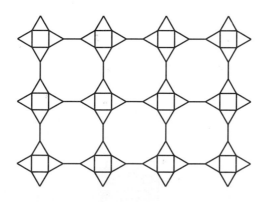

JUST FOR FUN 10.2

The winning strategy on a 3 by 3 or 5 by 5 grid is to occupy the center hexagon on the first move. On a 4 by 4 grid, the winning first move is any of those marked here.

4 by 4

ACTIVITY SET 10.3

1.

	NO. OF FACES	POLYGON
Tetrahedron	4	equilateral triangle
Cube	6	square
Octahedron	8	equilateral triangle
Dodecahedron	12	regular pentagon
Icosahedron	20	equilateral triangle

2. a. The tetrahedron has 4 triangular faces, and a rubber band holds 2 edges of 2 triangles together. The 4 triangular faces have $4 \times 3 = 12$ edges total, which are bound together in pairs, so there are $12 \div 2 = 6$ rubber bands needed. The cube requires 12 bands; the octahedron requires 12 bands; the dodecahedron requires 30 bands; and the icosahedron requires 30 bands.

3. a.

	VERTICES (V)	FACES (F)	EDGES (E)
Tetrahedron	4	4	6
Cube	8	6	12
Octahedron	6	8	12
Dodecahedron	20	12	30
Icosahedron	12	20	30

c.

	(1)	(2)	(3)	(4)
Vertices	5	10	12	10
Faces	5	7	8	7
Edges	8	15	18	15

5. b. Octahedron   e. Icosahedron   f. Cube
   g. Icosahedron or dodecahedron
   h. Dodecahedron   j. Cube or octahedron

ACTIVITY SET 10.4

1. a.

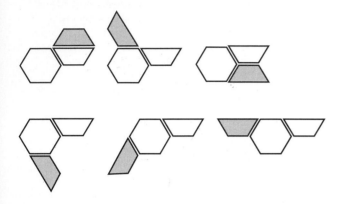

c. There are other ways besides the ones shown.

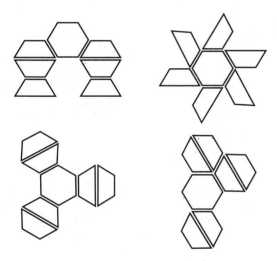

4. a. Angle *ABC* has a measure of 135°; *AD* = *DC* and *AB* = *BC*.

Angle *EFG* has a measure of 120°; *FG* = *HG* = *HF* and *EF* = $\frac{1}{2}$ of *FG*.

5. d. The eight-pointed wind rose.
   e. A regular 16-sided polygon can be obtained by cutting a 157.5° angle as shown here, with *AB* = *AC* = *AD*. *Note:* Some of the lines of symmetry are not crease lines.

ACTIVITY SET 10.5

3. These numbers limit the range of horizontal movement to between ⁻109 and 109 and the range of vertical movement to between ⁻59 and 59, so the targets remain on the screen.

ACTIVITY SET 11.1

3. a. 156 mm   **b.** 19 mm
7. a. A quart contains approximately 946 cm³. A liter contains slightly more than a quart.
   b. Approximately 10.9 cm

ACTIVITY SET 11.2

1. a. 9 sq. units   **c.** $7\frac{1}{2}$ sq. units   **e.** 8 sq. units

2. a. 9 sq. units   **c.** $10\frac{1}{2}$ sq. units   **e.** 6 sq. units

3. a. 3 sq. units   **c.** 1 sq. unit   **e.** 4 sq. units

4. a. 8 sq. units   **c.** $5\frac{1}{2}$ sq. units   **e.** 1 sq. unit

8. a. Parallelogram, 6 square units; triangle, 3 square units.
   c. Parallelogram, 9 square units; triangle, $4\frac{1}{2}$ square units.

9. The area of a parallelogram is equal to the length of a side multiplied by the height from that side. A triangle with base of length *b* units and height of length *h* units has half the area of a parallelogram with base length *b* and height of length *h* from that side.

JUST FOR FUN 11.2

4. The squares with an X in the following figure show one possible final move in the pentomino game.

5. Here are 5 pieces that work.

ACTIVITY SET 11.3

1. The volume of the crown was greater than the volume of the gold. King Hieron was cheated.

2.

	HEXAGONAL PRISM	HEXAGONAL PYRAMID	CYLINDER
Area of base	9.1 cm^2	9.1 cm^2	12.6 cm^2
Height (altitude)	5.0 cm	5.0 cm	3.0 cm
Volume	45.5 cm^3	15.2 cm^3	37.7 cm^3
Surface area	75.2 cm^2	38.7 cm^2	62.8 cm^2

3. Cylinder A: 1030 cm^3; cylinder B: 1342 cm^3

5. b.

	1	2	3	4	5	6
Central angle of disc	45°	90°	135°	225°	270°	315°
Base area (cm^2)	4.91	19.63	44.16	122.66	176.63	240.41
Height (cm)	9.92	9.68	9.27	7.81	6.61	4.84
Radius (cm)	1.25	2.50	3.75	6.25	7.50	8.75
Volume (cm^3)	16.24	63.34	136.45	319.32	389.17	387.86

   c. For central angles of less than 45°, the smaller the angle is, the smaller the volume is. For central angles of more than 315°, the larger the angle is, the smaller the volume is. The maximum volume of approximately 403 cm^3 occurs with a central angle of 294°.

6. c. A cone with a base of radius r and a height of h has a volume of $\frac{1}{3} \times \pi r^2 h$. The "half cone" has a base of radius $\frac{r}{2}$ and a height of $\frac{h}{2}$. Its volume is $\frac{1}{3} \times \pi (\frac{r}{2})^2 (\frac{h}{2})$, which is equal to $\frac{1}{3} \times \pi r^2 h \times \frac{1}{8}$. Therefore, the volume of the "half cone" is $\frac{1}{8}$ of the volume of the original cone.

7. a. 7235 cm^3

8. c. The volume of the 3 balls is $3 \times \frac{4}{3} \times \pi (3.15)^3 \approx 394$ cm^3. The volume of the can is $20 \times \pi (3.5)^2 \approx 769$ cm^3. Therefore, approximately $\frac{1}{2}$ of the space is wasted.

ACTIVITY SET 12.1

1. b. The points form 2 perpendicular lines that pass through the intersection of lines m and n and bisect the angles formed by the intersection of m and n.

2. a. The points form a circle with P as center and radius equal to the distance from P to the midpoint of the chords.

   c. The points form a circle whose center is the midpoint of segment $\overline{PS}$ and whose diameter is $\overline{PS}$.

4. A circle

6. a. A semicircle on diameter $\overline{PQ}$ (a circle if you reverse the card and repeat the process on the other side of segment $\overline{PQ}$)

ACTIVITY SET 12.2

1. a. The new figure will tessellate because the exact shape that has been adjoined to one edge of the rectangle was deleted from the opposite side of the rectangle.

ACTIVITY SET 12.3

1. a. Both triangles contain the angle at E, and the angles at A and A' are right angles. When two angles of one triangle are congruent to two angles of another, the triangles are similar.

2. c. Triangle E_1FE_2 is similar to triangle RFT. Therefore, $\frac{75}{7.5} = \frac{FT}{90}$ or $FT = 10 \times 90$

   e. When you are estimating large distances, the distance from eye to finger is relatively small and ignoring it will not significantly affect the estimate. However, when you are estimating small distances, which may be only a few times greater than the distance from eye to finger, ignoring the distance from the eye to the finger will give a larger error. In the latter case, the distance should be added to the estimated distance.

3. b. 20.25 m   **c.** 24.3 m

4. b. $\overline{ET}$ in the figure measures 80 mm. So 80 mm represents 60 m, or 1 mm represents .75 m. The height of the tree from T to R in the diagram is 24 mm, so the height of the actual tree between those two points is $24 \times .75 = 18$ m.

5. a. Approximately 33 m plus the height of the hypsometer above the ground.

6. b. Use a line from the land marker to the pine tree as a base line and measure the distance between these two points. From the pine tree, measure the 5 angles between the base line and the remaining 5 objects. From the landmark, measure the 5 angles between the base line and the remaining 5 objects. With the 10 angles, a map can be made of the locations of each object. Using the distance from pine tree to the landmark, a scale can be set up to determine all distances.

ACTIVITY SET 12.4

1. a. Bunyan   **b.** Two-sided
3. a. Two linked bands; the smaller is one-sided and the larger is two-sided.
5. Slip the string connecting the first person's wrists under the string that is around the wrist of the second person and over this person's hand.
6. *Hint:* Pull the strings through the hole in the panel.
8. No. If the arms are intertwined so that a knot is formed, this connection cannot be changed into a simple closed curve without breaking one or more hand grips.

JUST FOR FUN 12.4

Gale Game: There will always be a winner.
Sprouts: **1.** The greatest number of turns is 5 and the least number is 4.
3. The greatest number of moves is $3n - 1$ and the least number is $2n$. (*Note:* In some cases the least number of moves may appear to be less than $2n$. But remember, an arc can be drawn from a point back to itself.)

CREDITS

PHOTOS

Chapter 1

Page 8: Courtesy of British Information Service; **p. 12:** Ron Bergeron; **p. 12:** *Patterns in Nature* by Peter S. Stevens, Atlantic Monthly/Little Brown, 1974. Reprinted by courtesy of Peter S. Stevens.

Chapter 4

Page 81: Photo by Ron Bergeron; **p. 84:** Talbot Lovering

Chapter 8

Page 163: *Peanuts* reprinted by permission of United Feature Syndicate, Inc.; **p. 177:** Library of Congress

Chapter 9

Page 191: *Peanuts* reprinted by permission of United Feature Syndicate, Inc.; **p. 198:** Ron Bergeron

Chapter 10

Page 220: Courtesy of Museum of Comparative Zoology, Harvard Univ.; **p. 227, 228:** Talbot Lovering

Chapter 11:

Page 244: *Peanuts* reprinted by permission of United Feature Syndicate, Inc.; **pp. 260, 264:** Talbot Lovering

Chapter 12

Page 273: Talbot Lovering; **p. 292:** Ron Bergeron; **p. 293:** Courtesy of The B. F. Goodrich Company; **pp. 295, 296:** Ron Bergeron

ILLUSTRATIONS AND TEXT

Chapter 5

Page 94: Fraction Bar model from the Fraction Bars® materials by Albert B. Bennett, Jr., and Patricia Davidson © 1981. Permission of Scott Resources, Inc. Fort Collins, Colorado.

Chapter 6

Page 111: Decimal Squares model from the Decimal Squares® materials by Albert B. Bennett, Jr.,© 1981. Permission of Scott Resources, Inc. Fort Collins, Colorado.

Chapter 8

Page 178: Graphs from *A Guide to the Unknown,* by Frederick Mosteller et al., copyright 1972. Reprinted by courtesy of Holden-Day, Inc.

Chapter 12

Page 224: Line designs from *Line Designs* by Dale Seymour, Linda Libey, and Joyce Snider. Reprinted by permission of Creative Publications, Palo Alto; **p. 292:** Reprinted from Ford Times. Courtesy of Ford Motor Company; **p. 298:** Game of Sprouts from Martin Gardner, *Mathematical Carnival* (Knopf, 1975), Chapter 1.

MATERIAL CARDS

1. Rectangular Grid   (1.3)
2. Isometric Grid   (1.3)
3. Attribute-Game Grid   (2.1)
4. Two-Circle Venn Diagram   (2.1)
5. Three-Circle Venn Diagram   (2.1, 10.1)
6. Pica-Centro Recording Sheet   (2.3)
7. Coordinate Guessing and Hide-A-Region Grids   (7.2)
8. Table of Random Digits   (8.1, 8.3, 9.1)
9. Two-Penny Grid   (9.1)
10. Three-Penny Grid   (9.1)
11. Geoboard Recording Paper   (10.1)
12. Grids for Game of Hex   (10.2)
13. Perpendicular Lines for Symmetry   (10.4)
14. Metric Measuring Tape   (11.1)
15. Centimeter Racing Mat   (11.1)
16. Pentomino Game Grid   (11.2)
17. Attribute Label Cards and Circles for Wheels   (2.1, 2.2)
18. Logic Problem Clue Cards and People Pieces (Problem 1)   (2.3)
19. Logic Problem Clue Cards (Problems 2 and 3)   (2.3)
20. Logic Problem Clue Cards (Problems 4 and 5)   (2.3)
21. Object Pieces for Logic Problem 5   (2.3)
22. Mind-Reading Cards   (3.1)
23. Decimal Squares*   (6.1, 6.2)
24. Decimal Squares*   (6.1, 6.2)
25. Decimal Squares*   (6.1, 6.2)
26. Decimal Squares*   (6.1, 6.2)
27. Rectangular Geoboard Template   (6.4, 10.1, 11.2)
28. Algebra Pieces   (7.1)
29. Algebraic Expression Cards   (7.1)
30. Simulation Spinners   (9.2)
31. Trick Dice   (9.2)
32. Metric Ruler, Protractor, and Compass   (10.1, 11.1, 11.3, 12.1, 12.2, 12.3)
33. Circular Geoboard Template   (10.1)
34. Regular Polyhedra   (10.3)
35. Regular Polyhedra   (10.3)
36. Cube Patterns for Instant Insanity   (10.3)
37. Pentominoes   (11.2)
38. Prism, Pyramid, and Cylinder   (11.3)
39. Hypsometer-Clinometer   (12.3)

*Decimal Squares is a registered trademark of Scott Resources.

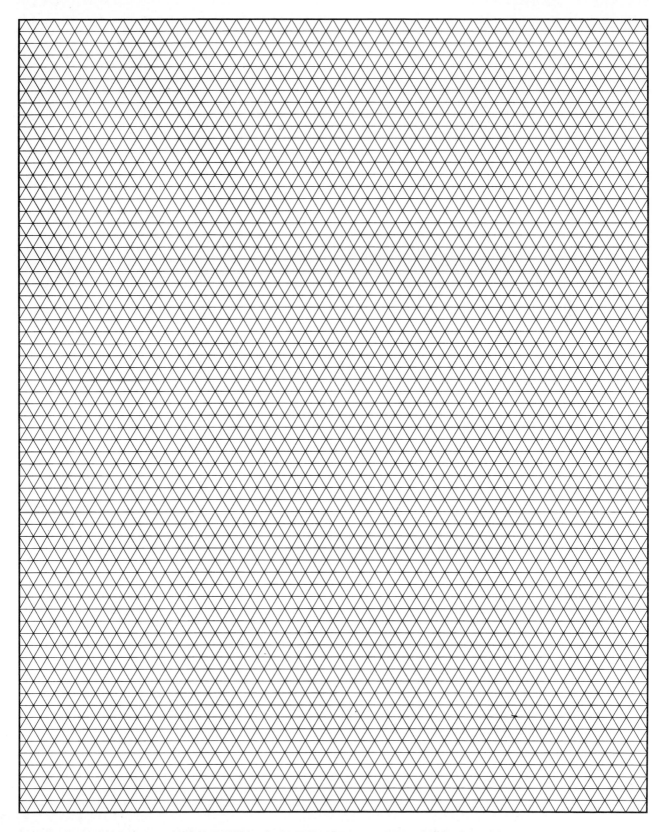

Rows, 1 difference (1 point)	Columns, 2 differences (2 points)	Diagonals, 3 differences (3 points)

		Place attribute piece here to start game		

THREE-DIGIT RECORDING SHEETS

FOUR-DIGIT RECORDING SHEETS

Coordinate Guessing and Hide-A-Region Grids

(Activity Set 7.2 JUST FOR FUN)

69588	18885	24831	28185	84019	91168	62187	69079	86492	24195
19797	27708	70288	72541	10576	79693	28704	97678	95777	46759
50212	65574	17333	21694	47617	71881	88513	62695	76222	42544
16380	57486	86835	82724	23964	77540	93652	75555	77283	29473
29826	51673	28082	85640	43062	21997	77247	14653	13471	03865
51427	10863	96787	43214	68955	13735	72107	63399	15951	53968
36037	55838	30244	28819	19794	72893	43642	89344	72686	17378
52421	74281	44363	37701	25103	06701	33100	00483	38208	57711
64936	77559	27432	27412	89263	50899	68524	54274	35905	40343
05013	22060	17792	96536	74156	88924	19652	84311	92236	18008
69970	37423	22837	28337	06347	84836	68812	06121	23216	64020
96601	64066	87785	41608	32193	67850	46509	70020	18435	75427
30984	17658	07126	96234	66401	05691	55657	29217	61037	83086
93775	97887	39692	84605	98008	43174	07226	17637	63106	11806
10975	47371	37928	71999	19339	87802	88208	23697	57359	64825
34487	51270	55303	80666	63115	97793	01883	46650	10668	04238
77876	02108	02420	23983	49776	29281	01665	04908	78948	09727
38781	58184	25008	00962	80002	22962	92127	49898	24259	61862
83788	62480	44711	21815	84629	06939	67646	06948	04529	45214
89704	30361	15988	83311	78147	00323	49940	68820	24291	44077
24113	92774	25852	01814	44175	64734	25392	58525	88314	97199
23041	81334	43410	28285	59247	22853	24395	17770	61573	38097
43123	25825	91840	79914	41137	99165	33796	95374	25960	35135
20585	11696	84826	43878	74239	98734	35854	82082	97416	20039
45699	87633	29489	57614	52384	88793	24228	60107	83502	28129
42060	77709	09509	58712	21415	38415	10841	93372	53568	70864
23038	92956	27304	20825	70350	33151	93654	81710	34692	58456
72936	52909	92458	61567	72380	00931	49994	38711	12237	49788
24631	18803	35690	70000	10040	38204	67146	85913	48332	86757
62397	54028	77523	24891	27989	02289	74513	26279	85382	82180
75724	78027	60675	01294	37607	84053	41144	94743	85633	50356
44997	49702	68073	99166	05851	22239	76340	79458	25968	75875
20733	42897	05445	46195	97046	16120	41546	04463	34074	05515
90448	49154	27693	90607	98476	50924	25067	01233	64588	31287
50151	76497	10878	87213	84640	35943	46320	03267	15324	95455
33944	22308	60879	07308	10759	75179	05130	66184	69554	65891
42837	55847	75893	54245	38752	68095	33158	81860	56469	84190
39357	40544	25447	96260	87283	22483	78031	91393	38040	82382
45673	87347	44240	61458	87338	62039	71825	52571	27146	86404
97714	52538	91976	52406	19711	99248	23073	43926	81889	47540

Cut out the five vertical strips and then tape or glue tab 2 under the edge labeled 2, tab 4 under the edge labeled 4, tab 6 under the edge labeled 6, and tab 8 under the edge labeled 8, to form a metric tape that is 100 centimeters long.

2	4	6	8	100 cm
15 cm	35 cm	55 cm	75 cm	95 cm
10 cm	30 cm	50 cm	70 cm	90 cm
5 cm	25 cm	45 cm	65 cm	85 cm
20	40	60	80	

Tabs ⟶

CENTIMETER RACING MAT

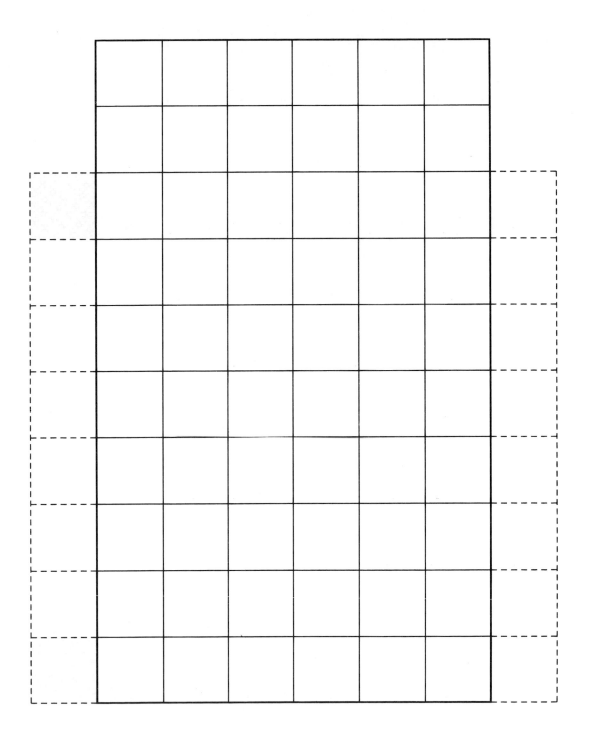

Attribute Label Cards and Circles for Wheels
(Activity Sets 2.1 and 2.2)

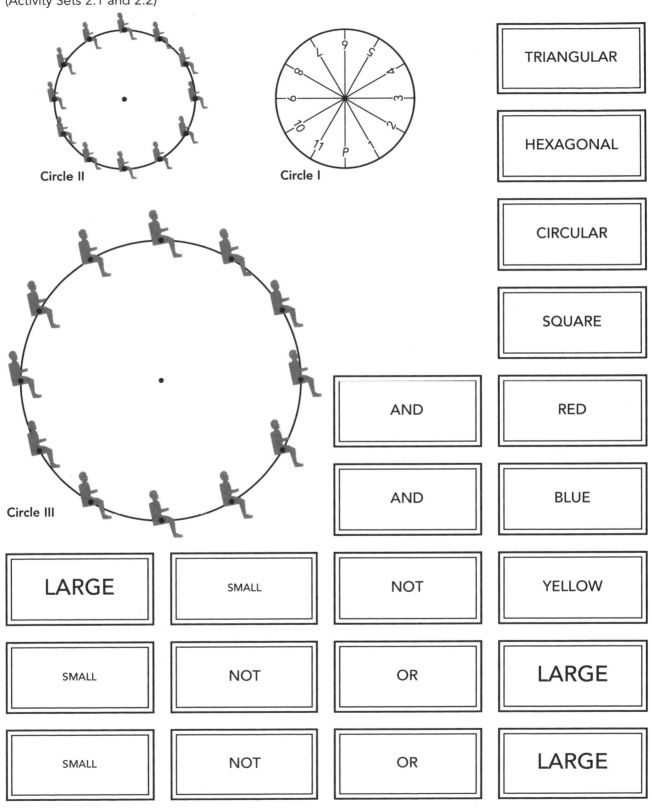

Circle II

Circle I

Circle III

TRIANGULAR

HEXAGONAL

CIRCULAR

SQUARE

AND

AND

NOT

RED

BLUE

YELLOW

LARGE

SMALL

NOT

OR

LARGE

SMALL

SMALL

NOT

OR

LARGE

Paul, Nicky, Sally, Uri, Jane, Veneta, Monty, Marc, and Edith are standing in a row according to height, but not necessarily in the order given.

Edith is closer to Sally than she is to Nicky.

LOGIC PROBLEM 1   CARD A

Veneta, Edith, Marc, Sally, Monty, and Jane are shorter than Paul, Nicky, and Uri.

There is just one person between Uri and Paul.

Name the 9 people in order from shortest to tallest.

LOGIC PROBLEM 1   CARD B

Edith, Marc, Monty, Jane, and Veneta are shorter than the other four.

Uri is between Sally and Nicky.

Monty and Paul have 7 people between them.

LOGIC PROBLEM 1   CARD C

Uri, Nicky, Jane, Paul, and Sally are taller than the others.

Veneta and Monty are the only two people shorter than Edith.

LOGIC PROBLEM 1   CARD D

Nicky

Paul

Sally

Marc

Uri

Edith

Jane

Monty

Veneta

Mr. Racquet is coach of the tennis team.

Susan said, "I won't play if Mike is on the team."

LOGIC PROBLEM 2   CARD A

Smith, Brown, Jones, and Robinson are told that they have each won one of four academic prizes, but none of them knows which, so they are speculating.

Smith thinks that Robinson has won the logic prize.

LOGIC PROBLEM 3   CARD A

John, Susan, Mike, Derek, Linda, and Anne play mixed doubles.

Mike said, "I won't play if either Derek of Linda is chosen."

LOGIC PROBLEM 2   CARD B

The four academic prizes are for outstanding work in mathematics, English, French, and logic.

Jones feels confident that Smith has not won the mathematics prize.

Who won each prize?

LOGIC PROBLEM 3   CARD B

How can Mr. Racquet select four compatible players (two men and two women) for a road trip?

Derek said, "I'll only play if Anne plays."

LOGIC PROBLEM 2   CARD C

Robinson is of the opinion that Brown has won the French prize.

The winners of the mathematics and logic prizes were correct in their speculations.

LOGIC PROBLEM 3   CARD C

John Said, "I'll only play if Susan plays."

Anne had no likes or dislikes.

LOGIC PROBLEM 2   CARD D

The English and French prize winners were not correct in their predictions of the prize winners.

Brown thinks that Jones has won the English prize.

The math prize was awarded to Robinson.

LOGIC PROBLEM 3   CARD D

On a plane, Smith, Jones, and Robinson are pilot, copilot and engineer, but not necessarily in that order.

The copilot has the same name as the singer living in the same town.

LOGIC PROBLEM 4   CARD A

The Chevrolet owner lives in the house next door to the house where the horses are kept.

The person in the red house is English.

The Japanese drives a Ford.

Each house is occupied by a person of different nationality.

The person in the ivory house does not drink milk.

LOGIC PROBLEM 5   CARD A

On the plane there is a singing group, The 3-Ms, whose names are M. Smith, M. Robinson, and M. Jones.

The copilot lives in the city between that of M. Jones and that of the engineer.

LOGIC PROBLEM 4   CARD B

The Plymouth driver lives next door to the person with the fox.

The Honda owner drinks orange juice.

The Norwegian lives next to the blue house.

Coffee is drunk in the green house.

Who owns the skunk?

LOGIC PROBLEM 5   CARD B

M. Robinson lives in New York City.

Jones consistently beats the engineer in racquetball.

LOGIC PROBLEM 4   CARD C

The Chevrolet owner lives in the yellow House.

Milk is drunk in the middle house.

The Norwegian lives in the first house.

The Spaniard owns a dog.

If each person has one home, one pet, one car, a different nationality and a different drink, who drinks the water?

LOGIC PROBLEM 5   CARD C

The singers each reside in a different city, New York, San Francisco and Chicago, as do the members of the plane crew.

What is the pilot's name.

LOGIC PROBLEM 4   CARD D

The Ukrainian drinks tea.

The green house is immediately to the right of the ivory house.

The Mercedes driver owns snails.

The fox lives with the owner of the house farthest from the green house.

The five houses are in a row.

LOGIC PROBLEM 5   CARD D

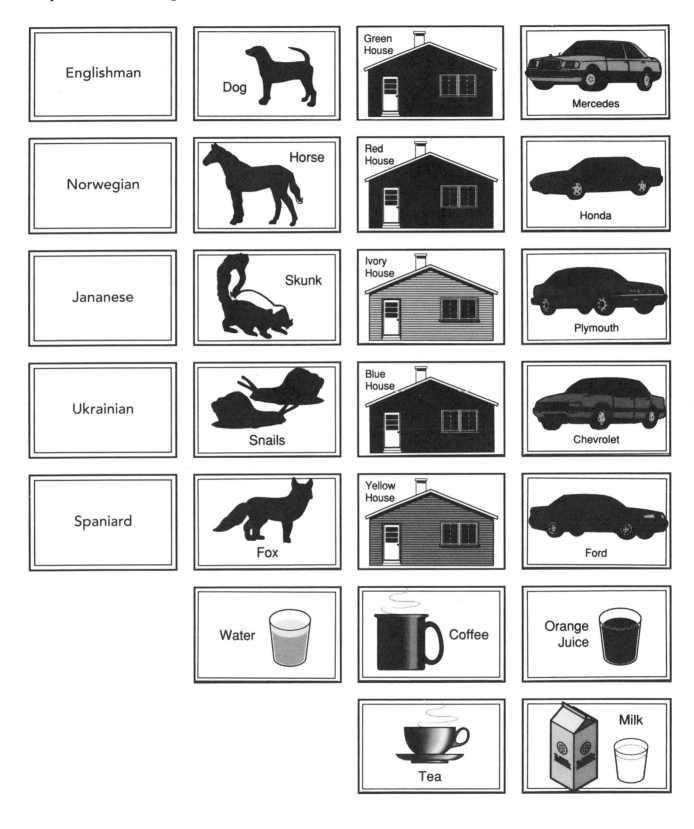

Englishman

Dog

Green House

Mercedes

Norwegian

Horse

Red House

Honda

Jananese

Skunk

Ivory House

Plymouth

Ukrainian

Snails

Blue House

Chevrolet

Spaniard

Fox

Yellow House

Ford

Water

Coffee

Orange Juice

Tea

Milk

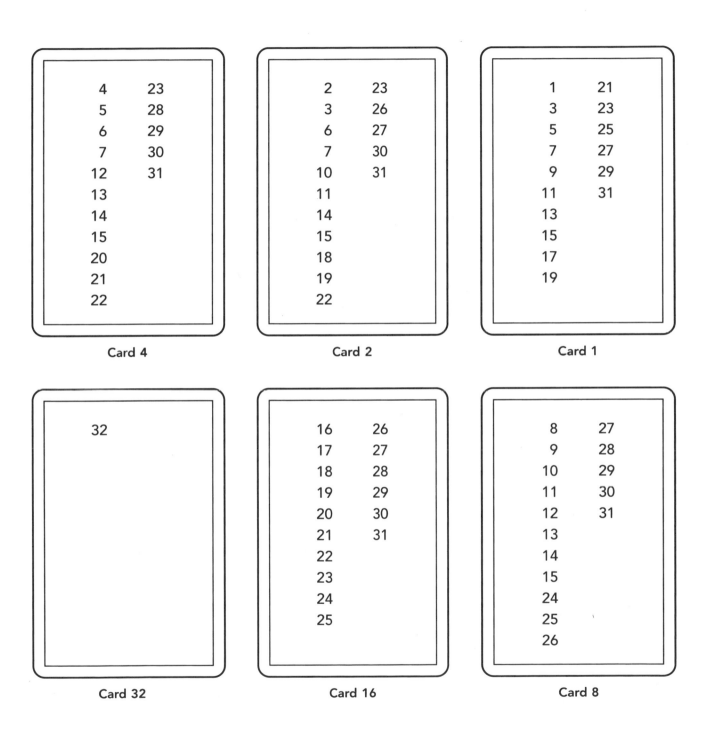

Card 4		Card 2		Card 1	
4	23	2	23	1	21
5	28	3	26	3	23
6	29	6	27	5	25
7	30	7	30	7	27
12	31	10	31	9	29
13		11		11	31
14		14		13	
15		15		15	
20		18		17	
21		19		19	
22		22			

Card 32		Card 16		Card 8	
32		16	26	8	27
		17	27	9	28
		18	28	10	29
		19	29	11	30
		20	30	12	31
		21	31	13	
		22		14	
		23		15	
		24		24	
		25		25	
				26	

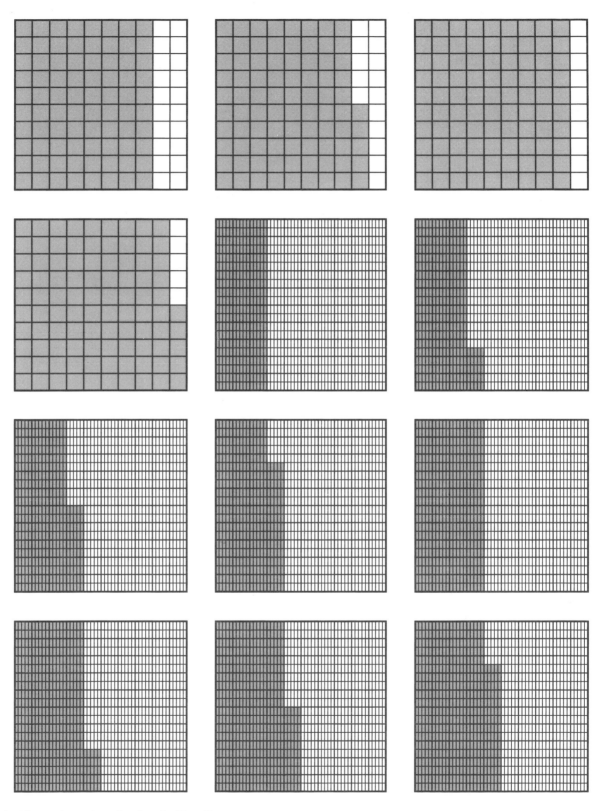

*Decimal Squares is a registered trademark of Scott Resources.

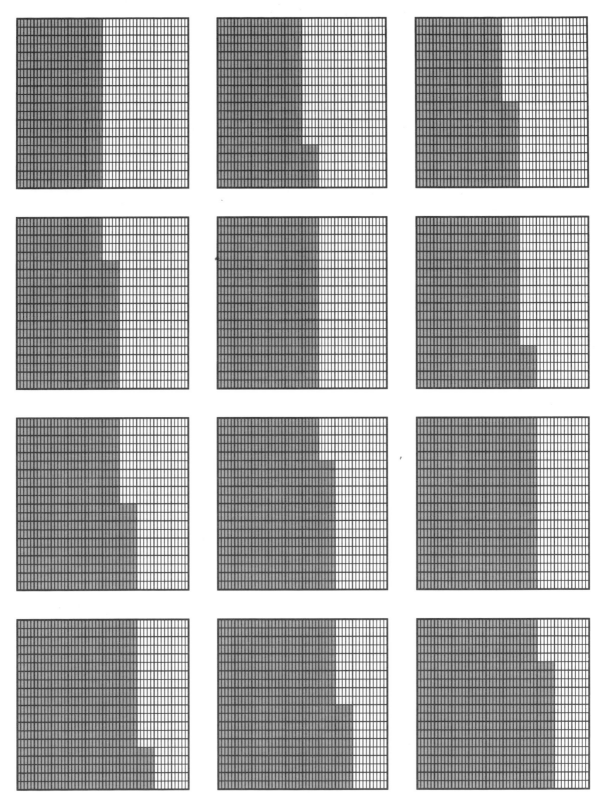

*Decimal Squares is a registered trademark of Scott Resources.

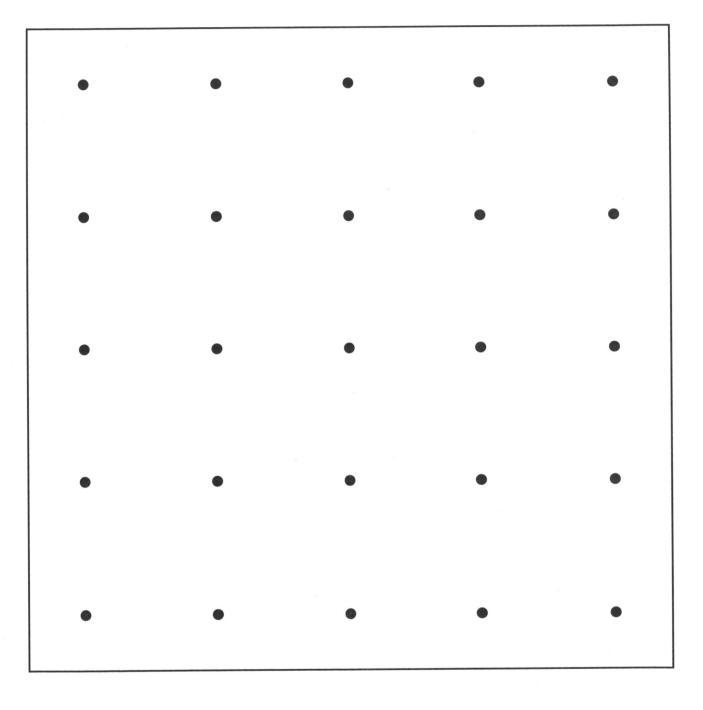

ALGEBRA PIECE

ALGEBRA PIECE

ALGEBRA PIECE

ALGEBRA PIECE

ALGEBRA PIECE

ALGEBRA PIECE

ALGEBRA PIECE

ALGEBRA PIECE

UNIT UNIT UNIT

UNIT UNIT UNIT

UNIT UNIT UNIT

UNIT UNIT UNIT

UNIT UNIT UNIT

UNIT UNIT UNIT

UNIT UNIT UNIT

UNIT UNIT UNIT

Team A		Team B	
I have $n + 1$ **Who has** two less than a number	**I have** $4n + 5$ **Who has** two more than the square root of a number	**I have** $n + 2$ **Who has** five less than a number	**I have** $5n + 3$ **Who has** one more than three times the square of a number
I have $n - 2$ **Who has** one more than two times a number	**I have** $\sqrt{n} + 2$ **Who has** five less than eight times a number	**I have** $n - 5$ **Who has** two more than three times a number	**I have** $3n^2 + 1$ **Who has** two more than one-third of a number
I have $2n + 1$ **Who has** five less than seven times a number	**I have** $8n - 5$ **Who has** one more than four times the square of a number	**I have** $3n + 2$ **Who has** five less than six times a number	**I have** $\frac{n}{3} + 2$ **Who has** six less than the cube of a number
I have $7n - 5$ **Who has** seven more than the square of a number	**I have** $4n^2 + 1$ **Who has** four more than one-third of a number	**I have** $6n - 5$ **Who has** eight more than the square of a number	**I have** $n^3 - 6$ **Who has** nine more than four times a number
I have $n^2 + 7$ **Who has** three more than half of a number	**I have** $\frac{n}{3} + 4$ **Who has** seven less than the cube of a number	**I have** $n^2 + 8$ **Who has** five less than half of a number	**I have** $4n + 9$ **Who has** seven less than half of a number
I have $\frac{n}{2} + 3$ **Who has** five more than four times a number	**I have** $n^3 - 7$ **Who has** one more than a number	**I have** $\frac{n}{2} - 5$ **Who has** three more than five times a number	**I have** $\frac{n}{2} - 7$ **Who has** two more than a number

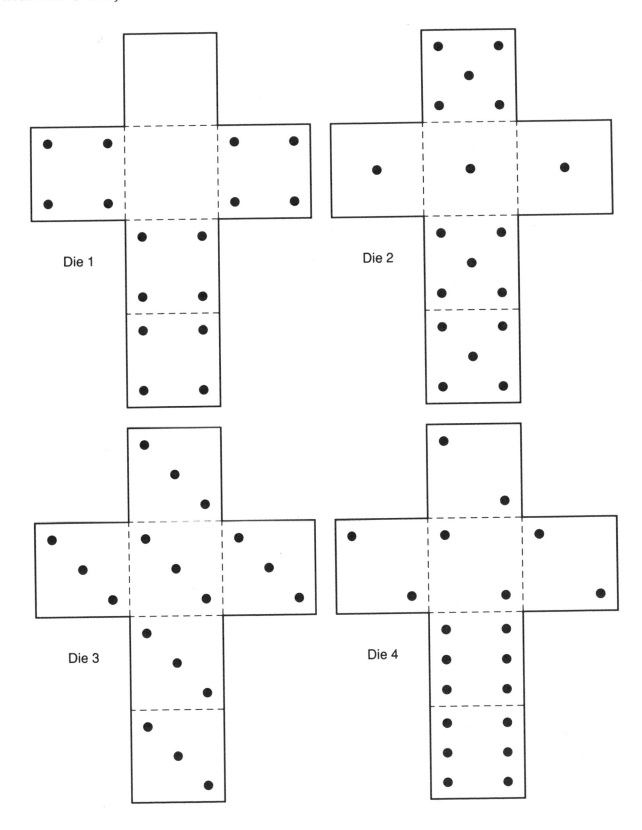

Die 1

Die 2

Die 3

Die 4

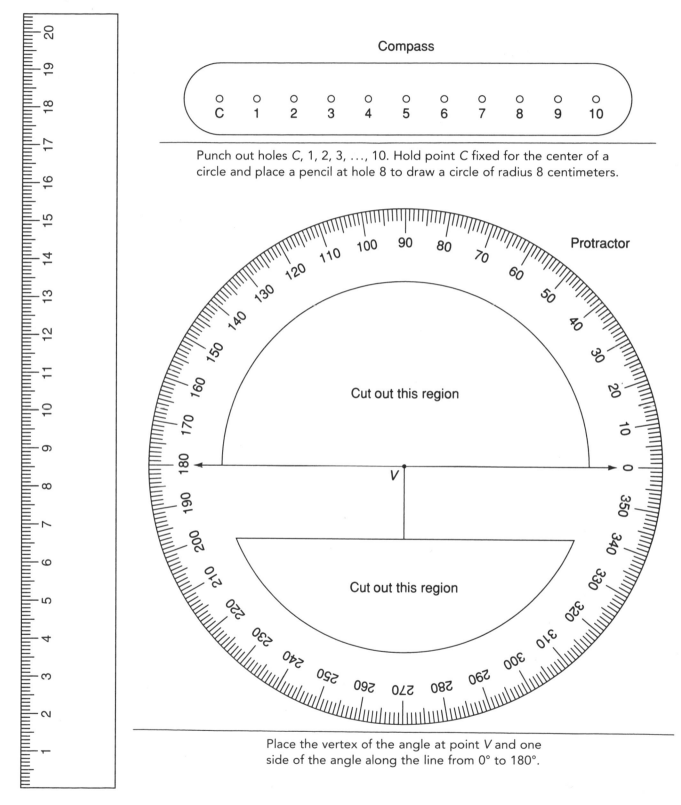

Compass

Punch out holes C, 1, 2, 3, ..., 10. Hold point C fixed for the center of a circle and place a pencil at hole 8 to draw a circle of radius 8 centimeters.

Protractor

Cut out this region

Cut out this region

Place the vertex of the angle at point V and one side of the angle along the line from 0° to 180°.

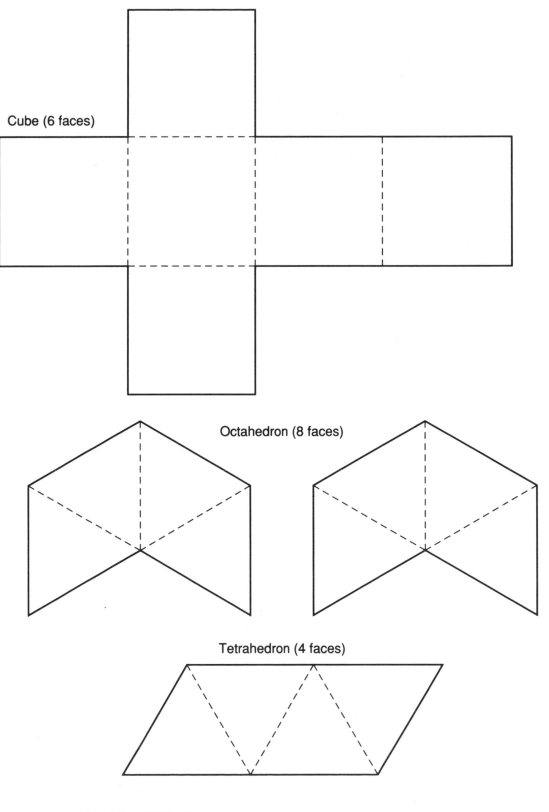

Cube (6 faces)

Octahedron (8 faces)

Tetrahedron (4 faces)

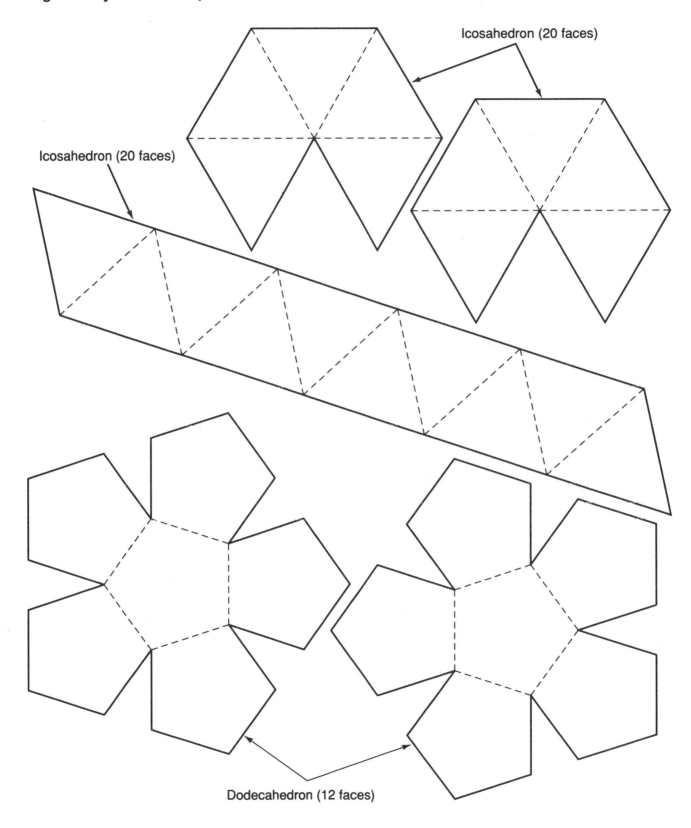

Icosahedron (20 faces)

Icosahedron (20 faces)

Icosahedron (20 faces)

Dodecahedron (12 faces)

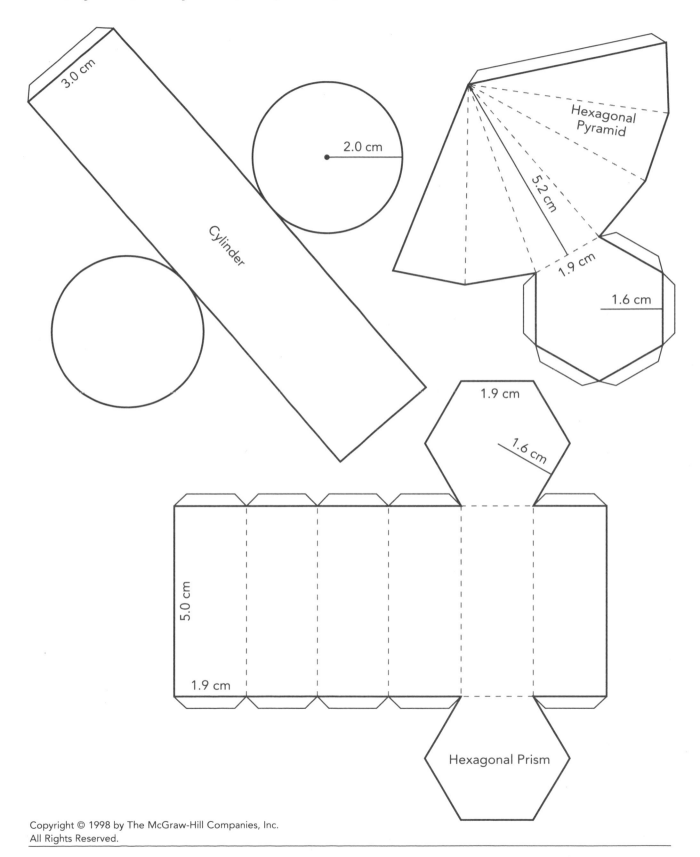

3.0 cm

2.0 cm

Cylinder

Hexagonal
Pyramid

5.2 cm

1.9 cm

1.6 cm

1.9 cm

1.6 cm

5.0 cm

1.9 cm

Hexagonal Prism

http://www.mhhe.com

WCB/McGraw-Hill
A Division of The **McGraw·Hill** Companies

P/N 006298-6
Part of
ISBN 0-07-913259-6

90000

9 780079 132598